Research in Contemporary Religion

Edited by
Carla Danani, Judith Gruber, Hans-Günter Heimbrock,
Stefanie Knauss, Daria Pezzoli-Olgiati,
Else Marie Wiberg Pedersen, Hans-Joachim Sander,
Trygve Wyller

Advisory Board
Siphiwe Dube (Johannesburg)
Andreas Mauz (Basel)
Cecilia Nahnfeldt (Turku)
Henrik Reintoft Christensen (Aarhus)
Ulrike Witten (Munich)

Volume 36

Vandenhoeck & Ruprecht

Meshack Edward Njinga

The Kingdom of God and the Poor

The Bible Reading of the Economically Underprivileged Christians in Tanzania

Vandenhoeck & Ruprecht

Published with the aid of the Institute of Missiology Missio e.V.,
The Lutheran World Federation (LWF),
The Church of Norway and the Faculty of Theology, University of Oslo.

This book is a revised version of Dr. Meshack Njinga's PhD thesis
The Kingdom of God and the Poor: The Bible Reading of the Economically Underprivileged
Christians in Tanzania,
defended at the Faculty of Theology, University of Oslo in April 2021.

Bibliographic information published by the Deutsche Nationalbibliothek:
The Deutsche Nationalbibliothek lists this publication in the Deutsche
Nationalbibliografie; detailed bibliographic data available online: https://dnb.de.

© 2024 by Vandenhoeck & Ruprecht, Robert-Bosch-Breite 10, 37079 Göttingen,
Germany, an imprint of the Brill-Group (Koninklijke Brill NV, Leiden, The Netherlands;
Brill USA Inc., Boston MA, USA; Brill Asia Pte Ltd, Singapore; Brill Deutschland GmbH,
Paderborn, Germany, Brill Österreich GmbH, Vienna, Austria)

Koninklijke Brill NV incorporates the imprints Brill, Brill Nijhoff, Brill Schöningh,
Brill Fink, Brill mentis, Brill Wageningen Academic, Vandenhoeck & Ruprecht, Böhlau
and V&R unipress.

This publication is licensed under a Creative Commons Attribution – Non Commercial
– No Derivatives 4.0 International license, at https://doi.org/10.13109/9783666503658.
For a copy of this license go to https://creativecommons.org/licenses/by-nc-nd/4.0/.
Any use in cases other than those permitted by this license requires the prior written
permission from the publisher.

Cover illustration: © Trygve Wyller, IR-Vicoba groups in Tanzania, 2017.
The groups meet regularly in the local village for Bible studies, taking point of
departure in one chosen pericope. The members are from the local community,
a person with some theological education chair the meetings.

Typesetting: le-tex publishing services, Leipzig
Cover design: SchwabScantechnik, Göttingen
Printed and bound: Hubert & Co, Göttingen
Printed in the EU

Vandenhoeck & Ruprecht Verlage | www.vandenhoeck-ruprecht-verlage.com

ISSN 2198-7556
ISBN 978-3-525-50365-2

Preface

Since many years, theology from below is a well-established slogan. This book makes this slogan concrete and alive. Dr. Meshack Njinga presents us with voices, practices and bodies of poor Tanzanian farmers and their struggle to handle all kinds of everyday challenges in their businesses and in their spiritual lives.

To encounter and to be taken into this everyday is a privilege for both scholars and all people interested in what is an organic entanglement of faith, politics, and business. From this entanglement we can learn a lot of how religion and politics co-practice and is really one act, and not two.

In this way, the book from Meshack Njinga is an important contribution to life-worlds where practices of liberation theologies are enacted, practices that research, so far, has rather little knowledge about. In this respect, Dr. Njinga's book opens new landscapes and brings the discussion on how faith, everyday and politics relate to new and significant levels. Transformative religion happens in many unexpected ways.

Oslo, May 2023

Trygve Wyller
Professor emeritus, Faculty of Theology, University of Oslo, Norway
Honorary professor, School of Religion, Philosophy and Ethics,
University of KwaZulu-Natal, South Africa

Acknowledgments

Writing a dissertation is not an overnight work; it is a gradual process that involves receiving support from many sources. The process brings together invaluable contributions from many persons to produce the completed form. It is not possible to give credit to each one by name. It must suffice to say thank you to everyone involved, each according to their input.

Nevertheless, I do wish to thank a few people in particular for their invaluable contributions to this project. First and foremost, I am grateful to the almighty God, for His presence and support over the time I have spent on this project. He has protected me from all danger and harm, enabled me, and given me good health and endurance to accomplish this project.

I am indebted to the Faculty of Theology at the University of Oslo for approving my research proposal, admitting me to the faculty, and granting me research travel finances. Without the provision of such financial assistance, the travels to the different places for research, presentations of part of my work, and buying books would have been impossible.

I am also indebted to the Norwegian Government through the Quota Funding Scheme (Lånekassen) for granting me a scholarship for 4 years. The scholarship made my life in Oslo possible. I promised to use the education I obtained through this scholarship to serve my people in Tanzania.

I am grateful to my church, the ELCT-KoD, for granting me permission to come to Norway to study despite the scarcity of workers. I know that, without that permission, it would have been impossible for me to come for the studies.

I am most grateful to the following institutions: The Lutheran World Federation (LWF), The Church of Norway, The Institute of Missiology Missio (MWI) and the Faculty of Theology, University of Oslo. These institutions have all given grants to finance this publication as an Open Access publication.

To my main supervisor, Prof. Trygve Wyller, I am grateful for his professional supervision, his thorough and meticulous reading, tireless support, guidance, and positive criticism. His visitation to Tanzania and to meetings with the IR-VICOBA groups gave a new impetus to the groups and my diocesan leaders. Moreover, it developed a new understanding of the projects. To you I say "tusen takk."

To my co-supervisors, Prof. Anders Runesson and Associate Prof. Rune Flikke, thank you very much for the critical, challenging, and yet supportive supervision shown through your professional guidance and positive criticism of my work. I greatly appreciate your valuable views and guidance, which led to the accomplishment of this work. I am thankful to Prof. Knut Holter for his critical reading of my entire work and to my colleague Helena Schmidt for reading one of the chapters during the maestro seminar. I appreciate their criticisms, challenges, and contributions, which helped strengthen this work. I would also like to thank other people who guided me at my initial study stage: Associate Prof. Nina Hoel, Associate Prof. Elizabeth Tveito, and Prof. Knut for their shortly arranged courses for methodology and dissertation writing skills. Moreover, I thank the Faculty of Theology, the Dean, Prof. Aud Valborg Tønnessen, the former leader of the Ph.D. Programme, Prof. Dianna Edelman, the present leader of the Ph.D. Programme, Prof. Marius Mjaaland, the Dean of Research, Prof. Anders Runessen, the Ph.D. Secretary, Dr. Helge, and all of the teaching staff, nonteaching staff, and students.

To the Amani and Agape-Upendo IR-VICOBA groups in ELCT-KoD, your Contextual Bible Study on the Kingdom of God and the poor texts was a main source of this work. Without it, I would not have been able to complete anything like this work. I am very grateful for your time, contributions, and kindness as I stayed among you in Tukuyu and Itete.

I am also grateful to the librarians at the Main Library (UiO), the Library of the Faculty of Theology UiO, the Iringa University Library, and the Tumaini-Makumira-Mbeya Centre Library and their team, for their willingness to assist me in accessing the literature for my study.

I am grateful to my Ph.D. colleagues: Gladys Wang Ekone, David Ocra-Stilles, Aba Anita, Helge Staxrud, Tonje Baugerud, and Helena Schmidt. Their presence, motivation, and encouragement played a great role in the accomplishment of this work in different capacities. Similarly, I am grateful to post-doc Kaia D. M.S Rønsdal. You people will never be forgotten.

I am very thankful to the Nordberg Parish, which spiritually nurtured me all the time I was studying in Oslo. I am grateful to Priest Kristin Stang Meløe, Priest Grundhild, and other priests as my pastors in the parish. My special thanks should go to Sister Aud Nottveit, who did the translations from Norwegian to English and sometimes to my own language Swahili. She made my being in church easy and communicable. Moreover, her several invitations to her home made me feel like having a mother in Norway. I will never forget her contributions.

Finally, yet importantly, I am indebted to my beloved wife, who has persevered with many difficulties stemming from my absence. Your invaluable contributions led this work to its completion. To you I say "Indagha sana." To my children, Noel, Alex the senior, Ansajiye, Alex the junior, and Baraka, I say "Asante sana."

List of Abbreviations and Acronyms

AIDS	Acquired Immune Deficiency Syndrome
ATR	African Traditional Religion
CBA	Central Bank of Africa
CBS	Contextual Bible Study
CCT	Christian Council of Tanzania
CDH	Council Designated Hospital
ELCT	Evangelical Lutheran Church in Tanzania
ELCT-KoD	Evangelical Lutheran Church in Tanzania-Konde Diocese
HIV	Human Immunodeficiency Virus
ILO	International Labour Organization
IMF	International Monetary Fund
IR-VICOBA	Interreligious Village Community Bank
MP	Member of Parliament
NBC Ltd	National Commerce Bank Limited
NT	New Testament
PCBS	Participant-Centered Contextual Bible Study
PLWHA	People Living with HIV/AIDS
REPOA	Research for Poverty Alleviation
SACCOS	Savings and Credit Cooperatives Societies
TF	Teologi Facultet
TNC	Transnational Corporation
Tshs	Tanzanian Shillings
UiO	University of Oslo
UN	United Nations
UN-FAO	United Nations Food Aid Organizations
UN-FOOD	United Nations Food
VICOBA	Village Community Bank

Table of Contents

Preface 5

Acknowledgments.. 6

List of Abbreviations and Acronyms 8

Chapter 1: Introduction 15
    1.1 Statement of the Problem and Aim of the Study................ 15
    1.2 Method 17
        1.2.1 A Short History of IR-VICOBA 18
        1.2.2 The Geographical Set-Up of the
              IR-VICOBA in Rungwe District........................ 18
    1.3 IR-VICOBA in the ELCT-Konde Diocese 19
    1.4 Background and Context... 21
        1.4.1 Liberation in Tanzania.. 21
        1.4.2 The Poor in Rural Tanzania and Bible Reading........... 26
    1.5 Liberation Theology Perspectives 29
    1.6 The Critical Reflection on Praxis 30
        1.6.1 The Poor in the Theology of Gutierrez and Sobrino 33
        1.6.2 Liberation Theology in the Theology of
              Gerald West 47
    1.7 Sources and Bible Study Participants................................ 55
    1.8 Organization of the Study... 55

Chapter 2: Facilitating Participant-Centered Contextual Bible
          Study with the IR-VICOBA Groups: Methodological
          Perspective.. 57
    2.1 The Methodology 57
    2.2 Why I Chose to Research on Participant-Centered
        Contextual Bible Study... 62
    2.3 Meeting with the IR-VICOBA Leaders: Meeting
        Amani IR-VICOBA Leaders in Tukuyu Town 66
    2.4 Traveling to Itete: Meeting the Leaders of the
        Upendo Agape IR-VICOBA Group................................. 69

2.5 Meeting with the IR-VICOBA Members Amani
IR-VICOBA.. 71
  2.5.1 Upendo (Agape) IR-VICOBA................................... 72
2.6 Research Ethics, Power Dynamics, and Positionality 73
2.7 Facilitation of the Participant-Centered
Contextual Bible Study in IR-VICOBA Groups 76
  2.7.1 The Facilitator's Task During the
  Participant-Centered Bible Study 78
2.8 The Problems Raised Within the IR-VICOBA
Participant-Centered Contextual Bible Study 79

Chapter 3: Presenting the IR-VICOBA Members' Reading of
the Synoptic Gospel Texts and the Poor................................. 83
3.1 Introduction 83
3.2 Discussion of Matthew 5:1-12 by Two Groups of
IR-VICOBA 86
  3.2.1 Participants and Their Discussion on Texts.............. 86
  3.2.2 Characters Review within the Text 87
  3.2.3 The Context Assessment 92
  3.2.4 Response of the IR-VICOBA Group Based
  on the Reading of the Beatitudes 96
3.3 The IR-VICOBA Members' Reading Intellectual
Activity: Mark 10:17-22.. 98
  3.3.1 Introduction.. 98
  3.3.2 Character Assessment during the Reading Process 99
  3.3.3 The Contextual Assessment.................................... 101
  3.3.4 The Response of the IR-VICOBA Based on
  the Reading Intellectual Activity 105
3.4 Discussion on the Reading Intellectual Activity:
Luke 16:19-31 107
  3.4.1 Introduction.. 107
  3.4.2 Character Assessment.. 108
  3.4.3 The Contextual Assessment.................................... 111
  3.4.4 The Response of the IR-VICOBA Based on
  the Bible Study Reading Intellectual Activity.............. 115
3.5 Conclusion 119

Chapter 4: Analytical/Thematic Interpretation of the Reading
of the Synoptic Gospels About the Poor by the
IR-VICOBA Groups.. 123
4.1 Introduction 123

4.2 Assessment of Characters by the IR-VICOBA
Members in Their Contextual Bible Study.......................... 124
    4.2.1 Jesus, the Poor, and the Rich..................................... 125
    4.2.2 The Downtrodden and the Blessings (Gifts).............. 128
    4.2.3 Classes of People Within the Context:
        The Last Judgment and Serving God Now 132
    4.2.4 Jesus, the Giver of Sight to the Blind 133
    4.2.5 Jesus, the Announcer of Freedom to Captives 135
    4.2.6 Jesus, the Teacher of Knowledge (Good News).......... 136
    4.2.7 Jesus and the Commandments................................... 137
4.3 Contextual Assessment of the IR-VICOBA
Members in their Participatory Bible Study....................... 139
    4.3.1 The Issue of Exploitation and Injustice in
        Society and the World at Large 139
    4.3.2 The Rich People, the Use of the Power of
        Money, and the Overriding of Justice........................ 142
    4.3.3 Disrespect Among Believers Because of
        Differences in Faith and Social Status 144
    4.3.4 The Issue of Gender as the Cause of Disrespect 147
    4.3.5 Environmental Degradation and Poverty 148
    4.3.6 The Gap Between the Rich and the Poor and
        Business Injustice... 152
    4.3.7 Lack of Knowledge as a New Blindness in
        the World Today 153
4.4 Conclusion 155

Chapter 5: The Analytical Interpretation of the Reading of the
IR-VICOBA Groups: Their Responses Based on
Their Contextual Bible Study 157
5.1 Introduction 157
    5.1.1 Self-Reliance and Empowerment 158
    5.1.2 The Dominating and Exploitative Nature of
        the Rich People in Society and the World 162
    5.1.3 Taking Care of the Needy: The Power of the
        Social Capital 163
    5.1.4 True Love Means Serving the Needy Neighbor........... 165
    5.1.5 Loving Wealth More Than Loving God and
        Neighbors Is Sin 165
    5.1.6 The Best Use of Resources: Empowering
        Through Teaching... 166
    5.1.7 Laziness as a Cause of Poverty 168

5.2 Conclusion 169

Chapter 6: The Profile of the IR-VICOBA Members' Bible
Reading in Tanzania: See-Judge-Act 171
    6.1 See-Judge-Act 171
    6.2 IR-VICOBA Participant Bible Study
        'See-Judge-Act' Is for Liberation 175
        6.2.1 The Fight for Economic Justice 178
        6.2.2 Social Justice and Gender Inequality in Society 181
        6.2.3 The Issue of Ecology and Environment Conservation .. 187
        6.2.4 The Issue of Caring for Others: Diaconia by
             the Victims of Poverty 189
    6.3 Conclusion 191

Chapter 7: See-Act-Judge: Theological Reflections on the
Reading of the IR-VICOBA Groups 193
    7.1 The Theology of Love 194
    7.2 Christological Approaches 195
        7.2.1 Jesus, the Empowerer and Liberator 198
        7.2.2 Jesus, the Teacher 201
    7.3 The IR-VICOBA Members' Theology on Poverty 202
    7.4 The Theology of Solidarity 204
    7.5 The Struggle Against Money-Theism 206
    7.6 Salvation Includes Human and Nonhuman Living Beings ... 208
        7.6.1 Enhancing Life 208
    7.7 Conclusion 210

Chapter 8: Liberation Theology of the IR-VICOBA Members
and the Tension Between the First and the Second Act 211
    8.1 IR-VICOBA Members Do Liberation Theology
        from Below 211
        8.1.1 The Relationship Between the Text and the
             Bible in the IR-VICOBA Groups 211
    8.2 From Local Perspective Liberation Theology to
        the Broad Perspective 220
    8.3 A Call for Further Research 224

Bibliography 225

Appendices

Appendix 1: Letter from NSD 233

Appendix 2: The Consent Form of the IR-VICOBA Groups 236

Index 238

Chapter 1:   Introduction

1.1   Statement of the Problem and Aim of the Study

This study investigates the specific Contextual Bible Study among particular groups of poor Christians in the Southwestern part of Tanzania. The main objective is to research and discuss the relationships between text and context when poor Christians undertake Contextual Bible Study. To this end, I use the Interreligious Community Bank Bible Study groups (IR-VICOBA)[1]. IR-VICOBA groups are groups of religious people who are relatively poor, mostly peasants or street vendors who earn just a loaf of bread each day through their businesses and low-paid work. These Christians come together to read the Bible with their pastors within the Evangelical Lutheran Church in Tanzania-Konde diocese.

They meet once a week to discuss the Bible readings on different themes within and outside of the Bible. At these meetings, the IR-VICOBA groups contribute at least a dollar per week. The money is kept in IR-VICOBA's account, and the account's records are well kept, so that, when a group member has problems or any other business, they are encouraged to come and take a loan. A member is allowed to borrow three times the amount of their savings and is expected to return the principal with a small amount of interest little by little each month (in many cases, the interest rate is about one-third of bank interest as agreed upon by the group). The IR-VICOBA groups are not allowed to have more than 30 members; groups are divided into smaller groups of five people who function as cells of the group. When they discuss matters, they use those cells. The cells function as follow-up cells for loans and interests among the respective members.[2] Section 1.2.3 provides more explanations of the IR-VICOBA. The project serves to answer the question: How do poor Christians in the Southwestern part of Tanzania reflect the relations between text and context in their Contextual Bible Study?

In my research, I observed how the IR-VICOBA, in their Contextual Bible Study, read the Bible together with the learned theologians in their groups. I studied how they relate their Bible study reading to the social context in which they are living.

---

[1] The acronym IR-VICOBA is an abbreviation of the phrase "Interreligious Village Community Bank." In Tanzania, there are many VICOBA groups that are not interreligious or religious-oriented. These VICOBA groups do not have Bible readings like the IR-VICOBA in the Konde diocese. Most VICOBA members are there only for economic and social empowerment.

[2] Unpublished Manuscript of IR-VICOBA, " Mwongozo wa kufundisha wawekezaji wa Vikundi vya IR-VICOBA" ("Instructions on How to Teach the IR-VICOBA"), unpublished material, p. 5.

Moreover, I searched how they relate their reading to their liberation from poverty and other predicaments that they are experiencing. Werner Jeanrond writes that

> Hermeneutics is more interested in the analysis of the dialectic between the reader and the text and in the effect of this dialectic for the self-understanding of the individual reader or groups of readers. Thus, hermeneutics reflects activities done through language rather than upon the history and grammar of particular historical languages.[3]

The IR-VICOBA members connect their reading in the text with their context. The context helps them to understand the text, and sometimes the texts help them understand the context. This will be reflected in this dissertation.

The research questions applied are the following. First, how do the members of the IR-VICOBA groups relate the relationship between the Bible and social reality? Second, what kind of Contextual Bible Study is practiced in the IR-VICOBA groups? Third, what are the main topics in their implied theology of the Bible readings?

The objective mentioned above and the study questions led me to probe how this type of Bible reading is used. One crucial aspect in the discussion will be how this kind of Contextual Bible Study (theology from below) is profiled, compared to other Contextual Bible Study readings, especially that developed by Gerald West in South Africa. Moreover, the works of Gustavo Gutierrez and Jon Sobrino[4] and Ernesto Cardernal on the theology of nonpersons, the crucified, and the poor, respectively, will be of much use. The issue of reflection and practices (praxis) on social, political, and economic reality have been viewed as a contributing factor to their liberation compared with the IR-VICOBA members' Contextual Bible Study. Their contextual theologies here serve as a working tool for this research.

---

3 Werner G. Jeanrond, *Theological Hermeneutics: Development and Significance* (London: SCM Press, 1994), p. 7.

4 Gustavo Gutierrez and Jon Sobrino are Latin American Theologians and Roman Catholic Priests. Gutierrez is a native of Peru (Helives) and worked among the poor of Rimac, a Lima slum. He is a Professor of Theology at the Catholic University. He is an author of *On Job: God-Talk and the Suffering of the Innocent: The Power of the Poor in History, We Drink from Our Own Wells, The Truth Shall Make You Free*; and *Las casas: In search of the Poor*. .Jon Sobrino worked in El Salvador. His books are Christology at the crossroads; Jesus in in Latin America; Spirituality of liberation; The murder and martyrdom of the Jesuits, Jesus the liberator; Christ the liberator and The Principle of Mercy.

1.2   Method

This study uses mainly field research as a method of collecting data. In the field, I used the observation method to collect data.[5] I observed how the IR-VICOBA members came up with their contextual interpretation from their context to the texts on the Kingdom of God in their "participant-centered Contextual Bible Study."[6] This interconnection between the texts and the context is the core topic of my research. In the field research, I attended the Bible study as a silent and passive listener, recorded and tried to perceive any nonverbal communication within the Bible study.

The research follows Bible study readings in the specially chosen groups in the role of silent participant observant. I chose the texts to be interpreted, but as a researcher, I never actively participated in their interpretation. I chose New Testament texts on the Kingdom of God and the poor for the groups to discuss. Knowing the people and their language, as both an insider and an outsider in the Bible study, I just recorded their interpretations and nonverbal communications in the groups during their contextual Bible study.

The reason for this focus is, first, that the Kingdom of God as portrayed in the Synoptic Gospels and as preached by Jesus proclaims justice, equality, righteousness, and the love of God to the poor by focusing on the liberation of the whole human being (mentally, physically, and spiritually). Furthermore, in the interpretation, I connect the kind of Bible reading of the IR-VICOBA members to their overall struggle in fighting poverty. The question is how and in which way one can see a connection between the fight against poverty and the specific Contextual Bible Study. In the community of believers, where people confront many socioeconomic difficulties, they try to fight to liberate themselves from those difficulties rule their lives. These difficulties may be a lack of justice, equality, rights, and love. When they come together as people of faith who use the Bible, they seem to use those texts to justify, measure, reflect, and commit more to their endeavors in socioeconomic reality. Sometimes the context shows a way forward or justifies and cements their endeavors for liberation and human emancipation, acting as a criticism of the Bible's texts. Both ways serve the liberation of the people. The relationship between the texts and the socioeconomic reality has meaning for the liberation of the people and the liberation of Biblical texts' interpretation.

Turning back to my main research question – How do poor Christians in the Southwestern part of Tanzania reflect the relations between text and context in their

---

5   The field research and observation are well discussed in Chapter 2 of the methodological section. Here, they are presented as a way of introducing them.
6   Gerald O. West, *Contextual Bible Study* (Pietermarizburg: Cluster Publication, 1993), p. 23.

Contextual Bible Study? – I also probe how Contextual Bible Study is empirically vital within the context of economically oppressed people like the IR-VICOBA members, and how it differs and relates with the Southern African and the Latin American theology of liberation. I discuss this more in Chapter 6, where I discuss the profile of the IR-VICOBA.

1.2.1 A Short History of IR-VICOBA

The inception of VICOBA occurred in Niger through *CARE Niger* in 1991. It was called Mata Masu Dubura (MMD). The aim was to empower women economically and socially. The process focused more on economic and social empowerment than on religious principles. VICOBA was introduced to Tanzania and its island of Zanzibar in 2000 by *We CARE Tanzania*. From there, many groups of women and youths in churches, mosques, and societal setups adapted the system to their respective environments for economic and social purposes. In 2011, the religious VICOBA groups met and formulated the now-called Interreligious Village Community Bank (IR-VICOBA) with the same intentions of dealing with economic and social challenges.[7]

1.2.2 The Geographical Set-Up of the IR-VICOBA in Rungwe District

The rural location of the IR-VICOBA is in Rungwe district, which lies between the latitudes 80 30' East at 90 30' South of the Equator and longitudes 330 and 340 East of Greenwich Meridian. The District shares borders with Kyela District in the South, Ileje District in the West, Makete District in the East, and Mbeya District in the North. The District headquarters is situated at Tukuyu, about 72 km from Mbeya District along Uyole Ibanda Highway, which passes Kyela District on route to Malawi.[8]

The District covers a total of 2,221 km^2, 1,668.259 km^2 or 75% of which is flat land. The remaining area is covered by 44.5 km^2 of forest and 498.3 km^2 of mountainous and residential area. The District covers 3.5% of the total Regional land area. The climate condition of the District is a function of altitude. The District is mountainous, with Rungwe Mountain and Livingstone ranges rising from an altitude of 770 m to 2265 m above sea level. The rainfall average ranges from 900 mm

---

7 "Mwongozo wa kufundisha wawekezaji wa Vikundi vya IR-VICOBA" ("Instructions on How to Teach the IR-VICOBA"), unpublished material, p. 1. See also Marie Ahlen, "Rural Member-Based Microfinance Institutions: A Field Study Assessing the Impacts of SACCOS and VICOBA in Babati District, Tanzania," Sodertorns University-School of Life Science (2012), pp. 13–14.

8 https://rungwedc.go.tz/history.

in the low-land areas to 2,700 mm in the highlands. Temperatures are generally modest and range from 18–25°C throughout the year.[9]

1.3   IR-VICOBA in the ELCT-Konde Diocese

In 2014, the directors for Women, Christian Education, Planning and Development, and Youth Departments were formed within the ELCT-Konde Diocese (ELCT-KoD). They wanted to include the VICOBA teachings within their groups across the entire diocese. The leaders gathered and jointly invited a facilitator from the Council of Churches of Tanzania (CCT) to demonstrate how to include the VICOBA in their Bible studies. ELCT-KoD is a system whereby groups of youths, women, and choirs meet together for Bible studies. These directors wanted to undertake Bible study while also securing money for the IR-VICOBA. Now, the objectives had increased. They sat as a Bible study group for 1 hour and a second hour for VICOBA.[10] Many parishes have IR-VICOBA, and their pastors are facilitators of those groups in the session on Bible Reading or Learning. However, during the microcredit session (VICOBA), pastors are just members, and its gatekeepers are the Chairperson, the Secretary, the Treasurer, and two Bookkeepers.

The increased objectives of IR-VICOBA have not undermined their Bible study objectives, but they have broadened their reasons for participation and created a greater awareness of their Bible and their context. The two main objectives of IR-VICOBA are to enable members to know the advantage of interfaith relations for creating a peaceful and lovely community; and to empower members of IR-VICOBA religiously, economically, and socially.[11]

Economically, IR-VICOBA members earn very little money, the average being less than $2 a day. That wage level qualifies them to be below the poverty standard established by the UN Food and Agricultural Organization. Such individuals depend primarily on agricultural pursuits and raising livestock. This approach does not yield much income, even in an area with adequate rainfall.[12] Some are street

---

9   Ibid.
10 Explanation from Pastor Melckzedeck Mbilinyi and Alice Henry Mtui after the IR-VICOBA session on 20 February 2017.
11 "Mwongozo wa kufundisha wawekezaji wa Vikundi vya IR-VICOBA" ("Instructions on How to Teach the IR-VICOBA"), unpublished material, p. 2.
12 José Luis Sánchez García, Sustainability as an Innovative Key Element, Another Perspective to Rethink the Problem of Hunger and Poverty in the World, *Journal of Innovation & Knowledge* 3, no. 2 (2018).According to a UN-FAO report in 2017, most people who suffer from hunger in the world live in developing countries. According to statistics from the UN-FAO in 2016, 815 million people go to bed hungry every night. This is up from 777 million in 2015. 98% of these people live in developing countries, and 75% live in rural areas, especially in Asia and Africa, where they rely

vendors who sell small goods to help support their families. Other workers produce cash crops like coffee, tea, and cocoa. However, through their agents, TNC buys their crops and adjusts prices, which do not adequately remunerate the farmers. The mark-up of their inputs sometimes provides less than their actual costs. These peasants have no capital to purchase even simple machines. For instance, those who grow tea, which must be picked once or twice a week, would need simple machines for picking the tea leaves. An example is that, during extended periods of rain, they are unable to harvest all of their tea leaves. Thus, a variety of economic factors result in their average daily income of less than $2 a day.

Religiously and socially, most of the VICOBA people are voiceless. For instance, in their parishes, they participate very little in the decision-making process of their churches. There is a Swahili saying, "*Masikini hana sauti*," which literally means "the poor are voiceless." When poor people seek to provide ideas in church and society, their suggestions are often not respected. Furthermore, their ideas are seen as valueless despite how they are presented. Church leaders tend to listen to people who contribute more to the church and social functions, for example, to those who contribute more during church fundraising, in marriage ceremonies, and other social contributions.

Often politicians seek support from indigent people like the IR-VICOBA members. They sometimes bribe them for their votes through modest monetary payments. Being less educated, the underprivileged may respond as requested, thereby promoting bad government by selecting corrupt leaders. Most rural people in Southwest Tanzania are deprived of excellent infrastructure and good services because of their remote locales. Politicians manipulate the rural population, albeit with little benefit for their communities.

There are many different groups of IR-VICOBA. These groups are self-monitored without the ELCT-KoD directly interfering with their Bible study and the socioeconomic themes they discuss.[13] However, pastors and evangelists in those areas are members of the IR-VICOBA alongside the elected leaders, who are gatekeepers. In the participant-centered Contextual Bible Study, leaders are chosen to facilitate the Bible study each time they meet. IR-VICOBA groups establish permanent leaders with different responsibilities. It is interesting to note that other members who are not Lutherans are invited to join the groups since the ELCT-KoD does not adequately control them. The ELCT-KoD is just nurturing these groups and coordinates other matters related to their interaction with outside people. For example, if the group aims to invite someone for fundraising purposes, the ELCT-KoD is

---

on locally grown food. See also Daniel Franklin Pilario, *Globalization and the Church of the Poor*, vol. 2015/3, Concilium (London: SCM Press, 2015), p. 19.

13 "Mwongozo wa kufundisha wawekezaji wa Vikundi vya IR-VICOBA" ("Instructions on How to Teach the IR-VICOBA"), unpublished material.

used as an inviting and hosting institution. I focus further on IR-VICOBA in the second methodological chapter.

1.4 Background and Context

1.4.1 Liberation in Tanzania

In this subsection, I want to introduce some of the essential recent history of Tanzania connected to liberation from ignorance, poverty, and diseases. This serves to enhance understanding of the IR-VICOBA people in Southwestern Tanzania and their endeavor of fighting against poverty.

During the time when Tanzania was practicing Socialism, by Nyerere's time, and Nyerere[14], the first president, fought the same enemies: ignorance, poverty, and diseases, declaring that *Ujamaa* by then was a liberation ideology to his people by his people, as is discussed in this section. This situation made some scholars from the West, like Per Frostin,[15] perceive this ideology as *liberation theology*. Not only Frostin but other theologians from Tanzania and elsewhere[16] implicitly perceived it similarly. Besides, there is a significant change in ideology and perception between the two times, although the enemies have remained the same.

Tanzania is among the developing countries in the world, and, according to the census of 2014, it has a population of almost 50.7 million. According to the headcount ratio of 2012, those of the poor population total 28.2 million of the 33.3 million living in rural areas.[17] These poor people in the Tanzanian rural areas are those who experience difficulty having a piece of bread each day, sending their children to school, failing to get proper treatment when they get ill, and dying before their time.

Tanzania started its liberation process as a nation immediately after independence, where it subscribed to the socialist ideology to liberate its citizens. The first

---

14 Julius Kambarage Nyerere was the first President of Tanzania after its independence in 1961.
15 Per Frostin, *Liberation Theology in Tanzania and South Africa: A First World Interpretation*, vol. 42, Studia Theologica Lundensia (Lund: Lund University Press, 1988).
16 Peter A. S.Kijanga, *Ujamaa and the Role of the Church in Tanzania* (Arusha: Evangelical Lutheran Church in Tanzania, 1978), p. 14. See also David Westlund, *Ujamaa Na Dini: A Study of Some Aspects of Socirty and Religion in Tanzania* (Stockholm: Universssity of Stockholm, 1980), p. 73. See Also Wilson Niwagila, *From the Catacomb to Self-Governing Church: A Case Study of the African Initiative and Participation of the Foreign Missions in the History of the Northwestern Diocese of the Evangelical Lutheran Church in Tanzania 1890–1965* (Hamburg: Verlag an der Lottbek 1991), p. 402.
17 Rural Poverty Portal at http://www.ruralpovertyportal.org/country/statistics/tags/tanzania. A point to note: The population likely grew to more than 60 million in 2019 using the population rate of 3.8%.

president declared: "We have been oppressed a great deal, we have been exploited a great deal, and we have been disregarded a great deal. It is our weakness that has led to our being oppressed, exploited and disregarded. We want a revolution – a revolution, which brings us to an end of our weakness, so that we are never again exploited, oppressed, or humiliated."[18] These words of President Nyerere aimed at liberating his people from poverty, illiteracy, and diseases. Nyerere believed in work and sharing, as he further writes, "The standard of living of masses of our people is shamefully low. However, if every man and woman in the country takes up the challenges and works to the limit of their ability for the good of the whole society, Tanganyika will prosper; and that prosperity will be shared by all her people."[19] Nyerere made clear what type of socialism he was targeting to build a nation of equal people, as in a familyhood.[20] He continues to write,

> '*Ujamaa*' then, or 'Familyhood,' describes our Socialism. It is opposed to capitalism, which seeks to build a happy society on the basis of the exploitation of man by man; and it is equally opposed to doctrinaire socialism which seeks to build its happy society on a philosophy of inevitable conflict between man and man.[21]

One finds brief parts of Nyerere's idea and belief in *Ujamaa* as a person reads the Arusha declaration and TANU's creed[22] and objectives[23] on Socialism and

---

18 Julius K. Nyerere, *Freedom and Socialism = Uhuru Na Ujamaa: A Selection from Writings and Speeches 1965–1967*, Eastern Africa (Dar es Salaam: Oxford University Press, 1968), p. 235.
19 *Ujamaa: Essays on Socialism*, Ujamaa (London: Oxford University Press, 1968), p. 9.
20 Ibid, p. 106. The term 'familyhood' here implies the African family, where the family members thought of themselves as one, and all their language and behaviour emphasized their unity. The basic goods of life were 'our food,' 'our land,' 'and our cattle.'
21 Ibid., p. 12.
22 Ibid., p. 13. TANU's creeds were the beliefs that (a) all human being are equal; (b) every individual has a right to dignity and respect; (c) every citizen is an integral part of the nation and has a right to take an equal part in Government at local, region, and national level; (d) every citizen has the right to freedom of expression, of movement, of religious belief and of association within the context of the law; I every individual has the right to receive from society protection of his life and of property held according to law; (f) every individual has the right to receive a just return for his labor; (g) all citizens together possess all the natural resources of the country in trust for their descendants; (h) in order to ensure economic justice, the state must have effective control over the principal means of production; and (i) it is the responsibility of the state to intervene actively in the economic life of the nation so as to ensure the well-being of all citizens and thus to prevent the exploitation of one person by another or one group by another, so as to prevent the accumulation of wealth to an extent inconsistent with the existence of classic society.
23 Ibid., p. 14. The objectives of the TANU were (a) to consolidate and maintain the independence of this country and the freedom of its people; (b) to safeguard the inherent dignity of the individual in accordance with the Universal Declaration of human Rights; (c) to ensure that this country shall be

self-reliance.[24] This is how *Ujamaa* was reflected in Tanzania. These creeds and objectives of *Ujamaa* were taught in all levels of the schools, from primary school to university level. Those who did not have a chance to attend those schools were taught in adult education. *Ujamaa* was decisive for the liberation of all citizens from poverty, ignorance, and diseases – which were said to be the nation's greatest enemies. According to Nyerere, education must lead to the total liberation of citizens and larger society by creating a sustained commitment to cooperative work, equality, and development. In this issue of education, as a liberation, Nyerere maintained:

> [Education] must also prepare young people for work they will be called upon to do in the society which exists in Tanzania – a rural society where improvement will depend largely upon the efforts of the people in agriculture and village development … It must produce good farmers; it has to prepare people for their responsibilities as free workers and citizens in a free and democratic society; albeit a largely rural society. They have to be able to think for themselves, to make judgement on all issues affecting them; they have to be able to interpret the decisions made through the democratic institutions of our society and to implement them in light of the local circumstances peculiar to where they happen to live.[25]

The Tanzanian ideology of *Ujamaa* resulted in the first Ecumenical Association of Third World Theologians (EATWOT) which took place in Tanzania in 1976. Per Frostin quotes the word of the Father of Liberation Theology, Gustavo Gutierrez, in the meeting:

> The first country to host these meetings (of EATWOT) was Tanzania, a small country inhabited by a poor, very poor population. Its people bear the marks of a harsh past

---

governed by the democratic socialist government of the people; (d) to cooperate with all political parties in Africa engaged in the liberation of all Africa; (e) to see that the Government mobilizes all the resources of this country toward the elimination of poverty, ignorance and diseases; (f) to see that the Government actively assists in the formation and maintenance of cooperative organization; (g) to see that, wherever possible, the Government itself directly participates in the economic development of this country; (h) to see that the Government gives equal opportunity to all men and women irrespective of race, religion, or status; (i) to see that Government eradicates all types of exploitation, intimidation, discrimination, bribery, and corruption; (j) to see that the Government exercises effective control over the principal means of production and pursues policies that facilitate the way to collectives ownership of the resources of this country; (k) to see that the Government cooperates with other states in Africa in bringing about African unity; (l) to see that Government works tirelessly toward world peace and security through the United Nations Organization.

24 Ibid., p. 13.
25 Julius K. Nyerere, *Education for Self-Reliance* (Dar es Salaam, Nairobi, London, New York: Oxford University Press, 1968).

involving colonial rule and racial contempt. But Tanzania has also shown much courage and creativity in undertaking a thoroughgoing process of liberation. Exploiting their native African tradition, they have set out on their construct a just and humane order. This accounts for the disproportionate moral authority exercised by the small nation and its president, Julius Nyerere, in the concert of nations. The achievements of the Tanzania people enable us to perceive and concretely experience the significance of the poor in history.[26]

If this was a situation in 1976, Tanzania used the liberation of its people to build a nation of equal and liberated people.[27] Writing on liberation theology in Tanzania and South Africa, Per Frostin called this type of liberation a "Third World experience,"[28] where, he indicated, "This brand of socialism understands itself as an ethic of liberation and emphasizing values which are essential in the struggle against colonialism and neo-colonialism."[29]

During this time, Tanzanians lived in Ujamaa village, owning most of their properties together. The government provided the necessary common goods, like schools, health facilities, infrastructures, and subsidies, to the peasants and Ujamaa village's farms. At that time, 90% of Tanzanians knew how to write and read, had free medication, and enjoyed free education. The Nyerere regime constructed several industries that aimed to make Tanzania more independent.

The question one may ask is why the significant levels of poverty shown above are still there? Did liberation under *Ujamaa* fail? If *Ujamaa* aimed at liberating the poor in a rural area, what went wrong to move Tanzania to shift from *Ujamaa* to the liberalization of trade policies? Shivji writes:

> I do not know if our world is better than it was 30 years ago. However, I do know that neither our country nor continent is. Structural Adjustment Programmes of the 1980s destroyed the little achievements in education, health, life expectancy, and literacy that we had made during the nationalist period. Neo-liberal policies of the last 10 years have destroyed the small industrial sector-textiles, oil, leather, farm implements and cashew nut factories – which had been built during the period of import – substitutions. Most important of all, we have lost the respect, dignity and humanity and the right to think for ourselves that independence presented. The larger majority of our people, workers

---

26 Frostin, *Liberation Theology in Tanzania and South Africa: A First World Interpretation*, 42, p. 19.
27 Meshack Edward Njinga, *The Shift from Ujamaa to Globalization as a Challenge to Evangelical Lutheran Church in Tanzania*, 1 vol. (Oslo: Theology Faculty, 2003), pp. 75–79.
28 Frostin, *Liberation Theology in Tanzania and South Africa: A First World Interpretation*, 42, p. 19.
29 Ibid., p. 34.

and peasants, as the ARUSHA Declaration dignified them, have been transformed into 'nameless poor.'[30]

Ujamaa did a lot by uniting the Tanzanians and making them live in rural areas. However, under the world economic crisis in the 1980s and 1990s, Tanzania found itself burdened by much debt and suffering as a result from the structural crisis of the IMF and World Bank. However, we now find the poor are still increasing in number. The number of poor people in rural Tanzania increases day after day because even the new policy is full of injustice. It remunerates much less to peasants than it does to business people and the TNC from outside of the country.

In the meeting held in Tutzing, Germany, the then ELCT director for Development, Rogate Mshana, mentions five causes of the government reforms which had long-term impacts on the Tanzanian economy:
1. The first and second round of oil price increases in 1973 and 1979;
2. The sharp decline in terms of trade since the end of the coffee boom in 1977;
3. Recurring poor climatic conditions;
4. The breakdown of the East African community in 1977, which necessitated substantial investments to provide service that was formerly rendered by the community using facilities located in Kenya;
5. The Idd Amin war imposed on Tanzania, which cost US $500 million.[31]

The new poor Christians who were formerly under *Ujamaa* – which external forces stopped from being liberated from poverty, diseases, and ignorance – are now going back to the 'book' they believe in – the Bible – to reread it for more liberation and in a new way and a new, challenging context. However, they are now challenged by the perplexity of trade liberalization, which causes them the difficulties of poverty, diseases, and ignorance again. Moreover, these poor people are more religious than one might think. In the rural areas, most people are Christians, Moslems, or members of African traditional religion. Those who follow a religion with sacred text, especially Christians, use the Bible in their daily study; they perceive and receive it as the Word of God, and sometimes that is the only book they have in their homes. Taking Christians as an example, they read the Bible in their homes,

---

30 Shivji, quoted by Athuman J. Liviga, "Economic and Political Liberation in Tanzania and Its Unintended Outcomes," *East Africa Social Research Review* 27.1, Organization from Social Science Research in Eastern and Southern Africa, pp. 1–31, here p. 7.
31 Rogate R. Mshana, "The Social and Economic Situation in Tanzania and Response of Civil Society. A Workshop of Civil Society in Africa: The Case of Tanzania Economic Situation," Tutzing 21–23 (1997), pp. 1–2. The reasons given here for reforms are also the reasons that indicate why poverty persisted in Tanzania during that period possible to this moment.

they also attend Bible study groups, and sometimes they can have more than one group.

These people read the Bible and reflect on the Kingdom of God and the poor. They read texts like "the Kingdom of God is for the poor" in the Beatitudes (Matthew 5:3; Luke 6:20), which make them reflect more and question the Bible, in light of their miserable situation.

1.4.2   The Poor in Rural Tanzania and Bible Reading

As indicated earlier, the poor in rural Tanzania diligently read the Bible, which might be the only book they have in their homes. They attend Bible studies to deepen their Biblical understanding; some attend more than one Bible study group weekly. The former ELCT Presiding Bishop once wrote that, nowadays, there is a revival of reading the Word of God. Christians are encouraged to read the Bible, to reflect on it in their groups, and to put what they read into practice.[32] The Presiding Bishop meant that the Church should encourage the members to read the Bible. He possibly wanted all Church readers and members to ensure they emphasized reading the Bible and putting it into practice. Below, I present several Bible studies that reflect upon my area of research.

Traditional Bible Reading in the Evangelical Lutheran Church in the Tanzania-Konde Diocese

In the Evangelical Lutheran Church in Tanzania-Konde diocese (ELCT-KoD), I am familiar with several types of Bible studies, including Alhamis Bible study, house-to-house Bible study, fellowship Bible study, women's group Bible studies, and youth-group Bible study, some of which are facilitator-oriented. These types of Bible study are among the Bible studies Elia Mligo calls "traditional Bible studies,"[33] since they still follow the 'facilitator-centered' method Paulo Freire calls the "banking concept of education," where students become depositories, and the teacher is a depositor.[34]

---

32   Kanisa La Kiinjili la Kilutheri Tanzania, *Nyumba Kwa Nyumba: Mwongozo Wa Masomo Ya Ibada, 2015* (Moshi: Moshi Printing Press, 2015), p. vii. The translation is mine from Kiswahili to English. These words of the Presiding Bishop Alex Gehaz Malasusa were written as a Preface to that book, which is used by Christians in the house-to-house Bible study.

33   Elia Shabani Mligo, "Jesus and the Stigmatized: Reading the Gospel of John in a Context of HIV/AIDS-Related Stigmatization in Tanzania," (2009), p. 117.

34   Paulo Freire, *Pedagogy of the Oppressed*, New rev. 20th-anniversary ed., Pedagogia Del Oprimido (New York: Continuum, 1993), pp. 52–53.

The previously mentioned Bible studies from the ELCT-KoD are examples I am familiar with. Other denominations, like the Moravians, the Roman Catholics, the Anglican Church, and the Pentecostal churches, too, have their own traditional Bible studies similar to those mentioned above. Some people meet in many groups hoping to meet their challenges spiritually, economically, and socially. Hasu puts it this way: "It asserts that God has met all human needs in suffering and death of Christ and that every Christian should share the victory of Christ over sin, sickness, and poverty. A true believer has the right to the blessing of health and wealth, and these can be obtained through a positive confession of faith."[35] Hasu is right to suggest that, since people read the Bible at home and convene in Bible study groups, they seek knowledge and the meaning of life by propagating their faith. This may be a rejuvenation of Max Weber's 'Protestant ethic,' where people were urged to accumulate wealth even though they were against consumption. Being rich became a sign of being blessed and saved – and not one of excessive use of profit but to fulfill God's will on Earth, something Weber calls "the ultimate purpose of life."[36] However, these underprivileged Christians in rural Tanzania do not know much about capitalism, though some have limited experience with capitalism because of Tanzania's socialist history. Those who remember the socialist history tend to carry a negative opinion about capitalism.

Most participants in rural areas attend different Bible study groups to seek meaning in life, which differs from the Calvinists, whom Weber describes as having the Protestant ethic. When these people acquire money, they consume *and* reinvest, not like Calvinists according to Weber, who only invest. Therefore, the poor in rural Tanzania go to those Bible study groups hoping to find solutions to their problems, poverty being the most significant problem. I now turn to discussing each sort of Bible study briefly.

Alhamis Bible Study

The Evangelical Lutheran Church in Tanzania-Konde diocese (ELCT-KoD) runs this Bible study, where members meet Thursdays for Bible study. The pastors are responsible for leading this Bible study or inviting another pastor to teach on the selected theme. In most cases, pastors are the teachers of the Bible studies. The emphasis lies on the 'themes' the host pastor prepares. The parish pastor is also

---

35 Päivi Hasu, "World Bank & Heavenly Bank in Poverty & Prosperity: The Case of Tanzanian Faith Gospel 1," *Review of African Political Economy* 33, no. 110 (2006), pp. 679–692 (here p. 679).
36 Max Weber and Anthony Giddens, *The Protestant Ethic and the Spirit of Capitalism* (orig.: Die Protestantische Ethik und der Geist des Kapitalismus) (London: Routledge, 1992), pp. xi–xii and p. 18.

responsible for making the timetable and inviting knowledgeable persons to teach members in the parish.

In Alhamis Bible Study, the members convene for one to two hours for Bible study, praises, and prayers. However, the methods are frequently one-sided, with the 'expert' spoon-feeding knowledge to the others. Class members are encouraged to ask questions for more clarification and understanding. Prayer accompanies the Alhamis Bible Study. The prayer sessions frequently focus on the sick, travelers, impoverished people, widows, and orphans. They also pray for people in authority so that to continue to exercise their authority with the wisdom of God.

House-to-House Bible Study

The Evangelical Lutheran Church in Tanzania (ELCT) administers this type of Bible study. Directives exist regarding how to conduct the Bible study church-wide. In this Bible study, 5 to 12 households gather in one Christian's house to discuss the Word of God to strengthen each other in faith, prayer, and knowledge of the Word of God.[37] Each group has its own leadership that plans and leads the Bible study. The designated leaders are the Chairperson, Assistant Chairperson, Secretary, and Treasurer.[38]

In these groups, one member (or a few members) read the given text, and afterwards they discuss what they have read. Everyone is encouraged to share their thoughts and perceptions and to ask questions. Everyone is to be respected within the Bible study. The difficult questions are supposed to be sent to the pastor or another Church leader.[39] These types of Bible studies encourage full participation. A lectionary, prepared by the Evangelical Lutheran Church in Tanzania and its weekly themes, is used.

There are many cells within one parish, and they are divided so that people can quickly meet within 30 to 45 minutes from their respective homes. The church elders generally appoint facilitators to lead these Bible studies. The house-to-house Bible study is also accompanied by prayers and intercession. The attendees also

---

37 Tanzania, *Nyumba Kwa Nyumba: Mwongozo Wa Masomo Ya Ibada*, 2015, p. ix. The objectives of house-to-house Bible study are 1. To encourage and strengthen the spirit of worshipping God together; 2. To encourage and strengthen Christians teaching of faith in the Word of God, sacraments, and intercession; 3. To enable Christians to know each other and strengthen the unity of the church (John 17:11; Acts 4:32; 1 Cor. 12:12-27); 4. To motivate Christians to grow in education, health, and development; 5. To develop the spirit of love and helping each other; 6. To work together, to give advice on spiritual matters, peace, and security; 7. To strengthen each other to like to do mission and evangelism; 8. To help Christians to grow spiritually and avoid them to turning to other spiritual sects and other denominations which are emerging every day; 9. To pray for one another.
38 Ibid., p. ix.
39 Ibid, p. viii.

pray for different prayer requests, as found in the Alhamis Bible study. In this Bible study, they also give an offering, which is kept in the account of the cell for use with social problems such as death, sickness, wedding ceremonies, and assisting the needy.

Church Groups Bible Studies: Youth and Women Bible Study

The youth groups and women's groups have their Bible studies Tuesdays and Wednesdays, respectively. They meet and follow the pattern of the Alhamis Bible Study. They set aside Tuesday for Bible study and prayers, while other days are for choir practices. When they meet for instruction, two presenters are present, one from within the parish and one from outside the parish. They discuss different themes like friendship, marriage, courtship, economy, and development as well as Bible themes that interest youth. They sometimes invite other professionals like doctors, lawyers, nurses, economists, and accountants to teach them topics relative to their professions.

The women also gather to discuss different themes, using the same method described for the Alhamis Bible Study, inviting a knowledgeable speaker. The women's Bible studies are well attended. In the Rungwe District in Tanzania, women outnumber men and as such constitute the pillar of the Christian Church.

The examples given above provide an overview of the regular Bible study process within different Tanzanian denominations. Church parishioners study the Bible hoping that their Bible study can provide solutions to their daily needs. The same process within the IR-VICOBA seeks to fight poverty through its Bible study process. I further discuss these findings in the methodological chapter (Chapter 2). Note that I have not included the Fellowship Bible Study because it is an ecumenical fellowship in which Christians from different denominations gather for Bible study.

1.5 Liberation Theology Perspectives

This section addresses my discussion of liberation theology as a tool for interpreting my data. I chose two groups of liberation theologians: The first group is the Latin American theologians; the second group is from Africa. I chose Gerald West and the Ujamaa Contextual Bible Study to represent this latter group and Gustavo Gutierrez and Jon Sobrino to represent the first group, although I know there are others, like Juan Luis Segundo, Leonard Boff, and Clodovis Boff. Especially as they describe the poor, Gutierrez and Sobrino keep similar track of their theology on liberation, mainly when they discuss the preferential option of the poor, the principle of mercy, or Jesus as a liberator. The classical Latin American theologians believe that liberation theology is a reflection on praxis, meaning the reflection of a reflection and the practices of poor believers, the theology of the nonpersons, as I discuss in the following sections. West and the Ujamaa Contextual Bible Study come from Africa and deal with the liberation theology bottom-up from an African perspective. My interest in using these theologians is that they all use the Bible as a liberating tool for the underprivileged, although they differ on substantial issues concerning *how* to make this interpretation. For Latin American classical liberation theologians, the first act of reflection and practices occur in the life and the commitment of the poor as they confront their socioeconomic or (sociopolitical) reality. The second act involves these people coming together, reflecting on those reflections and actions in light of the Word of God. The discussion on these differences is presented extensively within this section on the liberation theology perspective. Moreover, the Latin American theologians are the fathers of liberation theology. For West, all three stages are carried out within the Bible study venue, as I explain further in the discussion on their implementing theology from below.

Further, I show that, according to liberation theologians, the poor are the source of liberation theology. They employ "see-judge-act"[40] accordingly when facing their socioeconomic reality, which is full of injustice, and once again when they meet together to reflect according to the Word of God where theology takes its part. However, this study reveals that the Latin American liberation theologians, particularly Gutierrez and Sobrino, have two acts: First, since when the poor see, judge, and act in their context; second, when they meet in the Bible study, they act in light of the Word of God. For Gerald West, see, judge, and act moments occur within the Bible study venue, then going to the context.

1.6 The Critical Reflection on Praxis

Liberation theology has always focused on the responsibility of reflecting critically on praxis and social reality. Describing critical reflection on praxis, Gutierrez argues, "Theology must be a critical reflection on humankind, on the basic human principles."[41] To emphasize this attitude, Gutierrez continues, saying critical reflection refers to "a clear and critical attitude regarding economic and socio-cultural

---

[40] The explanation of "see, judge act" is given in the following section under the heading "Critical Reflection on Praxis."

[41] Gustavo Gutiérrez, *A Theology of Liberation: History, Politics, and Salvation*, Revised version. ed., Teología De La Liberación (London: SCM Press, 1988), p. 9. See also Jon Sobrino, *The Principle of Mercy: Taking the Crucified People from the Cross*, Principio-Misercordia (Maryknoll, NY: Orbis Books, 1994), pp. 37–39.

issues in the life and reflections of the Christians community."[42] To emphasize the theory, Gutierrez writes, "It is – at least ought to be – real charity, action, and commitment to the service of others. Theology is a reflection, a critical reflection attitude. Theology follows; it is a second step."[43] In many writings by Gutierrez, he comments on theology as a second act following on from commitment:

> Theology is a reflection – that is, it is a second act, a turning back a re-flecting, that comes after action. Theology is not a first; the commitment is first. Theology is the understanding of the commitment, and the commitment is action. The central element is charity, which involves commitment, while theology arrives later.[44]

Latin American liberation theologians describe this pattern in their writing. The second act is reflecting on the light of the Word of God – what one has acted on before. Moreover, he maintains:

> As a critical reflection on society and the church, theology is an understanding which both grows and, in a certain sense, changes. If the commitment of the Christian community, in fact, takes different forms throughout history, the understanding which accompanies the vicissitudes of this commitment will be constantly renewed and will take untrodden paths.[45]

Brown, quoting from Gutierrez's Job, writes: "Contemplation and practice together make up the first act; theologizing is a second act. We must first establish our-

---

42 Gutiérrez, *A Theology of Liberation: History, Politics, and Salvation*. See also Alfred T. Hennelly, *Liberation Theology: A Documentary History* (Maryknoll, NY: Orbis Books, 1990), p. 63.
43 Gutiérrez, *A Theology of Liberation: History, Politics, and Salvation*, p. 9. See also Sobrino, *The Principle of Mercy: Taking the Crucified People from the Cross*, p. 30.
44 Hennelly, *Liberation Theology: A Documentary History*, p. 63. See also Gutiérrez, *A Theology of Liberation: History, Politics, and Salvation*, p. xxxiv. In most of his writings, Gutierrez silences the seeing stage by describing only the judging and action-commitment and prayers then following with judging, which he calls undertaking a critical reflection on the first act, which is action. It means that, in every incident, one sees the situation, whether political, economic, or sociological, and then acts upon it – and later reflects on what they have done. Sturla J. Stålsett, *The Crucified and the Crucified: A Study in the Liberation Christology of Jon Sobrino. Studien zur interkulturellen Geschichte des Christentums* (Bern: Peter Lang, 2003), pp. 80–83. Stålsett describes that the first act has two aspects, the foundational experience, i. e., the mere being affected by the suffering of the innocent 'other' (which he calls "passive"); and the other aspect in the first act is the struggling for liberation (which he calls "active"). Then, finally, the second act is theologizing.
45 Gutiérrez, *A Theology of Liberation: History, Politics, and Salvation*, p. 10.

selves on the terrain of spirituality and practise; only subsequently is it possible to formulate discourse on God in an authentic and respectful way."[46]

In one way, Gutierrez indicates that theology, as a critical reflection having the two acts, has to make some changes in its course of action in society and in the Church. "It is in this reference to praxis that an understanding of spiritual growth based on scripture should be developed and it is through this same praxis that faith encounters the problems posed by human reason."[47] Turning to theology, Gutierrez writes that "theological reflection would then necessarily be a criticism of society and the church insofar as they are called and addressed by the Word of God; it would be a critical theory, worked out in light of word accepted in faith and inspired by a practical purpose – and therefore indissolubly linked to historical praxis."[48] Describing the theology of liberation of Segundo, Hewitt writes, "The critical theory embodies a consciously critical attitude toward society that struggles to change the course of history … Thus critical theory social theory is understood as a practical, transformative activity with an emancipatory intent."[49]

Therefore, according to Gutierrez and other Latin American liberation theologians, liberation theology follows this theory effectively, and if it divorces from the action, then it is not fit to be a theology of the people. It is a reflection on the praxis, the first acts, of the people. Liberation theology took the issue of the poor seriously, the 'nonpersons' who suffer from many problems in the world but also who see, judge, and act in their respective societies. Stålsett writes:

---

46 Robert McAfee Brown, *Gustavo Gutiérrez: An Introduction to Liberation Theology* (Maryknoll, NY: Orbis Books, 1990), p. 77.

47 Gutiérrez, *A Theology of Liberation: History, Politics, and Salvation*, p. 11. See also Judith Gutierrez and Judith Condor, *The Task and Content of Liberation Theology* (2007), pp. 27–29. See also Brown, *Gustavo Gutiérrez: An Introduction to Liberation Theology*, pp. 65–68. Brown gives a meaning of praxis by referring to its Greek translation; it goes beyond setting a contrast between theory and practices, but, in the application by liberation theologians, it is where theory and practices are inseparable. Each continually influences and is being influenced by the other. As mutual interchange continues, they are not continually transforming one another but are transforming the overall situation as well. To illustrate this, Brown gives an example of the hungry two donkeys tired in one lope with two piles of hay. He continues to give a summary on praxis as follows: 1. Praxis avoids abstraction; it is grounded in the experience of the world; 2. The thought is for change, of transformation. Truth is something that is 'done'; 3. People are empowered to change their situations rather than having solutions imposed on them; 4. The best praxis situation is communal reflection and action; 5. Praxis is never completed; it contains the tools for ongoing correction and avoids settling into a rigid orthodoxy.

48 Gustavo Gutiérrez, Caridad Inda, and John Eagleson, *A Theology of Liberation: History, Politics and Salvation*, Teologia De La Liberacion, Perspectivas (London: SCM Press, 1974), p. 11.

49 Marsha Aileen Hewitt, *From Theology to Social Theory: Juan Luis Segundo and the Theology of Liberation*, vol. 73, American University Studies. Series 7, Theology and Religion (New York: P. Lang, 1990), p. 5.

On a more profound level, 'the poor' can be interpreted politically in this act as 'potentially revolutionary', socioeconomically as 'dependent' and 'oppressed', pastorally as 'neighbor' calling for Christian love and care, philosophically as 'other' coming from 'beyond' and calling for 'service' and theologically as 'the poor of Yahweh', 'people of God', the other, who in their need for liberation reveal the other God.[50]

Moreover, liberation theology took the issue of poor participation in self-liberation very seriously, in all aspects of human life in their society and local churches.

1.6.1 The Poor in the Theology of Gutierrez and Sobrino

This section regards another thing than the first/second act. The issue of the poor is also important from another perspective besides the first/second act perspective. The 'poor' are a central epistemological figure for both Gutierrez and Sobrino. By giving strong significance to the poor, the Latin Americans develop a theology of the poor by reflecting on their reflection and praxis as they struggle (their first and second acts). It will be interesting to see in my analysis of the IR-VICOBA whether they share that theology of the poor or not.

On the issue of the poor and other downtrodden, Sobrino quotes Mendellin: "Christ our saviour not only loved the poor but also, 'being rich, become poor', lived in poverty, centered his mission on proclamation to the poor of their liberation and founded his church as a sign of this poverty among human beings."[51]

According to Sobrino, "The poor are those who hunger and thirst, who go naked, strangers, the sick, those in prison, those who mourn those weighed down by real burdens (Luke 6:20-21, Matt 25:25)."[52] In the quotation above, Sobrino indicates that the poor are those who suffer from socioeconomic need, and one may conclude they suffer by lacking the basic needs every human being is supposed to have.

Sobrino continues to describe more than the poor as "those despised by the ruling society, those considered sinners, republicans, the prostitutes (Mark 2:16; Matt 11:19; 21:23; Luke 15:1ff), the simple-minded, the little ones, the least (Mark 9:36; Matt 10:42; 18:18-14, 25:40-45), those who carry despised tasks (Matt 12:31; Luke 18:11)."[53] In this sense, "the poor are the marginalized, those

---

50 Stålsett, "The Crucified and the Crucified: A Study in the Liberation Christology of Jon Sobrino," p. 83.
51 Jon Sobrino, *Jesus the Liberator: A Historical-Theological Reading of Jesus of Nazareth*, Jesucristo Liberador (Maryknoll, NY: Orbis Books, 1993), p. 18. Jon Sobrino is a Jesuit Priest and a theologian who teaches at the Central American University in San Salvador.
52 Ibid., p. 80.
53 Ibid.

whose religious ignorance and oral behaviour closed, in the conviction of the time, the gate reading to salvation for them."[54]

The poor are the crucified people who endure much suffering. To show the relationship between Jesus and the poor, Sobrino uses the term "the crucified."[55] The crucified are poor in all senses of the word poor. On this situation, Sobrino writes:

> It is, then, to these poor that Jesus says the Kingdom of God belongs: those for whom the essential things of life are so hard to achieve, those who live despised and outcast, who live under oppression, who, in short, have nothing to look forward to; those who furthermore, feel themselves cut off from God, since religious society forces them to introject this understanding – it is these whom Jesus tells to have hope, that God is not like their oppressors have made them think, that the end of their misfortune is at hand, that the Kingdom of God is coming and is for them.[56]

In another book, Sobrino writes:

> Thus the language of 'people' and 'peoples' is laced with death, not natural but historical death, which takes the form of crucifixion, assassination, the active historical deprivation of life, whether slowly or quickly. That death, caused by injustice, is accompanied by cruelty, contempt, and also concealment. I usually add that the crucified people are also denied a chance to speak and even to be called by name, which means they are denied their existence. The crucified people 'are not' and the affluent world prohibits or inhibits them from 'becoming.' The affluent world can thus ignore what happens to them, without any pangs of conscience.[57]

---

54 Ibid., Jon Sobrino quoting J. Jeremiah in *Teologica del Nuevo*, 5th ed. (Salamanca), p. 35.
55 Jon Sobrino, *No Salvation Outside the Poor: Prophetic-Utopian Essays* (Maryknoll, NY: Orbis Books, 2008), pp. 3–7. See also Stålsett, "The Crucified and the Crucified: A Study in the Liberation Christology of Jon Sobrino," pp. 22–23. This term made Sturla Stålsett come up with the title "the crucified and the crucified" while studying the liberation Christology of Jon Sobrino. Describing the term 'crucified,' Sturla says the term is not an easy catchword or merely pious talk. Rather, the term expresses nothing less than the theological significance of contemporary suffering in Sobrino's theology. He continues to give the fundamental challenges which bring the whole issue of praxis to the center of that reflection. The two main questions are: How to do theology when faced with the reality of the crucified peoples? How can theology help to bring the crucified down from the cross(es)? Sturla also writes that this Christological theology of the crucified is a 'theologoumenon,' using E. Schillebeeck's term, which tries to respond to the question 'Who is Jesus to the crucified?' Besides the Trinitarian relatedness of Jesus often taken into account in Christologies, Sobrino insists that this must be complemented by analysis of historical relatedness.
56 Sobrino, *Jesus the Liberator: A Historical-Theological Reading of Jesus of Nazareth*, p. 82.
57 *No Salvation Outside the Poor: Prophetic-Utopian Essays*, p. 4.

The poor are vulnerable to many things, like lack of enough food and a balanced diet, lack of shelter, lack of medication, and lack of security, and sometimes they have been affiliated with all evil occurrences within society. When they scrutinize their situation, they think God has forsaken them, and that he is on the side of the rich people because he has blessed the rich so abundantly and left the poor to suffer. Sturla J. Stålsett, in his research on Sobrino, writes, "It is new, and yet old: to recognised the face of Jesus the crucified in the faces of the humiliated and downtrodden of today, and to signal this recognition by naming their suffering 'Crucifixion.'"[58] Stålsett continues asking about the suffering of this world and suffering people as he asks what possible meaning it can have to speak of the crucified people and crucified history. What purpose can it serve? He mentions that it is "to restore the dignity and to uphold their hope, another one closely related, is the mobilization for a merciful intervention for their justice and freedom, a praxis of liberation."[59] Sobrino writes that this reality helps to remove "mendacity and blindness toward the crucified people in the world."[60] Sobrino, quoting Ellacuria, describes how the issue of poverty is an issue of all times and eras, which the powers of this world continue to create. Sobrino writes:

> Among the signs that are always appearing, some striking and others barely perceptible, there is an outstanding one in every age, in whose light all the others must be discerned and interpreted. That sign is always the historically crucified people, which remains constant although the historical form crucifixion is different. Those people are the historical continuation of the servant of Yahweh, whose humanity is still being disfigured by the sin of the world, whom the powers of this world are still stripping of everything, taking away everything including his life, especially his life.[61]

Like Sobrino, Gustavo Gutierrez[62] deals with the issue of liberation theology, the central issue of which is about the Kingdom of God and the liberation of the poor, the marginalized, and the downtrodden in their historical setups. He refers to such individuals as the 'nonperson': "The term *poor* might seem not only vague and churchy but also somewhat sentimental and aseptic. The poor person today is the oppressed one, the marginalized from the society, the member of the proletariat

---

58 Sturla J. Stålsett, *The Crucified and the Crucified: A Study in the Liberation Christology of Jon Sobrino* (Universitetet i Oslo, 1997), p. 1.
59 Ibid, p. 2.
60 Sobrino, *The Principle of Mercy: Taking the Crucified People from the Cross*, p. 6.
61 *No Salvation Outside the Poor: Prophetic-Utopian Essays*, p. 3.
62 Gustavo Gutierrez is a Peruvian Priest, theologian, and writer born on 8 June 1928 in Lima Peru.

struggling for the most basic rights; the exploited and plundered social class, the country struggling for its liberation."[63]

The poor, according to Gutierrez, "is the product or by-product of an economic and social system fashioned by a few for their own benefit."[64] For Gutierrez, the explosion of the poor in Latin America is the great source of liberation theology because it changes how Christianity, history, and theology are viewed. Writing in the Foreword of Gutierrez and Cardinal Gerhard Ludwig Muller, Robert A. Krieg writes, "Gustavo Gutierrez has founded a theology that takes its point of departure from the experience of the poor with God and God's experience with the poor. It asks how can we speak about the love of God in light of the misery of the poor? And how can hope exist among the poor?"[65] In the theology of Gustavo Gutierrez, we find a critical reflection on, and by, the poor of Peru (and the rest of the world) concerning their past, their present, and their future.[66] Describing the world of the poor, Gutierrez continues:

> The world of the poor is a universe in which the socio-economic aspect is basic but not-all inclusive. In final analysis, poverty means death: lack of food and housing, the inability to attend properly to health and education needs, the exploitation of workers, permanent unemployment, the lack of respect of one's human dignity, and limitations placed on personal freedom in the areas of self-expression, politics, and religion.[67]

Looking critically at the quotation above from Gutierrez, we see how the poor are affected in all spheres of their life, whether economic, social, political, or religious. In this sense, being poor means being entirely deprived in all human spheres of life. A poor person is almost like a living dead or a person who lives a meaningless life since there is no value in the life of a poor person.

The poor are those who fight for their rights and dignity, and it is a way of life, as Gutierrez argues:

> At the same time, it is important to realize that being poor is a way of living, thinking, loving, praying, believing, and hoping, spending leisure time and struggling for a livelihood. Being poor today is also increasingly coming to mean being involved in the struggle for

---

63 Gutiérrez, *A Theology of Liberation: History, Politics, and Salvation*, p. 173.
64 Ibid.
65 Gustavo Gutiérrez et al., *On the Side of the Poor: The Theology of Liberation* (original: An der Seite der Armen) (Maryknoll, NY: Orbis Books, 2015), pp. x–xi.
66 Ibid., p. xi.
67 Gutiérrez, *A Theology of Liberation: History, Politics, and Salvation*, p. xxi.

justice and peace, defending one's life and freedom, seeking more democratic participation in the decision made by society, organizing to live their faith in an integral way.[68]

The two quotations above are contradictory, since it would seem as if poverty is indeed a way of life. However, Gutierrez here means that, whatever the situation in history, the struggle for life still goes on and people continue to live. Being poor, they reflect upon their own life and ask critical questions about why it is like that. As portrayed by Gutierrez above, the history of Latin America is an accurate picture of life in developing countries. According to Gutierrez, the above vignette has contributed more to liberation theology, "which is an expression of the right of the poor to think out their faith."[69] He continues, saying that "the fact that misery and oppression lead to cruel, inhuman death, and [are] therefore contrary to the will of God of Christian revelation, who wants us to live … They reveal a human depth and toughness that are a promise of life."[70] Gutierrez means that the Church has to change in its Christianity, theology, and evangelization. Gutierrez explicitly discusses the critical reflection theory in his writing, as I have discussed above. Jon Sobrino uses that theory in his theological writings, albeit without discussing it. However, when one reads his writings, one recognizes how he uses it – mainly, when he writes about Jesus as a liberator, about the preferential options for the poor, and the principle of mercy.

The Poor Are the Source of Liberation Theology (See, Judge, Act)

As I have discussed before, the see, judge, act philosophy forms the whole liberation theology of Gutierrez and other classical Latin American liberation theologians. This process builds on the praxis of the poor people in their society, which in this study is the first act and also follows the second act, which involves reflection on the praxis of the poor people now in light of the Word of God. Gutierrez writes that the situation of the poor and their participation in reflection upon being human during their Bible reading make them the real interlocutors of liberation theology.[71] They are the ones who have a connection with Jesus, the Liberator, who

---

68 Ibid., pp. xxi–xxii. See also Gustavo Gutiérrez, *The Truth Shall Make You Free: Confrontations*, Verdad Los Hará Libres (Maryknoll, NY: Orbis Books, 1990), p. 10.
69 *A Theology of Liberation: History, Politics, and Salvation*, p. xxi.
70 Ibid., p. xxii.
71 Sergio Torres and Virginia Fabella, *The Emergent Gospel: Theology from the Underside of History: Papers from the Ecumenical Dialogue of Third World Theologians, Dar Es Salaam, August 5–12, 1976* (Maryknoll, NY: Orbis Books, 1978), p. 241. Here, Gutierrez discusses the difference between progressive theology and liberation theology. Gutierrez says that liberation theology is the theology of the nonperson, the nonhuman, who calls on social, economic, and political injustice in their

did not come to save the healthy and the rich but the poor. Because theology begins with these people in their reflections on their actions and reflections on different matters concerning their socioeconomic reality, it becomes a liberation theology. Connecting with Sobrino, then, the crucified people are, like Jesus himself, the source of liberation. As was stated earlier, and to reiterate the words of Gutierrez, liberation theology is a theology of the poor.

The poor people have the privilege and power to come together to theologize, which is the second act of the liberation theology, "for there is a dialectic between the life of faith and the life of the body, between faith in the resurrection and our temporal death. In this dialectic, liberation theology represents the poor's right to think."[72] Gutierrez continues by arguing that the right of the poor to think is the right to express – to plumb, comprehend, come to appreciate, and then insist upon other rights an oppressive system denies them.[73] To make somebody think – that is, for a person to reflect on their ontology – means empowering somebody regardless of the socioeconomic system. Liberation theology emphasizes this since it is a starting point for reflecting on the context of poor people. Experience is an excellent teacher when confronted with reality; sometimes it is challenging to think differently while occupied with what you conceive. The poor, before coming together to do the theology of nonpersons in Contextual Bible Study, act and reflect (praxis) on their socioeconomic reality.

In Contextual Bible Study, the poor and marginalized now become the interlocutors of the theology; they are making theology reflected in their context and the precarious situation they are facing. The right to think makes them ask *why* they are in that situation, and they can even ask difficult questions regarding the Bible, the Church, and even God. However, they still become more strong and faithful Christians within their context. In most cases, this is their second stage of doing theology – the second act – and they ask *why* they have seen what they saw, judged as they judged, and acted as they acted by coming to Contextual Bible Study.

In the second act, the poor become critical thinkers, making critical reflections on their context, which can be any context in which they happen to be living. This understanding of Gutierrez portrays his theology as "see, judge, act." He puts it as follows: "The first stage or phase of theological work is the lived faith that finds expression in prayers and commitment. To live in faith means to put these

---

context without questioning their faith, while progressive theology is a theology of nonbelievers who question our religious world.
72 Gustavo Gutiérrez, *The Power of the Poor in History: Selected Writings* (original: Fuerza Histórica De Los Pobres) (London: SCM Press, 1983), p. 90.
73 Ibid., p. 90.

fundamental elements of the Christian faith into practice, in light of the demands of the reign of God."[74] As quoted by Stålsett, Gutierrez writes:

> We will have an authentic liberation theology when the oppressed themselves can freely raise their voices and express themselves directly and in a creative manner both in the society and within the people of God; when they 'give account of the hope' which they bear, and become promoters of their own liberation.[75]

He continues:

> The second act of theology, which of reflection in the proper sense of the term, has for its purpose of reading the complex praxis in the light of God's word.[76]

Gutierrez emphasizes reflection, which is viewed as a judgment on what someone experiences and does. This is what the liberation theologians call "see-judge-act."[77] A 'see' moment is when people suffering from hardship see the problems in their socioeconomic (and sometimes sociopolitical) reality. They come to reflect on it, which is a 'judging' moment, and they 'act' to solve the problem and reflect and practise repeatedly. This repeated reflection and practice, according to classical theologians, is called the *first act*. When the poor come to discuss in the Bible groups where they theologize, they now also reflect theologically, according to the Word of God. That is the *second act*. As I have discussed above, Gutierrez calls "theology" the second act. It is applied to critical issues someone is facing (or their context),

---

74 Gutiérrez, *A Theology of Liberation: History, Politics, and Salvation*, p. xxxiv.
75 Stålsett, "The Crucified and the Crucified: A Study in the Liberation Christology of Jon Sobrino," p. 82.
76 Gutiérrez, *A Theology of Liberation: History, Politics, and Salvation*, p. xxxiv. Stålsett, "The Crucified and the Crucified: A Study in the Liberation Christology of Jon Sobrino," pp. 79–81. On the issue of critical reflection in light of the Word of God, Stålsett describes the theory of critical reflection on praxis according to the liberation theologian Gutierrez. It involves two acts: The first act, which he prefers to as the "passive act," has two aspects: the foundational experience, which is the mere being affected by the suffering 'other'; and the aspect of discovery or the foundational experience inactive, which is characterized by commitment. It concerns the discovery that the poor are not just suffering but are struggling for liberation. (This makes the poor the main actors and protagonists.) The second act is that involving theology.
77 Sands Justin, "Introducing Cardinal Cardijn's See-Judge-Act as an Interdisciplinary Method to Move Theory into Practice," *Religions* 9, no. 4 (2018), pp. 1–3. This method was introduced and proposed by Cardinal Joseph Cardijn, who used this method when working with the Young Trade Unionists in 1924 (later to become the Young Christian Workers, JOC). During this period the see-judge-act notion was used to address inequality, employing it with the success of JOC he had developed.

and then it has to be judged in light of the Word of God to make a theological reflection.

All the lives of believers become the source of a theology of see-judge-act. Gutierrez, quoting Chenu, writes of the participation of Christians in critical social movements: "They are active *loci theologici* for the doctrine of grace, the incarnation, and redemption."[78] Moreover, Gutierrez puts it this way:

> Theology must be a critical reflection on humankind, on basic principles. Only with this approach will theology be serious discourse aware of itself, in full possession of its conceptual elements. However, we are not referring exclusively to this epistemological aspect when we talk about theology as critical reflection. We also refer to a clear and critical attitude regarding economic and socio-cultural issues in the life and reflection of the Christian community.[79]

Liberation theology expresses the faith and acts of the poor in their society of the poor – it is a second act. A theology that breaks with the theology of the dominator to maintain continuity with the history of the poor – a history all but unknown but rich and full of promise. Here is genuinely a 'theology oppressed,' rejected by the authorities, in complicity with powerful elements in the Church.[80] Although the poor are not academics, rich, or even influential, their experience with suffering and difficulties makes them contribute more to this area of theology, liberation theology. They reflect every situation and moment in this way of doing it. Boff and Boff write about where to find liberation theology: "You will find it in the base. It is linked with a specific community and forms a vital part of it. Its service is one of theological enlightenment of the community on its pilgrim way. You can find it any weekend in any slum, shantytown, or rural parish."[81] Curt Cadorette, writing on Gutierrez, puts it in this way:

> There can be little doubt that Gustavo Gutierrez has had one overriding purpose – to study, explain and strengthen the potentiality of the poor, and his theology is essentially that potentiality expressed in written form. It is a statement of solidarity with the poor, a protest of their oppression, and an affirmation of the invincibility of their God-given hope.[82]

---

78 Gutiérrez, *A Theology of Liberation: History, Politics, and Salvation*, p. 6.
79 Ibid., p. 8.
80 Gutiérrez, *The Power of the Poor in History: Selected Writings*, p. 94.
81 Leonardo Boff, Clodovis Boff, and Paul Burns, *Introducing Liberation Theology*, vol. 1, Como Fazer Teologia Da Libertaçao (Tunbridge Wells, Kent: Burns & Oates, 1987), p. 19.
82 Curt Cadorette, *From the Heart of the People: The Theology of Gustavo Gutiérrez* (Oak Park, IL: Meyer Stone Books, 1988), p. 115.

Cadorette continues to argue, "Gutierrez's theology is a mixture of feeling and analysis guided by a vision of what it means to be a Christian in a world sadly by systematic oppression. It is a theology of experience, his own and that of the poor, along a long and sinuous road toward liberation."[83]

The poor and marginalised rich in their experience easily articulate this type of theology by any means since it is embedded in them and is part of them. It is not a dogma taught but an expression of the experiences, rites, mores, traditions, sufferings, and hardships they have passed through. It reflects joy in faith in God (regardless of what is mentioned above) and in the joy that God is on their side. When theology is put into practice like this, it touches the lives of people and makes poor people privileged to participate in the expression of their faith and put that expression into praxis.

The poor people who read the Bible no longer depend on the learned scholars or the interpretation taught by the Church or orthodoxy; now, they want to go further to discover more reflections on the Word of God. They put more into orthopraxis, where theology becomes more a part of them and becomes more practical than only mental reflections and contemplations. Reflections become more helpful to the poor to come up with liberating praxis. The poor reflect on issues like justice, equality, and freedom. Indeed, they might go further, even reflecting on their poverty, their economic problems, and their hindrances.

Liberation theology transcends the world of other theologies from the 'realm of ideas' to that of real history, where persons and social groups live in confrontation. For example, in modern society, within the social classes that maintain modernity, there is a difference in religious convictions that creates a division among those who share the same social world, similar lifestyles, and quality of life. This might be an environment where progressive theology elaborates its answers from their critiques and questions, but liberation theology deals with the society of nonpersons since the rift that separates individuals is not religious, but economic, social, and political and should not be tolerated.[84]

'The Gospel in Solentiname' by Ernesto Cardenal: Liberation Theology to Fight Poverty and Hardship in Life

The Gospel in Solentiname is a collection of readings conducted by Ernesto Cardinal in a remote archipelago in Lake Nicaragua. The Bible studies were conducted every Sunday by the 'Campesinos' in the church or in a gathering place near the

---

83 Ibid., p. 115.
84 Gutiérrez, *The Power of the Poor in History: Selected Writings*, p. 93.

lake or in thatched houses.[85] After reading several commentaries within the book, I found that they present different opinions and ones that can easily describe the sociopolitical and socioeconomic situation they were passing through. Through their interpretation of the Bible, one finds that they were in a struggle with the dictatorship leadership, and that they were after communalism, believing that it was their destination for a utopia egalitarian society and a solution for ending poverty.

Their commentaries present different perspectives of the members doing the Bible reading with Cardenal. Cardenal writes:

> Not everyone who came participated equally in the discussion. Some spoke up more often than others, Mercelino was a mystic. Olivia was more theological. Rebeca, Mercelino's wife, always talked about love. Laurereano saw everything in terms of revolution. Elvis was always thinking about the perfect society of the future. Felipe, another youth, was constantly aware of the proletarian struggle. His father, old Tomas Pena, couldn't read but spoke out of a deep wisdom. Alejandro, Olivia's son, was a youth leader; he had guidance to offer everyone, especially other young people. Pancho was a conservative, but later took a different position. Julio Meirena was a staunch defender of equality. His brother Oscar always talked about unity ...[86]

The description given by Cardenal above portrays how the Bible readers came to the Bible with their knowledge and practice from their socioeconomic or sociopolitical environment. Interestingly, the Bible readers had a notion of being connected by the Holy Spirit in their Bible interpretation. An example is their perception of the Holy Spirit in their readings: "Oscar called the spirit of unity, Alejandro called the spirit of service to others, Elvis called it the spirit of future society, Felipe called it the spirit of proletarian struggle, Julio called it the spirit of equality and community sharing, Laureano called it the spirit of the revolution and Rebeca called it the spirit of Love."[87] These are interpretations made by Cardenal from the group he was reading the Bible with. Moreover, these are themes one finds when reading the commentaries. Nevertheless, you find that unity, a spirit of service to others, and love portray one thing from a different angle.

When one reads these commentaries of the Gospel sees a lot of these reflections, and you can come up with different themes. Having sat with the IR-VICOBA

---

85 Ernesto Cardenal (2010), *The Gospel in Solentiname* (Eugene: Wipf & Stock Publishers), p. xi. Father Ernesto Cardenal was a Nicaraguan priest and internationally acclaimed poet who lived in Managua. For 10 years he lived on the Solentiname Islands in Lake Nicaragua, where he established a community of artists, writers, and peasants later destroyed by the military during the Somoza dictatorship.

86 Ibid., p. xii.

87 Ibid., p. xiii.

members in their contextual Bible study, I found a lot of parallel similarities with these people who were reading the Bible with Cardernal regardless of the difference in time and socioeconomic difficulties they were fighting against. One of the similarities is fighting poverty, ignorance, and diseases.

The Issue of Revolution and Liberation

One hears a lot of reflection on revolutions as one reads different commentaries of the texts, as a way of fighting ignorance and poverty. For example, reading Luke 6:24-26, with the title "Woe unto You Rich …" Felipe says, "It seems to me that here Jesus has put himself on the side of the poor. But the Gospels can also be the liberation of the rich. Because this changes, whether they like it or not, will make them fulfill the Gospels, even though by force. But we Christians must not wait for God to do this. We have to work for it."[88] The language of Felipe makes someone who hears this ask why the poor and the rich should make those changes. The rich share what they have with others, and the poor gain from the share they get from the rich. This is a sense of equality in the society of the new Kingdom of God.

Commenting on Luke 12:13-21 about 'Riches,' Felipe continues with his idea that "Jesus was coming to divide all the wealth of the world among all people."[89] Felipe commented that, after hearing the comment from Cardernal himself, who said, "The man saw that Jesus was just, and that's why he wants to set him up as a judge. But he didn't know that Christ's justice was another kind of revolutionary justice. Even now there are Christians who think that Christ's justice is the justice of capitalism."[90]

Discussing Luke 18:18-30, about the rich young man who wanted to inherit the Kingdom of God, Felipe says, "It seems to me that he's also showing them that there are two kinds of actions: God's action and human action. People with their own human ideologies can't do this, share what they have. But with God's ideology they can indeed do it."[91] This comment made other participants comment that, even from that perspective, even the rich can be saved if they share what they have. Otherwise, salvation and justice are far from them. Nevertheless, they also commented that there are some poor who like the rich act selfishly and cannot share even the little they have.

Therefore, anyone who interprets these Bible readings of 'Campesinos' finds that most of their comments on revolution require acts of God and acts of man. In many comments, you see many acts that bring them together, knowing that they depend

---

88 Ibid., p. 91.
89 Ibid., p. 343.
90 Ibid.
91 Ibid., p. 498.

on their actions to make the kingdom come among them. Their big enemy is the selfishness and injustice the rich and some poor people exhibit. Moreover, these enemies are being engineered by the Somoza's dictatorship, where many were forced to live a very precarious life and many times bringing them under cruxification to martyrdom.

Equality (Perfect Society) and Love to the Neighbors

According to the 'Campesinos,' equality and love were ways of creating a perfect society without poor people. These people, being poor and living under the dictatorship of Somoza, portray how life was difficult for them, and they needed a second hand to lift everybody up. Discussing the beatitudes of Matthew 5:1-12, Julio comments that the rich cannot practice love because they are selfish and exploit others, whereas the poor can love since they are less selfish and full of love.[92] Adding to the comments, Cardenal says, "… the rich in some ways made money out at the cost of the poor, making other people work for them, and using the money from that work to make more money at the cost of more work by others."[93] On the same thought, Alejandro says this:

> What we see here is that there are two things. One is the Kingdom of God, which is the kingdom of love, of equality, where we must all be like brothers and sisters; and the other thing is the system we have, which isn't brand new, it's a century old, the system of rich and poor, where business is business. And so we see that they're very different things. Then we have to change society so that the Kingdom of God can exist. And we're sure that the kingdom will have to be established with the poor, right?[94]

Alejandro puts two things together, the issue of love and the issue of revolution, where the poor bring about the Kingdom of God since it belongs to them. The Kingdom of God is for the poor people and not for the rich because the latter cannot practice love. Therefore, the beatitudes speak of bringing the Kingdom of God to the poor because it is theirs. The Kingdom these 'Campesinos' were discussing has nothing to do with heaven. To them, the Kingdom is here, a revolution kingdom full of love and a sense of humor toward everybody's neighbor. Discussing the Last Judgment, Matthew 25:31-46, Felipe comments that "He says that it will be when he comes as a king, that's is, when the kingdom is established and since we know that the kingdom will be here on Earth, the judgment will then be here on

---

92 Ibid., p. 83.
93 Ibid.
94 Ibid, p. 84.

Earth."[95] Along the same line, Gigi comments, "One very important thing that I find in this Gospel is that it's an announcement of the definitive triumph of love, of justice, of the new society, and the defeat of capitalism."[96] For these 'Campesinos,' capitalism was like a devilish system led by the rich. To them, the rich belonged to the punishment in the Last Judgment. Possibly they were the source of the hard life (poverty) people endured. Ending capitalism, the system of the rich, means ending poverty and the perilous life people were enduring.

The Monetary System and the Socioeconomic System (Capitalist System)

The Bible readers seem to be very aggressive when they talk about 'the love of money.' They refer to the love of money as going against the will of God. Regarding Matthew 6:24-34, "Look at the lilies in the field …," the Bible readers vehemently discuss that the love of money makes people selfish, isolates people, and keeps people from loving. Jose Espinosa comments that "Love of money makes you proud. You want to excel over others, to be more than the other fellow, and that is why people get split into classes."[97] Therefore, for these Campesinos Bible readers, you can't be a Christian *and* be rich. Some others had another notion that you can be rich but use your richness to assist others. Felix, who always defended the rich though he was poor, commented that "There are rich people who aren't servants of money but use it to do good for others, although there aren't many rich people like that."[98] Commenting on money and love, William asserts that "to serve means to love, and what Christ is saying is that you can't love God and love money. The Bible readers here commented that Jesus was against the love of money. But Jesus wanted people to go against the love of money, which is a service to god mammon the god of wealth, an idol, which is idolatry."

The Campesinos also commented on the issue of the monetary system as part of slavery, which undermines whatever people do. The poet Coronel said that banks are temples of god mammon and he continued to comment that

> But as long as we are under the control of money we are part of a system of slavery, although the relations between masters and slaves are given another name today. Slavery is now in its capitalistic phase, but the slavery is more gigantic. I imagine the money which goes hand to hand to be like a long, a long chain that links everybody's neck together and winds up on Wall Street, which is where all the money ends, as you know. The Pesos that

---

95 Ibid., p. 486.
96 Ibid., p. 488.
97 Ibid., p. 111.
98 Ibid., p. 112.

you have in your wallet (fortunately I don't have any at the moment) don't belong to you. They belong to Wall Street. You can believe you've earned them and that they belong to you, but they'll go from hand to hand until they get to Wall Street. As these revolutionary faithful have made clear to us here, to serve money is to serve slavery, while to serve the opposing master is to be free.[99]

When one reads those words above, it turns out that Coronel was talking about the socioeconomic system that prevailed during the Somoza regime. The system under the capitalistic type of economy controlled the country's monetary system. By then, the power of money led the economy in that country, although it was a dictator-type capitalistic economy. The rich controlled everything, so that Campesinos rose to fight and opted for another type of economy, a communalism they believed would end their poor life. That is why they kept saying, "You do not need money to serve others." They put together two things to fight for their freedom: the love of money and the rich people in power.

Conclusively, I find that the Campesinos were like the IR-VICOBA discussed in this book who read the Bible with their pastors. If you read between the lines of their commentaries, you find they were fighting the same enemies IR-VICOBA did, namely, poverty and the lack of freedom in socioeconomic and sociopolitical life. The Campesinos were fighting against a capitalism entangled with Somoza regime's dictatorship. They were calling for revolution and for change to the socioeconomic and sociopolitical system that undermined them. In great pain, Felipe, Elvis, and Donald among the Bible readers died as martyrs while fighting as revolutionary fighters, as Cardernal writes.[100] This is another proof that they put into action every word they had discussed in their Bible study with Cardernal. These Bible readers believed that communalism was in line with the Bible, and that capitalism went against love and thus against God. It was their way of fighting the capitalistic system, which they thought was devilish. That was their praxis – putting their reading into practices and putting into their Bible study into what they practiced in their socioeconomic societies.

One can deduce many themes from these Bible commentaries of the Campesinos. It depends on what one wants. The selection above is just a few of those select themes.

In my study in Tanzania, the members of IR-VICOBA are Christians who have a praxis model of doing theology. They put words and actions together. This goes with the agreement of what the Third World theologians (EATWOT) suggest. Gutierrez also attended this meeting in Dar es salaam-Tanzania, where it was said, "We reject as irrelevant an academic type of theology that is divorced from the action. We

---

99   Ibid., p. 113.
100 Ibid., p xv.

are prepared for a radical break in epistemology which commits to the first act of theology and engages in critical reflections on the praxis of the reality of the Third World."[101]

Against this background, one important question is the following: Does the IR-VICOBA follow the same patterns of see-judge-act as the Latin American theologians? Or are they alternatively following another pattern of reading the Bible like the see-judge-act the *Ujamaa* and others in South Africa follow? Once these questions have been responded to, we may be able to better specify the relationship between text and context in the IR-VICOBA groups. Therefore, we now need to summarize how see-judge-act develops in the contextual Bible study of Gerald West.

1.6.2 Liberation Theology in the Theology of Gerald West

The question I ask in the following subsection is how West differs from the Latin American theologians Gutierrez and Sobrino on the first/second act issue. The *Ujamaa* Contextual Bible Studies in South Africa perform see-judge-act, but their emphasis on 'act' relates to the action taken *after* the Bible study. Gerald West describes one of these Bible studies: "In addition to the renewed relevance of the Bible in the experience of individual workers, there is also the ongoing use of the Bible in the see-judge-act structure of the YCW [Young Christian Workers] reflections."[102] For Gerald West, theology from below is a process first of reflection on the Bible reading, and then from the Bible reading comes the action.

West writes: "Contextual Bible Study is a South African contribution to the trajectory of Biblical liberation hermeneutics … Briefly, Contextual Bible Study is a form of liberation hermeneutics that emerged in South Africa in the 1980s."[103] He emphasises how the underprivileged and the marginalised require Contextual Bible Study for their liberation and emancipation. He writes:

> The cry and need of ordinary people, poor people, being among them, is curbed by this Contextual Bible Study, where the trained Biblical scholars read the Bible with the poor

---

101 Frostin, *Liberation Theology in Tanzania and South Africa: A First World Interpretation*, 42, p. 3.
102 West, *Biblical Hermeneutics of Liberation: Modes of Reading the Bible in the South African Context*, 1, p. 185. The see-judge-act of *Ujamaa* has been well explained in the introductory chapter with the title "Liberation Theology in the Theology of Gerald West."
103 Gerald O. West, "Locating 'Contextual Bible Study' within Biblical Liberation," *Hermeneutics and Intercultural Biblical Hermeneutics: Original Research*, 70, no. 1 (2014), p. 1. See also Gerald West, "Locating Contextual Bible Study Within Praxis," *Diaconia* 4, no. 1 (2013).

and marginalised people. As claimed by experts of Contextual Bible Study groups, this way is used as a liberating and emancipatory method to the poor.[104]

In my view, West has a vital liberation hermeneutical point in this passage. The poor and marginalised people live in a difficult situation and try to read the Bible to seek the answer from the Word of God for their challenges. When the poor read the Bible with learned theologians, it brings many transformations to their lives. The Word of God now illuminates them to come to the 'act' moment of transformation. The poor and downtrodden now start finding some solutions for the challenges in their lives. This is the basic stance of the liberation theology of West. Liberation starts *after* Contextual Bible Study. For this reason, the texts illuminate the context of the downtrodden.

Besides the importance of the Bible as a liberating and emancipatory tool, West also describes the other side of the Bible, which is used as an oppressing and enslaving tool. West takes an idea from Mofokeng to accuse the "oppressor-preachers of misusing the Bible for their oppressive purpose and objectives, which indicates that the Bible is an essential book for liberation but can, however, be misused."[105] The misuse of the Bible has enslaved people up to this moment in African Christianity. One can give different examples, the most terrible among them being the way Apartheid justified its evil practices by using the Bible.

Gerald West and his colleagues in South Africa started a Contextual Bible Study called *Ujamaa*[106] in South Africa as a continuation of liberation activity after Apartheid. West describes the importance of the Contextual Bible Study in the South African post-Apartheid context. He writes:

> God does speak to us in our context in various ways. The Bible is one of the primary ways in which God speaks to us, but we often cannot hear what God is saying because we think we already know what the Bible says. We have domesticated the Bible; we have tamed it. If we are to hear God speaking into our South African context these days, then we must be willing to return to the Bible with open ears, eyes and hearts.[107]

---

104 Gerald O. West, *Biblical Hermeneutics of Liberation: Modes of Reading the Bible in the South African Context*, vol. 1, Cluster Monograph Series (Pietermaritzburg: Cluster, 1991), p. 68.
105 *The Stolen Bible: From Tool of Imperialism to African Icon*, vol. 144, Biblical Interpretation Series (Leiden: Brill, 2016), pp. 328–329.
106 The term *Ujamaa* is a Swahili word meaning 'familyhood'. The Ujamaa Centre borrowed it from Swahili since they use Swahili in their practices, too. If one visits their website, one finds that they have included a version of Swahili homepage.
107 West, *Contextual Bible Study*, p. 7.

These words from West provided a starting point in understanding why he and his colleagues started the *Ujamaa* Centre, where they practised the Contextual Bible Study in 1985.[108] West writes, "Those who have heard the cry of the people for God to speak to them in their struggle and suffering have begun to develop a new way of reading the Bible. We call this Contextual Bible Study because we are trying to understand what the Bible is saying to our South African context today."[109] The emphasis of Contextual Bible Study readings is to listen to what God's word is to them (the reader) in their contemporary context. West writes:

> Those who are committed to the contextual Bible study process have decided to choose to read the Bible from a particular perspective within the South African context, the perspective of the poor and oppressed. The poor and oppressed are those who are socially, politically, economically or culturally 'marginalised and exploited. We have made this choice because we believe God is mainly concerned for the poor and oppressed. Our reading of the Bible and our concern for justice and righteousness in South Africa indicate that God is mainly concerned for the marginalised and vulnerable. Throughout the Bible, we read that God hears the cry of the widows, orphans, women, strangers, the disabled, the poor and oppressed. God sees the suffering and hears the cry of the slaves in Egypt (Exod 3:7), the prophets continuously speak and act against injustice to the poor (Isa 58:6-12; Amos 5:11-12).[110]

West continues to write that even Jesus was born among the poor and oppressed in Palestine. Jesus chose to remain with and work among the poor and oppressed. He was oppressed and died on the cross. This suggests that justice and righteousness will come only after the needs of the oppressed and the poor have been addressed.[111]

---

108 For more discourse on Ujamaa Contextual Bible Study, see http://ujamaa.ukzn.ac.za/WHATisUJAMAA.aspx, http://ujamaa.ukzn.ac.za/WHATisUJAMAA/commitments.aspx and http://ujamaa.ukzn.za/whatUJAMAAdoes.aspx. The mentioned commitments for Ujamaa Bible Centre are as follows: "1. Our core purpose is to mobilise, train, support and empower the poor, the working-class, and the marginalised. We work specifically with women, youth, people living with HIV/AIDS, and the unemployed. We work for the values of the Kingdom of God and for a society in which all have abundant life (John 10:10); 2. Where these values and commitments are shared by other religious communities, government, and civil society, we collaborate and work together for social transformation; 3. Our primary resources for this work are Biblical and theological, making particular use of Contextual Bible Studies (CBS) and the See, Judge, and Act method. We work, wherever possible, in the languages of the local communities with whom we collaborate; 4. We are committed to the ongoing cycle of action and reflection known as praxis."
109 West, *Contextual Bible Study*, p. 7.
110 Ibid., p. 13.
111 Ibid.

Writing for the 70th anniversary of the HTS Teologiese Studies/Theological Studies, Gerald West comments that Contextual Bible Study has been a contributor to the trajectory of Biblical liberation hermeneutics in South African scholarship over the past 70 years, and it has rendered its distinctive brand. West indicates that the 1985 Kairos Document has influenced these hermeneutics.[112] The reasons for reflections are three-fold: First, the Kairos Document came from below, and many people were involved in the South African struggle for liberation by words and deeds; second, the Kairos Document emerged through an extended communal, collaborative, and diaconal process that brought the poor and oppressed, organic intellectuals, and socially engaged theologians together; third, the Kairos Document provided new theological categories forged from their (Southern African) context. These distinguish between 'State Theology,' 'Church Theology,' and 'Prophetic Theology.'[113]

This is the environment within which West and other theologians developed their interactive and liberating Contextual Bible Study in South Africa. West indicates that all the groups, including the poor, marginalised, and women, depend on the Bible as a tool for liberation. It is their symbol for the presence of the God of life and resource in their struggle for survival; reflections on the Biblical teachings are significant to them.[114] Therefore, 'reading with' the poor and marginalised, according to West, "involves an epistemological paradigm shift in which the poor and 'marginalised are seen as primary dialog partners in reading the Bible and doing theology. Liberation hermeneutics begins with the reality, experiences, needs, interest and questions and resources of the poor and 'marginalised"[115] According to West, the Contextual Bible Study in South Africa

> is a Bible reading process that takes place within the framework of liberation hermeneutics. The framework of commitments that encompasses contextual Bible study include: First, a commitment to begin the reading process from the experienced reality of the organised

---

112 The Kairos Document was a Christian, Biblical, and theological comment on the political crisis in South Africa published in 1985. It was an attempt by concerned Christians in South Africa to reflect on the situation of death in their country. It analyzes the current theological models that determined the type of activities the Church engaged in to try to resolve the problems of the country. It was an attempt to develop, out of this perplexing situation, an alternative Biblical and theological model that, in turn, should lead to forms of activity that make a real difference to the future of their country. See *The Kairos Document: Challenge to the Church*, 2nd ed. (Grand Rapids, MI: Eerdmans, 2017), p. vii.
113 West, "Locating 'Contextual Bible Study' within Biblical Liberation Hermeneutics and Intercultural Biblical Hermeneutics: Original Research," p. 1.
114 Gerald West, *The Academy of the Poor: Towards a Diagonal Reading of the Bible* (Pietermaritzburg: Cluster Publications, 2003), p. ix.
115 Gerald West, *The Academy of the Poor*, p. xiv; see also West, *Contextual Bible Study*, p. 15.

poor and marginalised, including their language, categories, concepts, needs, questions, interests and resources; second, a commitment to read the Bible communally 'with' each other, where power relations are acknowledged and equalised as far as possible: third, a commitment to read the Bible critically using whatever critical resources are available, including local critical resources of the Biblical scholarship; and the critical resources of the Biblical scholarship; and fourth, a commitment to social transformation through the Bible reading process.[116]

This extensive overview by West focuses on four critical terms, within the Contextual Bible Study. However, it is important to see that these critical terms are all related to the Bible reading, not an interpretation of the social reality. Here is the main difference to Guttierez and his distinction between the first and the second act. The interpretation starting with the reality is not the difference; the difference is how one should act in this given reality, from which sources one finds the interpretation. Gutierrez finds it from the social praxis of the poor, while West finds it in the Bible (no first act) providing a way forward to act from the Bible study.

According to West, the critical terms for Bible study are *commitment, critical, communal*, and *social transformation*. The first term, *commitment*[117], means that both 'ordinary readers'[118] and trained theologians need to commit themselves to reading the Bible seriously to make changes within themselves and within the framework of their community. Without that commitment, nothing can be achieved. The changes from within help create changes in the whole community since change starts within a person and then proceeds outwardly to the community. Personal commitment is one of the assumptions Gerald West and his colleague in Ujamaa make regarding Contextual Bible Study.

According to West, ordinary and trained readers are encouraged to listen to each other. Unless that happens, the trained readers will dominate the Bible study as it is experienced during the colonial type of Bible study, in which ordinary readers tend to be silenced. West says 'reading with' means that the trained readers acknowledge

---

116 Gerald West, *The Academy of the Poor*, pp. 5–6. See also ibid., pp. 11–12.
117 Mligo, "Jesus and the Stigmatized: Reading the Gospel of John in a Context of HIV/AIDS-Related Stigmatization in Tanzania," p. 124. Philpott defines the meaning of the term *commitment* as "an entrusting of oneself to a particular value or group of people and pledge to perpetuate the value or the well-being of that group of people."
118 West describes the term 'ordinary readers' to mean those Bible readers who read the Bible precritically and also those readers who are poor and marginalized. See Gerald West, *The Academy of the Poor*, p. x. See also Gerald West, *Reading Other-Wise: Socially Engaged Biblical Scholars Reading with Their Local Communities*, vol. no. 62, Semeia Studies (Leiden: Brill, 2007), p. 2. *Contextual Bible Study*, pp. 8–9.

and recognise the privilege and power their training gives them in the group. It also means that they have to empower ordinary readers in the group to discover and then to acknowledge and recognise their own identity and value and significance of their contributions and experiences.[119] The word 'empower' means there is one side with 'power' and the other side is on the receiving end. West defends his position, indicating that trained readers have the privilege of their education; however, they may lack the experience of the suffering, and trauma, which ordinary readers may have experienced. Nevertheless, the challenge lies in balancing these differences, coming to the dialog, and contributing as equal partners in the Bible study.

The Ujamaa Contextual Bible Study is committed to reading the Bible 'critically.' West writes that critical consciousness is just that – *critical* – and he describes what that means: Critical consciousness includes asking 'why?' questions. Moreover, it involves probing beneath the surface, being suspicious of the status quo. We must ask questions like 'Why do poor people have no food?' However, according to West, this does not make the Bible insignificant; instead, it remains an essential resource to ordinary people in the Church and community. West maintains that reading the Bible critically is important since history shows that the Bible has been used to legitimize oppression, for example, during the Apartheid era. It is the responsibility of the Contextual Bible Study Group to ensure that 'critical consciousness' is built among the members of the group.[120]

West provides three ways of reading the Bible critically: 1. In its historical and sociological context; 2. Carefully and strictly in its literary context; 3. In its thematic and symbolic context as a whole. West suggests that these approaches might overlap

---

119 Mligo, "Jesus and the Stigmatized: Reading the Gospel of John in a Context of HIV/AIDS-Related Stigmatization in Tanzania," p. 15.
120 West, *Contextual Bible Study*, pp. 17–19. Gerald West, "Reading the Bible with the Marginalised: The Value/s of Contextual Bible Reading," *Stellenbosch Theological Journal* 1, no. 2 (2015), p. 239. Mligo, "Jesus and the Stigmatized: Reading the Gospel of John in a Context of HIV/AIDS-Related Stigmatization in Tanzania," p. 127. Mligo gives a warning on West's of the terms *critical* and *precritical* with connection to African scholarship. The concern here is whether the two terms have their etymology in Western scholarship (Enlightenment), for example, in the historical-critical method or critical thinking. Does Mligo probe the question of how an ordinary reader can use the term *critical* in their process of reading? The asking of the question 'why,' as West suggests, is hard for a typical ordinary reader. I am not undermining the ordinary readers, but I try to put myself in their shoes. I agree with Mligo that the term *critical* is more Western toward any writings or conversation. However, this does not make it wrong to use here since, as an African, I know we do not have this attitude of probing believed norms, rituals, or traditions. We are used to accepting these as they are. This notion applies to the Bible, the Word of God, the revelation from God, the voice of God: How can we probe and ask questions? So, we have to copy from other scholarship, and this helps us now since even what we call democracy, development, or justice is copied from other scholarship to facilitate our understanding of the familiar world we want dialogically to build.

and can be used together in Bible study.[121] West here employs what Paulo Freire writes, namely, that "only dialogue, which requires critical thinking, is also capable of generating critical thinking."[122] Therefore, when trained readers/theologians and ordinary readers read the Bible critically, they develop powerful and liberating insights by reading the Bible together. Writing on the Contextual Bible Study method, Gerald West suggests the following:

> Socially engaged Biblical scholars have always accepted the parameter of the contextual Bible study process; that the Bible must be read from the perspective of the organised poor and marginalised, the Bible must be read together with the poor and marginalised, that the Bible reading is related to social transformation and significantly that the Bible must be read critically.[123]

When the poor and marginalised read the Bible critically, it helps them to recognise the theological nature of the Biblical text and develop critical tools, enabling them to critically analyze the text.[124]

Personal and social transformation through Contextual Bible Study is of vital importance. Bible readers strive to transform from one stage to another as themes are discussed. This transformation includes the existential, political, economic, cultural, and religious spheres of life.[125] This transformative commitment to the Contextual Bible Study is critically important. Without it, the previous three commitments become meaningless. This broad-based transformation makes the Ujamaa Contextual Bible Study unique and essential to today's South African world.

West adds another essential ingredient to the Contextual Bible Study, namely, *facilitation*. In one of their workshops, West and his colleagues agreed on the five most important characteristics of the facilitator: The facilitator should use methods that encourage the whole group to participate; the facilitator should manage conflict and make the group a safe place for member contributions; the facilitator should train others to become a facilitator; the facilitator should clarify what is not clear and summarize the discussion; and the facilitator should enable the group to be aware of, and be involved in, the needs of the community. A facilitator, then, is someone who helps facilitate the progress and empowerment of others, making it easier for others to act, to contribute, and to acquire skills.[126] This role of the facilitator does

---

121 West, *Contextual Bible Study*, pp. 19–20.
122 Freire, *Pedagogy of the Oppressed*, p. 73.
123 Gerald O. West, *The Academy of the Poor: Towards a Dialogical Reading of the Bible*, vol. 2, Interventions (Sheffield: Sheffield Academic Press, 1999), p. 63.
124 Ibid., p. 66.
125 West, *Contextual Bible Study*, pp. 21–22.
126 Ibid., p. 22.

not allow them to dominate the Bible study or to become authoritarian, as it does in other Bible studies.

Despite West's arguments when presenting the facilitator role, he has been criticized for not giving ordinary people enough authority in the Contextual Bible Study. One critique comes from Elia Mligo[127], who questions the Contextual Bible Study practice. In the response from West, he once again summarizes his position by not distinguishing between the first and the second act.

Responding to the criticism of Elia Mligo in an article "Christian Social Practise in a Context of HIV/AIDS-related Stigmatization in Tanzania" in the journal *Diaconia*, Gerald West writes, "The most significant contribution of Contextual Theology, the theological trajectory that was given institutional form through the Institute for Contextual Theology, has been the See-Judge-Act process. The process is central to Contextual Bible Study. It is not a methodological technique, but it is an emancipatory process."[128] Making it clear, West describes that the 'see' moment involves the social analysis where the poor and marginalised examine their reality, and the Ujamaa Centre is called to focus its attention on this reality. In the second stage, the 'judge' moment, both the critical reading and the products of critical reading are essential. In the 'see' moment, the reality is understood, and the 'judge' moment flows from the critically read Biblical perspective. West writes:

> The see moment of social analysis generates a particular contextual concern that becomes the 'theme' for the Bible study. The engagement with the Bible (The judge component) begins with a community's 'thematic' appropriation of the Biblical text being used (community-consciousness), allowing every participant to share their particular understanding of the text.[129]

The process then ends with the 'act' moment, which constitutes the actual responses of the community following the 'see' and 'judge' moments. These are the outcomes of Contextual Bible Study.[130] Here one sees clearly how the "act," in West's perception of it, is a Bible-informed act. In other words, the second act – and not the first act – in Gutierrez's version.

In Chapters 6 and 7, I explore these differences and similarities in theology and the profile of the IR-VICOBA groups with a comparison between Ujamaa and Latin American approaches.

---

127 Elia Mligo, *Jesus and the Stigmatized: Reading the Gospel of John in a context of HIV/AIDS-related Stigmatization in Tanzania,* Oslo: University of Oslo, pp. 128–134.
128 West, "Locating Contextual Bible Study Within Praxis," pp. 43–48.
129 "Reading the Bible with the Marginalised: The Value/s of Contextual Bible Reading," p. 244.
130 "Locating Contextual Bible Study Within Praxis," pp. 43–48.

1.7 Sources and Bible Study Participants

The recorded documents and the written materials from the field constitute the primary resources for this study. In the field, I recorded participant Contextual Bible Study results from two selected groups of IR-VICOBA. These groups, among the many in ELCT-KoD, are the Amani and (Upendo) and the Agape IR-VICOBA groups. The Amani IR-VICOBA comes from the small town of Tukuyu in the Rungwe District and the Upendo (Agape) IR-VICOBA group from the Itete village, 45 km from Tukuyu in the Rugwe District. These two groups are a sample of the many groups of IR-VICOBA in ELCT-KoD. The participants in those groups comprise people of different ages and sex. Interestingly, regardless of the African patriarchal culture, women chairpersons led the two groups.

As a member and minister of ELCT, I have some knowledge about these people, though it is limited knowledge and not like that of a full participant of the IR-VICOBA groups. However, I do not use my insider/outsider role to influence the study subjectively. I strive to approach the study objectively.

After recording the participant Bible study, I transcribed the interactions from Swahili to English from my mobile phone. The IR-VICOBA members use Swahili in their Bible study. The secondary written sources are books, articles from journals and books, internet materials such as research papers, and dissertations from different libraries.

In my discussion of Biblical texts in this study, the Bible citations are taken from the NRSV (with Apocrypha). However, the IR-VICOBA members used the Swahili Union Version for their participant-centered Bible study.

1.8 Organization of the Study

In this first chapter, I have presented the problem as well as the aim and general background of the study. I also presented theoretical and theological perspectives that are used in the following analysis and interpretation. I have given some context regarding the liberation of the poor in Tanzania after and during independence. This chapter details the context of Bible reading within the Tanzanian context and the short history of the IR-VICOBA groups within ELCT-KoD. I have also presented the issue of the other contextual Bible studies.

In the theological and theoretical perspectives of the liberation theologians, Gutierrez and Sobrino in particular, we see how they use the see-judge-act approach, albeit as a critical reflection upon the reflections and practices of what the poor and the needy do in their lives. Therefore, they indicate that – to them – doing theology is a 'second act' (cf. Section 1.3 above), meaning that the first act of the see-judge-act takes place within the lives of the poor. The second judging moment, which they call the 'second act,' is now done according to the Word of God. The formation of this theology is a reflection upon the reflection and practices of the people in their context, while in Gerald West's context, the formation of liberation is the product of the Contextual Bible Study of the poor.

In Chapter 2, I present my methodological approach in detail. I reveal how I entered into the field and how I observed the IR-VICOBA members in their Contextual Bible Study interpreting the Bible texts on the Kingdom of God and the poor. Moreover, I explain and discuss how I collected the data.

Chapter 3 presents the IR-VICOBA members' interpretation of the selected texts. Chapter 4 includes my discussion and interpretation of their Bible interpretations and the double interpretation of the IR-VICOBA members, where I present the discussion of their interpretation of text and two contexts: that of the Bible and that of the IR-VICOBA members. In these two chapters, I ask how the members of the IR-VICOBA groups relate the relationship between the Bible and their socioeconomic reality. Chapter 5 discusses and interprets their responses to the learning process in the participant-centered Contextual Bible Study. That is where I reflect more on my research question: How do the members of the IR-VICOBA groups relate the relationship between the Bible and their social reality?

Chapter 6 is devoted to interpreting the intellectual activity carried out as IR-VICOBA. There, I discuss their profile by considering some similarities and differences with other contextual or liberation theologians referred to in this study, like the Latin American theologians presented in the theology and theory section of Chapter 1 and the Ujamaa Contextual Bible Study described in the methodological chapter (Chapter 2). In Chapter 6, I reflect on the research question: What kind of Contextual Bible Study is practised in the IR-VICOBA groups? The aim here has been to see how they build their profile of reading and from below. There, I also look at which patterns of liberation theology the IR-VICOBA groups are trying to follow. Is it the see-judge-act approach of the Latin Americans or a "see-judge-act" approach emerging from the Ujamaa Contextual Bible Study from South Africa?

In Chapter 7, I reflect on the research question: Which are the main topics in their implied theology of the Bible readings? Do the poor employ any theology while reading the Bible together in their Contextual Bible Study? I also reflect more on the theology they are doing, regardless of the fact that the IR-VICOBA members do not think they are addressing theology in their Bible reading. As a theologian, I see a specific theology from below.

I conclude and make my concluding remarks of the study in the last chapter, Chapter 8.

Chapter 2: Facilitating Participant-Centered Contextual Bible Study with the IR-VICOBA Groups: Methodological Perspective

2.1 The Methodology

This study is qualitative research on how poor Christians of the IR-VICOBA selected groups to read Biblical texts and move from the text to their context, also especially from context to the text, as mentioned in Chapter 1. I say "especially from context to the text" since, in most cases, the IR-VICOBA members interpret texts using their experience, which prompts them to start reflecting on the text from their context, as I discuss in Chapter 3. Stausberg and Engler maintain that "qualitative methods tend to investigate the meaning that individuals and groups ascribe to human or social phenomena."[1] As Mouton and Marais write, comparing qualitative research and quantitative research, "The qualitative approach has been chosen because qualitative approaches are relatively more open and broader in the way in which they tackle problems of human experiences than quantitative approaches."[2] For this reason, I choose qualitative research that fits with the aims of my project.

In gathering data for this study, I did fieldwork research, whereby I collected data through observation and conducted a "participant-centered Contextual Bible Study"[3] to produce contextual theology results from the IR-VICOBA groups.[4] On the issue of participation observation, scholars describe the method in many ways. Graham Harvey writes: "Field research in the study of religion is the practice of observing religious groups, communities, or activities, sometimes for sustained periods, sometimes in a series of shorter visits. It entails attempting to understand as fully as possible what people do, when, where, and how and (possibly) why

---

[1] Michael Stausberg and Steven Engler, *The Routledge Handbook of Research Methods in the Study of Religion* (London, New York: Routledge, 2011), p. 7.
[2] J. Mouton and H. C. Marais, *Basic Concepts in the Methodology of the Social Sciences*, p. 163.
[3] I borrow this phrase "participant-centered Contextual Bible Study" from Elia Shabani Mligo, *Jesus and the Stigmatized: Reading the Gospel of John in a Context of HIV/AIDS-Related Stigmatization in Tanzania* (2009), p. 136.
[4] Stephen B. Bevans discussed doing contextual theology and argued that "doing theology contextually means doing theology in a way that takes into account of two things. First, it takes into account the faith experience of the past that is recorded in the scriptures and kept alive, preserved, defended-and perhaps even neglected or suppressed-tradition ... Second, contextual theology takes into account the experience of the present, the context." See Stephen B. Bevans, *Models of Contextual Theology*, Rev. and expanded ed., Faith and Cultures Series (Maryknoll, NY: Orbis, 2002), p. 5.

they do it."[5] He continues, "Sometimes while in the religion 'field' among religious practitioners, researchers attempt to observe without intruding too much on what would happen if they were not there."[6] Dewalt and Dewalt write that, "for anthropologists and social scientists [including religious scholars], participant observation is a method in which a researcher takes part in daily activities, rituals, interactions, and events of a group of people as one of the means of learning the explicit and tacit aspects of their life routine and their culture."[7] However, in my research, I remained silent, only observing their interpretation of the Bible texts on the Kingdom of God and the poor without interference.

In the field, I researched how IR-VICOBA groups read the Bible critically within their socioeconomic context. This critical reading, their transfer of knowledge, and their application to their own context are central aspects of this participant-centered Contextual Bible Study and thus central parts of my research. Ira Shor and Paulo Freire write:

> Reading is not just to walk on the words, and it is not flying over the words either. Reading is re-writing what we are reading. Reading is to discover the connections between the text and the context of the text, and also how to connect the text/context with my context, the context of the reader.[8]

Using the participant-centered contextual model suggested by Shor and Freire above, I investigated how the Amani and Upendo (Agape) IR-VICOBA groups interpret Biblical texts using their life experiences where they face many difficulties. Moreover, I investigated how they fought against the causes of their poverty, themselves being poor Christians. More specifically, I researched how they critically reflected on Biblical texts[9] and developed a position independent from current contextual theology.

In this, the study involves the *hermeneutics* of the IR-VICOBA members. Ingvild Sælid writes, "Hermeneutics is derived from a Greek word *hermeneuein*, which means to 'express,' 'translate,' 'interpret.'"[10] She continues to describe that

---

5 Stausberg and Engler, *The Routledge Handbook of Research Methods in the Study of Religion*, p. 218.
6 Ibid., p. 219.
7 Kathleen M. DeWalt and Billie R. DeWalt, *Participant Observation: A Guide for Fieldworkers* (Walnut Creek, CA: AltaMira Press, 2002), p. 1.
8 Paulo Freire and Ira Shor, *A Pedagogy for Liberation: Dialogues on Transforming Education* (London: Macmillan, 1987), pp. 10–11.
9 Ibid., p. 11. I maintain the meaning of reading critically in the sense Freire and Shor maintained in the above quotation. That attitude creates the necessary intellectual discipline, asking questions about the reading, the writing, the book, and the text. Here, the book and the text in question is the Bible.
10 Stausberg and Engler, *The Routledge Handbook of Research Methods in the Study of Religion*, p. 275.

"the sources of hermeneutics are the text and other utterances, and the goal is to achieve an understanding of their meanings. In a religious studies the study of texts and utterances is not an end in itself, but a means to say something about religion and religious processes in a society."[11] John W. Creswell and Cheryl N. Poth describe hermeneutic phenomenology as "oriented toward lived experience (phenomenology) and interpreting the texts of life."[12] In addition, I interpret the readings of the IR-VICOBA members' own interpretations in my analysis, which make them 'double interpretations.'

The IR-VICOBA members read the Bible together with trained pastors who are members of those groups. This shows how the poor lay Christians read the Bible together with trained theologians and how the Bible becomes a liberating tool to both parties. As West writes:

> A hermeneutic of engagement emphasizes both accountabilities to present communities of faith and struggle, by accepting that the Bible is a significant text for them and continuity with the past poor and marginalized communities of faith and struggle by not abandoning their traces in the Bible. Recognizing the damage done by the Bible, socially engaged Biblical scholars insist on critical modes of reading; recognizing that the Bible still possesses the power to orient life in a meaningful, trustfully, powerful way, socially engaged Biblical scholars insist on a critical appropriation.[13]

This quotation overtly describes how a living faith community of laity and socially engaged Biblical scholars come together during Bible study to achieve an exceptional understanding of the Bible's power, which orients the life of people. In this study, I investigate the Bible reading of the poor people of IR-VICOBA; Bible study is then applied as a tool of education for both socially engaged theologians and the laity as well as a tool to empower the poor. "Socially engaged Biblical scholars believe

---

11 Ibid., pp. 276–278. Here, Gilhus gives the six guidelines of interpretation: 1. Read the text slowly and thoroughly, 2. Apply everything one knows about the language and context of the text, where in the case of a text, the context includes especially its social and cultural background and surroundings. Different contextualization leads to different readings. 3. Keep an eye on the possibilities of cultural comparison. 4. Be aware that textual meaning is always in flux. The text can be studied both concerning their origin and concerning how various communities have used them over time. 5. Ask whose interests are promoted in a text. Writing texts and making interpretation of them are practices connected to groups and their interests. 6. Try to pose new questions to a text.
12 John W. Creswell and Cheryl N. Poth, *Qualitative Inquiry & Research Design: Choosing Among Five Approaches* (4th ed.): *international student ed. ed., Qualitative Inquiry and Research Design* (Thousand Oaks, CA: Sage, 2018), p. 77.
13 Gerald O. West, *The Academy of the Poor: Towards a Dialogical Reading of the Bible*, vol. 2: *Interventions* (Sheffield: Sheffield Academic Press, 1999), p. 66.

that empowering and liberating interpretation of the Bible is still possible."[14] The IR-VICOBA groups consist of trained pastors, trained evangelists, and trained Christian education teachers who are members of those groups (there are one or two in each group). The rest of the group consists of poor lay Christians.

In my fieldwork, I observed how the members of Amani IR-VICOBA and Upendo Agape IR-VICOBA,[15] within ELCT-KoD, read the Bible and interpret the selected texts on the Kingdom of God and the poor. I selected the texts to enhance my research on this subject. The selected texts are those narratives that explain poverty or richness, and I wanted to research how these poor people interpret them while themselves struggling with poverty. I took the example of Matt. 5:3, where Jesus said that "blessed are the poor in spirit"; I wanted to know if these members of the IR-VICOBA would interpret that Jesus *wanted* them to be poor to enable them to inherit the Kingdom of God.

Moreover, I listened to how they as groups of poor Christians reflected on and put into action the hermeneutical reading of the Bible. I did not contribute to the ongoing Bible study reading process but rather only recorded what they discussed. I also observed and interpreted the nonverbal communication among the group members. I learned much when they laughed, nodded, or shook their heads as one was contributing a point. Those nonverbal communications reflected the message of my study. In general, my passive presence helped me strive toward a more objective understanding of how the members related their impoverished situation with economic and social injustice and what measures they took to fight the situation they were facing as poor Christians in their context. Moreover, it assisted me in knowing the power relations between the trained scholars and the ordinary readers, and between the ordinary readers within the group. The power relations in the group impacted the results of the Bible studies.

My passive presence in the Bible study caused me to struggle to remain objective within my career as pastor, theologian, and church worker of the same church. I know that practice participant observation is founded on the necessity of participation. Graham Harvey quotes Droogers: "We must acknowledge the role of the body as a research tool ... [We] should recognise the bodily presence and participation, even among believers will help scholars to understand what (particular) experience means to them."[16] However, because of the nature of my research and my being a minister in this church, being anything other than silence would not

---

14 Ibid., p. 66.
15 The word 'Amani' is a Swahili word meaning 'peace' and the word 'Upendo' means 'love'. IR-VICOBA is an abbreviation of the phrase "Interreligious Community Village Bank." IR-VICOBA are groups of Christians who are relatively poor, largely peasants, street vendors, and low-paid civil and church workers.
16 Stausberg and Engler, *The Routledge Handbook of Research Methods in the Study of Religion*, p. 226.

have worked well. I discuss this dilemma in Section 2.5 on Power Dynamics and Positionality.

In most cases concerning difficult theological issues, I observed that members relied on theologians for clarification. This would appear to be a positive thing; however, it changed the interpretation because the learned theologians impacted the discussion and used their power to influence opinion. The members have a different level of education, and those few with high levels of education, like degrees and diplomas, had more influence on the Bible study because they had knowledge that gave them power within the group. Nevertheless, the facilitator was obliged to orchestrate this power for the betterment of the Bible discussion by ensuring all voices were heard within the Contextual Bible Study.

To reach my study objectives and research questions, I gave the six texts I had selected from the Bible (see below) to the gatekeepers within the IR-VICOBA groups, which describe the Kingdom of God and the poor. This was my contribution to their participant-centered Contextual Bible Study. The intention was to see how these particular Christians interpreted the texts as poor people aiming to fight poverty. Therefore, this study concerns doing theology from below – the grassroots theology of the people – using Gutierrez's words of "theology of the nonperson,"[17] referring to people the progressive theologians cannot understand and agree on whether they are theologizing. The IR-VICOBA members, to which the pastors and other theologians belong, play a significant role in this Bible reading. The relevant questions are: "Are they doing theology from below?" "Is there any indication of liberation and total emancipation in their reading?" Yet, in the following chapters, I present, discuss, and interpret their theology to see whether and how they are similar to that of other liberation theologians and how they differ and form their own profile of the theology 'from below.'

The members of the Amani IR-VICOBA and Upendo IR-VICOBA discussed the texts from the Synoptic Gospels regarding the poor. The texts selected[18] from the Synoptic Gospels were Matt 5:1-12, the Matthean Beatitudes; Matt 25:31-46, about a range of poor people; Mark 10:17-22, the rich man; Luke 4:18-19, Jesus and the Kingdom of God to the poor; Luke 16:19-31, the rich man and Lazarus; and Luke 6:20-21, Luke's Beatitudes. The readings from the Synoptic Gospels have been of great significance to me and were used to indicate how the members deal with their economic and social context, how they understand and interpret what Jesus said, and how they understand the characters and their contributions in the Gospels as recorded by the evangelists. Reading texts about the Kingdom of God and the

---

17 Per Frostin, *Liberation Theology in Tanzania and South Africa: A First World Interpretation*, vol. 42, Studia Theologica Lundensia (Lund: Lund University Press, 1988), pp. 7–8.
18 I objectively selected these texts to make my research viable. Since I chose to work with two different groups of the IR-VICOBA, it was essential that I selected the texts.

poor provided insights into how the readers, together with learned theologians, interpret the Bible texts and deal with theological issues like liberation, love, justice, solidarity, self-empowerment (power), and freedom. Furthermore, I investigated how the members related to the texts about the Kingdom of God and the poor within their own context.

The texts were selected to qualitatively observe the critical interpretation by the members. For instance, the two Beatitudes, where Matthew writes "poor in spirit" and Luke writes "the poor," were not read sequentially but thematically, for example, starting with Matt 5:3-12, and then, in the following Bible study, they read Luke 6:20-21. Thematic readings were as follows: Luke 4:18-19, followed by Mark 10:17-22, and then Matt 25:31-46. This 'poor-poor-poor-rich-poor/rich relationship' pattern created a thematic correlation of discussion and led to further reflections by the members on the selected themes. The selected texts shed much light on how the IR-VICOBA members, being poor individuals themselves, interpret texts about the Kingdom of God and the poor according to their own socioeconomic context. My selection of the texts did not contribute to the contents of the reading of the groups. But it did help me focus only on the issue of the poor and the Bible reading. The IR-VICOBA members could use any text, and I still would research their way of reading and how it impacts their lives since they start their interpretation from their context toward the text besides the learned theologians who are facilitators giving the historical background of the texts.

I passively participated in the Bible study with each of the IR-VICOBA groups selected for this study for 6 months. I met with them once a month regarding the matter of recording, and for the other 3 weeks, I attended to see if there were any differences if their own regular Bible study were not being recorded. Moreover, I did this to give them a chance to do other things they were used to doing. Thus, I learned many things, for instance, that when they did not read Bible texts, they introduced a different theme from life, such as how to start a project or how to record all the activities and costs of the project. Sometimes the groups learned more about family relations, which was of much interest to me as a pastor and a theologian.

2.2 Why I Chose to Research on Participant-Centered Contextual Bible Study

There are many reasons why I have chosen participant-centered Contextual Bible Study as a preferable hermeneutical method to investigate the impact of Bible reading among poor Christians in Tanzania, using a sample of the IR-VICOBA people. First, after reading about Gerald West's Ujamaa Contextual Bible Study, I saw that the IR-VICOBA groups within ELCT-KoD were following a similar method of reading the Bible as other Bible study groups within ELCT-KoD, as discussed in Chapter 1. The IR-VICOBA members' motives for fighting poverty and their style of their using Bible studies and discussing other matters – like how to deal with financial matters, home economics, how to do business, how to care for business, entrepreneurship, health issues, social issues, and political issues – made me prefer them as study objects. This was my rationale for choosing them to be involved in my research on the Kingdom of God and the poor and trying to investigate the impact of their Bible reading.

Second, I chose to investigate the IR-VICOBA participant-centered Contextual Bible Study because it is claimed to be an example of liberating hermeneutics that connects the people's struggles in life and their Bible reading, meaning that their faith is connected with their struggle and makes them fight within their respective context. To substantiate this, West writes, "A hermeneutics of engagement emphasizes both accountabilities of present communities of faith and struggle, by accepting that the Bible is a significant text for them, and continuity with the past poor and marginalized communities of faith and struggle, by not abandoning their traces of the Bible."[19] Therefore, since there are many poor people in the world today, I thought that this method would enable me to see how poor people in rural areas of Tanzania reflect on this situation as part of their reading process of the Bible together with learned theologians.

Dickson A. Kwesi commented on Biblical interpretation in African Christianity that still applies Western methods, which are not really relevant for laypeople but only learned individuals who practice theology. This is because African theologians have been trained in that theology and do very little contextualization thereof.[20] Being an ordained minister within my church, I have seen how downtrodden people are not listened to and their voices go unheard. But when I visited the IR-VICOBA members near my church, I found these people have many ideas and sometimes create many challenges to clergies and the prevailing scholarship. I learned that this was the right method, and that the VICOBA members were the right people to participate in my research, given that the poor people were being given a voice to theologize with within the groups. My choosing the VICOBA groups related to how I perceived them to conduct their Bible study, and how they made the group more challenging, even for the trained theologians there. This, then, was my third reason for selecting them. The words of Bevans and Tahaafe hold much water here: "In the past, the majority of Christians lived in the most affluent areas of the world. Now the majority of Christians live in the poorest part of the world: the church

---

19 West, *The Academy of the Poor: Towards a Dialogical Reading of the Bible*, 2, p. 48.
20 Kwesi A. Dickson, *Theology in Africa* (Maryknoll, NY: Orbis, 1984), p. 144.

of the 21st century is and will continue to be a poor church."[21] If the center of the church has shifted from the North to the South, the method of doing theology has to be one that pertains to the people of the South, even though they are poor.

How these people relate to theology can give us a snapshot of how the world needs to do theology, especially the grassroots theology of those who make up the majority of the modern church. I found that one of these methods of doing theology was the participant-centered Contextual Bible Study. I asked myself whether this Bible-reading method would provide a real picture of the impact of 'the Bible reading of the poor' while still experiencing the present Kingdom of God in the world. Moreover, I asked whether this type of Bible reading could emancipate the poor from themselves or teach them how to liberate themselves from negative socioeconomic phenomena. I believed that investigating the IR-VICOBA groups would help me to answer these questions.

Fourth, I find that the African culture is based primarily on oral tradition and not on literary tradition, making the downtrodden free to theologize in their participant-centered Bible study together with the learned theologians. The participant-centered Contextual Bible Study is well structured to include all people in its theologizing. The IR-VICOBA use much of their experience to interpret the Bible; nevertheless, I find that it is still well-rooted in African soil. Themes that arise in the Bible study reflect the needs of the people, not as rational theological interpretations, but as immediate critical reflections from the Bible related to their needs within their respective context.[22] I agree with Mbiti on the above idea; nevertheless, I know it cannot be generalized, since there are groups that do not agree with this strand of viewing the Bible. They look on it as a tool of enslavement and feel they do not need to cite some of its verses in their rituals[23] However, in many cases, Bible study

---

21 Stephen B. Bevans and Katalina Tahaafe-Williams, *Contextual Theology for the Twenty-First Century* (Cambridge: James Clarke, 2012), p. 7.

22 Rosino Gibellini, *Paths of African Theology*, Percorsi Di Teologia Africana (London: SCM Press, 1994), pp. 27–39. Mbiti here describes the importance of the type of Bible study that includes all people, whether literate or illiterate, since the illiterate hear the Bible when it is read aloud in churches or at home. In this sense, they also interpret the Bible by using their own experience after hearing it in hymns, in the storytelling of Bible stories, by memorization of the Bible passages and verses, or from Biblical plays.

23 Matthew Engelke, "Text and Performance in an African Church: The Book, 'Live and Direct,'" *American Ethnologist* 31, no. 1 (2004), pp. 76–91. See also *A Problem of Presence: Beyond Scripture in an African Church*, vol. 2: *The Anthropology of Christianity* (Berkeley, CA: University of California Press, 2007). In these two works, Engelke writes on the Apostolic Church called the Masowe Wechisanu Church in Zimbabwe. The church was established in the 1930s by Shoniwa Masedza (who was called Johane Masowe, John of the Wilderness), especially for Christians who do not read the Bible. The claims of these people not reading the Bible according to Engelke is that the book is not 'divine'; it is just a mere book, and it can be worn away or used as toilet paper. To them, in order for the word to be considered divine, it should not be copied; the one directed to other people, in this case, the

in Africa has become a liberating tool, a helping tool, and empowering tool, even though it is not well structured and does not use the 'right' scholastic language. Nevertheless, it touches the hearts and needs of people in need. This may also be found in the words of Paul Freire:

> The insistence that the oppressed engaged in reflection on their concrete situation is not a call to armchair revolution. On the contrary, reflection – true reflection – leads to action. On the other hand, when the situation calls for action, that action will constitute an authentic praxis only if its consequences become the object of critical reflection.[24]

The IR-VICOBA groups undergo training on how to equip themselves to solve the socioeconomic challenges that confront them in the world economy. This marks the rationale of my preference for choosing this method for my study, and the groups go well with the above words of Freire. As a community of believers, they have the right to interpret and learn how to understand the real meaning of the texts about their lives. Jonathan Draper, writing on the issue of readers having their own rights, says: "Every positive meaning is determined by the cultural construction of the interpretive community to which the reader belongs, which may or may not include the author."[25] Therefore, I found the participant-centered Contextual Bible Study fulfills this notion, especially relative to the poor and the Kingdom of God in their societies.

Fifth, participant-centered Contextual Bible Study does not discriminate against those who do not know how to read and write. In this case, those IR-VICOBA members who did not know how to read and write were nevertheless able to theologize. They contributed to intellectual activities during the Bible study; they were not silent and always kept sharing their ideas and experience with one another. This is supported by what John Mbiti described some years ago, namely, that Christianity in Africa had three types of theological trends in the communities: the written theology, which was for trained clergy; and the oral and symbolic theologies, which were for the lay Christians.[26] Today's theologians think they go with the

---

Israelites, should be 'live and direct'. Therefore, Engelke tries to present that issue that the Bible in that church in Africa is present through its *absence*; the Bible is significant without contributing significations.

24 Paulo Freire, *Pedagogy of the Oppressed*, new and rev. 20th-anniversary ed., Pedagogia Del Oprimido (New York: Continuum, 1993), p. 48.
25 J. A. Draper, "African Contextual Hermeneutics: Readers, Reading Communities, and Their Options between Text and Context," (2015), pp. 3–22 (here p. 18).
26 John S. Mbiti, *Bible and Theology in African Christianity* (Nairobi: Oxford University Press, 1986), pp. 46–47.

waves of today's technology; they forsake the oral and symbolic theologies, which close the gap between the learned theologians and the lay Christians.

2.3 Meeting with the IR-VICOBA Leaders: Meeting Amani IR-VICOBA Leaders in Tukuyu Town

I reached Mbeya city on 2 December 2016, where I had to take a holiday of one month, as it was where my family resided. It was good to be with my family since it had been a long time since I left them in January 2016. After my holiday, I started planning for my fieldwork since I was supposed to be in the field for some time. I started planning the research with the two IR-VICOBA groups on the 2 January 2017, by communicating with the IR-VICOBA leaders to arrange when to meet them and their groups. I communicated by mobile phone since they were 70 km (for Amani IR-VICOBA) and 105 km (for Upendo (AGAPE) IR-VICOBA) from Mbeya City where I lived. In particular, I arranged to meet with pastors, evangelists, chairpersons, and secretaries of the two groups. I wanted to meet with them because I did not want to change their way of doing the Bible study and VICOBA sessions or introduce any new ways of doing it.

As I was traveling from Mbeya to Tukuyu, I boarded a bus going to Kyela, and I paid Tshs3000 (€1.40)[27] for the bus fare. I sat next to a lady who was very charming and welcomed me with the greeting *"habari za asubuhi kaka?* (Good morning, brother). I replied, *Nzuri dada yangu.* (It is well, my sister). *Pole Kwa safari?* (How is the journey?) So she said, *Namshukuru Mungu* (I thank God).[28] I conversed with this woman the whole way to Tukuyu, where I was dropped off to go to the ELCT-KoD head office.

We talked of many issues on our way as we were traveling downward to Tukuyu –about the situation of the inhabitants of the Mporoto hills and down the Rungwe Mountains, their daily activities, and how they were dutiful. We talked about natural vegetation, planted forestry, and different crops. The challenging thing was why these people were still poor despite their efforts. I had all the questions in my mind as to why these people were still challenged by poverty when the vegetation was so beautiful and the crops were very promising in the fields. Starting from Isyonje, where the Rungwe District starts, there were pine trees and fields with good maize

---

27 The exchange rate during the research was €1 = Tshs 2200 (Tanzanian shillings).
28 In Tanzania culture, if not in African culture in general, a person is greeted according to his or her age. Greetings and relationship are fraternal – you call a person according to their age within your own family (e. g., brother, father, mother, and sister), even if you are not related and even if it is the first time you've met the person. Therefore, a sister can be anyone at the age of my sisters, a mother anybody at the age of my mother, and a father a person at the age of my father.

and potatoes. When I crossed the River Kiwira, the weather and the vegetation changed; we started seeing many banana trees, coffee, tea, and some little potatoes and maize on small farms.

When we reached Kiwira Bus Station, the bus stopped for a long time by a market. There, we saw many women running businesses, most of them selling bananas, pineapples, mangoes, and groundnuts; some were selling used clothes. She told me that those young women did not depend on the bananas they got from their farms but rather went to remote areas where they could buy bananas more cheaply and came to sell them there. I was curious to know how much they could buy in the remote area and how much per bunch they would receive when sold. She told me that it depended on the season. A banana plant produces fruit over the whole year, and in the high season, they buy at around Tshs 3,000 (€1.40) per bunch and sell them for about Tshs 10,000 (€4.50). In the low season, they may buy for around Tshs 7,000 (€3.20) and sell them for about Tshs 15,000 (€6.8) per bunch. I told her that, if that were the case, they were receiving much higher profits than the peasants. She agreed, saying that the people in the middle of these business exchanges always got more than the producers. She added that some peasants, however, ask *bodaboda*[29] people to go to their area and take bananas to sell directly to the market. They pay the *bodaboda* people after selling their bananas. A *bodaboda* can take five to eight bunches of bananas per trip, and a peasant with many banana bunches needs two or three *bodabodas*.

I was still curious to ask her who their customers were when they reached Kiwira's markets. The lady told me that ripe bananas were sold to travelers in buses. For the plantains and other unripe bananas, people from other cities came to buy there, and then went on to sell them to those cities. Sometimes people from nearby countries (i. e., Malawi, Zambia, and Botswana) came to buy bananas there. She said, "I do not know how much they sell when they reach cities and big municipalities, but what I know they get much profit."

The bus conductor requested the driver to continue with the journey because all the passengers had exited with their luggage. These passengers were coming from Mbeya. They were street vendors who came to sell different goods in the Kiwila market, like new and used clothes and home utensils. They bought new and used clothes from wholesalers in Mbeya city and came to sell them in Kiwila market. Some with little capital bought used clothes from other people who sold in Mbeya and came to sell them in Kiwila. These street vendors come to sell their goods at this particular market because most peasants from remote rural areas come here to sell their crops, especially bananas, and in return, they buy some used clothes, new

---

29 Bodaboda is a name given to motorcycles made in China, which are used for transportation everywhere in Tanzania, other than in areas where they are not permitted by law, like town centers.

clothes, home utensils, and other necessities like salt, sugar, matches, cooking oil, and kerosene. The street vendors sold goods at low prices since the government had exempted them from paying taxes as small business people.

As we departed the Kiwira market, we saw tea and banana fields. I showed the lady that these people were wealthy; they had tea fields where they picked tea leaves every day. She exclaimed, "Brother, even if you gave me a tea field for free, I would not take it. Tea does not benefit the peasants; it is better to grow bananas, which you can eat with your children." She went on, "I do not know the price, but peasants complain every time that the price is low, and it is very laborious to pick the tea leaves." She said she would like to grow cocoa, which seemed to remunerate peasants a little more than tea, and cocoa plants were not so difficult to tend to compared to picking tea leaves.

I reached Tukuyu at noon, a journey that took us at least 2 hours, and I thanked the lady as she continued going to Kyela District, 56 km from Tukuyu. I went directly to the ELCT-KoD headquarters, where I was to meet with the leaders of the VICOBA group and some pastors who were members of the Amani IR-VICOBA group. I went directly to the Dean, the assistant to the Bishop's office, who would be my host in Tukuyu. I wanted to meet other people in the office because I had not seen many of them since I had arrived from Oslo. When I met the Dean and told him that I would be part of the family that day, I left the office and visited other offices to greet other people, especially those I had not met since I came from Oslo. The assistant to the Bishop was my friend, and I would stay at his house.

I met with the Amani IR-VICOBA's leaders, pastors, and evangelists on Thursday, 12 January, at 16:00 hours. There was a chairperson, a female secretary, a female treasurer, three pastors (one male pastor and two female pastors), and a male discipline master of the Amani IR-VICOBA. I told them about my intention to do research while attending their Bible study days as a requirement for my Ph.D. project. In principle, they agreed to allow me to do research, but they wanted me to meet the members first to seek their consent for the research. We agreed that I would attend a Bible study where I could ask the groups for their consent. We also arranged the date, which they chose as Monday, 16 January 2017, at 16:00 hours, which was when they met for their next Bible study and VICOBA contributions. I left there and went to the Dean's residence since I was to stay there overnight. On the following morning, I went to Itete to meet the leaders of the Upendo Agape IR-VICOBA group.

2.4 Traveling to Itete: Meeting the Leaders of the Upendo Agape IR-VICOBA Group

I left the Dean's home around 10:00 hours since traveling to Itete by *daladala* during the rainy season takes 3 to 4 hours. The roads are rough, with many trenches full of water. Itete lies some 10 km from the Ukinga mountains[30] (which used to be called the Mount Livingston ranges).

On my way to Itete, I looked at the Kimbila Tea plantation, which was formerly a Moravian Church-owned plantation, and then it belonged to Muhamed Enterprises, who own several fields of different cash crops, like sisal and tea, and factories in Dar es Salaam. I saw people who were laborers in those fields and asked my neighbor in the *daladala* if he knew how much they earned. He told me he did not know, but another traveler did: "They are paid TZS 120 (€0.05) per kilogram of green tea leaves." I asked how many kilograms a person could pick per day. According to their experience, during the rainy season, more experienced people could pick up to 20 kg, but in most cases, they picked an average of 10 kg. This meant a person received an average of Tshs. 1,200 (€0.50) per day, meaning they would get a total of Tshs 20,000 (€8) at the end of the month. This was indeed low-paying work. A man told me that they came only four times a week since they had distributed days according to plots within the plantations. Some owned their own fields and picked from those on the other days.

The area near Kimbila was not as fertile as that in Tukuyu. They had bananas but not the varieties we saw at Kiwila and Tukuyu. I saw maize, groundnuts, beans, peas, sugarcane, and mangoes in the fields. After we crossed the River Mwatisi, where I saw very attractive vegetation with a different crop, I spied bananas like those in Tukuyu or Kiwila, avocados, sugarcanes, small fields of tea and coffee, and many mango trees full of mangoes because it was 'mango season.'[31] When we crossed the River Mbaka,[32] I saw other crops – cocoa trees. This area was a little warmer than

---

30 I prefer these ranges to be called 'Ukinga mountains' instead of 'Livingstone Mountains' because the Kinga lived there even before Dr. Livingstone passed there and renamed those mountains the Livingstone Mountains. He took the privilege of naming them since the Wakinga, who were living there, had no knowledge of writing.

31 In Tanzania, fruits are referred to in relation to their season of harvest. For example, people will tell you this is mango season, orange season, or pineapple season. A person is not supposed to ask for a mango in orange season. This is because people have no facilities to keep those fruits. For example, during that time, I passed a 20-liter plastic container full of mangoes that sold for just Tshs 2,000 or less than a single US$ (US$1 = Tshs 2,200).

32 Kanisa la Kiinjili la Kilutheri Tanzania-Ukanda wa Kusini, *Karne Ya Kwanza Ya Injili (1891–1991)* (Dar Es Salaam: Dar es salaam University Press, 1991), p. 17. Mwakisunga describes the River Mbaka as the river the Moravian Missionaries and Berlin Missionaries agreed not to pass through when doing missionary work. A station was supposed to be built 5 km from the river, and the real border

Tukuyu, which was higher; this was low land, very close to Lake Nyasa, and was warm, a requirement for successfully growing cocoa trees.

Itete is a small village where the Lutheran missionaries moved their station after their first station encountered problems with local chiefs and had a climate unconducive to missionaries from Germany. Some of them died because of tropical diseases, especially malaria. In this village, the missionaries built a hospital, which is now a Council Designated Hospital (CDH) and belongs to the ELCT-KoD, although the government has entered into a partnership to run it. The government provides the hospital with medicine, personnel, and other medical equipment; the ELCT-KoD provides infrastructure and some personnel.[33] Therefore, there are many people of different backgrounds in this place, although it is situated in a rural area. However, peasants make up the majority of the people living in the neighborhood with the hospital.

The peasants in this area grow cocoa and tea as cash crops as well as bananas, maize, beans, sugarcane, groundnuts, and avocados to earn a living. The hospital employs doctors, clinical officers, nurses, nurse assistants, gardeners, and some church workers. Some depend 100% on farming, but they subside with animal husbandry (cows, pigs, and chickens). The reason for keeping cows is to sustain their fields since the manure from the cow can be spread on the banana and cocoa fields. Some people held more than one job, for example, dealing with farming, animal husbandry, *and* running a small business (e. g., selling goods like sugar, salt, and soap).

My first-born son, who was working at Itete hospital as a business administrator, came to receive me at the bus station. I reached Itete at about 13:30 hours. I was dirty and tired from 3-hour trip of 46 km. We went to his house, and I stayed there during my research. After I took a shower and had some lunch, I met with the IR-VICOBA leaders as agreed at 16:00 hours.

I met with the Upendo (Agape) IR-VICOBA's leaders, pastors, and evangelists on 12 and 14 January. I told them about my intention of doing research while attending their Bible study. They agreed that I could research with them; however, like Amani IR-VICOBA leaders, they wanted me to meet the members first to seek their consent for doing that research with them. We agreed that I would attend a Bible study, where I was required to ask the groups for their consent to the research and the date. They chose Monday 23 January 2017 at 16:00 hours, the day they were scheduled to meet for their Bible study and VICOBA contributions. I returned to

---

was put to be 34 degrees. The Lutherans were supposed to go the East and the Moravians to the West.

33 Conversation with Lee Mwakalinga, the doctor in charge of Itete Hospital during my research.

stay with my son for that night; early in the morning, I returned to Mbeya to meet with the groups.

2.5 Meeting with the IR-VICOBA Members Amani IR-VICOBA

I met with the Amani IR-VICOBA members for the first time on Monday, 16 January. The Amani VICOBA comprised a group of 30 people who met every Monday for Bible study and VICOBA sessions. On the day I met them for the first time, there were 17 people in the room, 5 men and 12 women. Though I did not ask their age, they ranged from approximately 20 to 55 years. In that group, there were two pastors, a Christian Education Educator, two nurses, and other individuals who dealt with nonformal activities, meaning they were either peasants or small business vendors. However, most of them did both. Even church workers also did farming activities to subsidize the salary they received from the church.

They asked me many questions about why I chose them when there were many other Bible study groups to choose from, and why I was researching Bible study at all. I responded to all of their questions that it was a requirement for a Ph.D. student to do research, and I chose Contextual Bible Study as a way to collect data by observing how they read the Bible. I also told them there were indeed many Bible study groups, but I chose them because they had put the issue of their economy with Bible study, an act I saw as a matter of putting into praxis what they read. They appreciated my choosing them in this regard.

They consented to the research on their Bible study; however, their concern was the time dedicated to the research would not be enough. They told me they met for 90 minutes, during which they had the Bible study and the collection for their VICOBA session. After the discussion, we agreed to meet on another day at a convenient time for about 2 hours. They chose every first Saturday of the month from 12:00 to 14:00 hours, and during this meeting, they would have only Bible study. I found the idea to be very promising. They alerted me that this would be the case with the exception of March, where the first week would be devoted to their annual general meeting. Therefore, the agreement between us was that, if there was anything that would cause an inconvenience, they would let me know beforehand so we could reschedule. However, I told them that I would also be coming to their regular Monday session to see how they did their normal Bible study and VICOBA sessions, as long as I was not in Itete, where I would be conducting the same research as I did with them. They welcomed me openly.

2.5.1 Upendo (Agape) IR-VICOBA

When I met the Upendo (Agape) IR-VICOBA for the first time, the group also had 30 Lutheran[34] members. It is a rule in IR-VICOBA meetings that there be no more than 30 members. According to the register, which I later saw, there were 11 men and 19 women in the group of 30. With the exception of two pastors and two nurses, many members were peasants or employed in informal jobs, like street vending. A few who were above the age of 50 had children employed elsewhere and received some support from them financially or of another nature. After staying for some time, some members told me that they had biological or related children who were caring for them since these members contributed to their education. They would occasionally send money to them either to assist them in paying school fees for their young sisters and brothers or their daily lives. When I later visited their homes, I also saw that some members owned various animals, like cows, goats, sheep, and chickens.

In our first meeting, I asked the group leaders to give me time to discuss my research. I did not want to be asked questions when I was with the Amani Group. This group was also grateful that I chose them for research. Unlike the Amani IR-VICOBA group, when I met with the Upendo IR-VICOBA group on the 23rd, they agreed to meet with me on the same day they always meet for VICOBA. They arranged that they would extend this Bible study for an hour before they started their regular session. Therefore, they agreed to meet at 14:00 instead of the usual 15:00 hours.

On that day, 19 members were in the room: 13 women and 6 men. Their ages were between 20 and 56 years, much like the age range I saw in Amani IR-VICOBA. After I had stayed for some time and visited some of the members' homes, I came to discover that most of the families around Itete, where the Upendo Agape IR-VICOBA was held, had many children. There were families with between 5 and 10 children. In their streets, one would find so many children that one would not know whose those children were without asking. In that area, like other rural areas, children were a "symbol of richness" and "a bright future," as they believed that "children would care for them when they are old." John Mbiti describes that, in Africa, children are held to be significant because they are the seal of marriage, the prolonger of the family name, and the glory of the family. All in all, children are

---

34 More than 85% of the population the Itete area have been Lutheran since the missionary era. During the colonial regime, people who were required to live in this area were the African converts. Non-Christians lived far from this area. The members of VICOBA are the children, grandchildren, and great-grandchildren of those first converts. The group is inspired by the Lutheran Church, which minority faith-based people, like those of the Pentecostal church, cannot join; instead, they must try to find another way of establishing the same group within their own faith community.

required to care for their parents and grandparents in the future.[35] Some people in the area put more emphasis on educating their children; some did not. As a result, in families that did not educate their children, they were confronted by more problems than blessings with their children. This was vividly the case in a rural area like Itete, where one could see those who had educated children. Even their lifestyles were different because they cared more than those who were not educated.

People of other denominations and religions, like the few Pentecostal members, Roman Catholic, and African traditional religion members, surrounded the Agape Upendo IR-VICOBA people. Extremely few Muslims worked in the area, and they did not have a place of worship because the mission had oriented the area: The Lutherans were the first to do missionary work in the area, so Lutheranism seemed to be the leading Christian denomination of the area.

2.6 Research Ethics, Power Dynamics, and Positionality

The ethical research challenges relating to this thesis occur on two levels, formal and informal. The formal one relates to procedures and formal regulations for empirical research.

According to the research ethics regulations in Norway, I notified the Data Protection Services (NSD) before initiating the fieldwork. The NSD is the institution that has the mandate to approve empirical research when personal data are being processed in research. I received the approval from NSD on 17 October 2016.[36] At the time of the NSD application, the title of my thesis was a different one than the title that became the final one. However, the plan for the fieldwork in the application was the same as that actually planned. NSD gave their approval on the condition that there was informed consent among the participants of my research. Upon arriving in the field, I obtained informed consent from the participants in the group.[37] Nowhere in this work are the names of the participants mentioned; instead, I use general terms such as 'a member' or 'the IR-VICOBA member.'

During my visits with the two VICOBA groups, I taped the group discussions on my password-restricted mobile phone and later copied them to a USB stick. Later on, I transferred the audio files and the transcriptions to my password-protected area on the University of Oslo server, according to the recommended guidelines for research data management and storage. The audio files and the data on the USB stick have since been deleted.

---

35 John S. Mbiti, *Introduction to African Religion* (London: Heinemann, 1975), pp. 108–109.
36 See Appendix 1.
37 See Appendix 2.

According to NSD conditions, all lists with names and other information concerning identity must be kept separate from the transcriptions during the project time. The lists of names is to be deleted as soon as the project ends.[38]

The ethical challenges in my work, however, emanate not just from formal approvals and procedures. Issues of positionality and power also belong to fieldwork. As a pastor, theologian, and middle-class Tanzanian, I envisaged experiencing some differences between myself and the participants in my field research because of differences in education, economy, and experience. I was aware of the people who were going to be undertaking the participant-centered Contextual Bible Study with me. Therefore, with this knowledge, I made sure that all members knew from the beginning that I was researching so that they would not hesitate to contribute their knowledge and experience on the Bible study in the chosen texts on the poor when they saw me being a silent observer. Moreover, I let the gatekeepers know beforehand that I needed their full understanding of the Gospel in the selected Synoptic Gospel texts without any discrimination of gender, education, or age. This forced me to fulfill the act of research accountability. "Accountability refers to the researcher's commitment to not reproduce the divisions of gender expressed within the dominant paradigms, consequently reinforcing stereotypes about a particular group of [people].[39] That does not mean that a researcher is not supposed to take note of the experiences of the marginalized or experience power imbalances among the respondents.[40] I took notes regarding all nonverbal communications during the Bible study while recording all verbal communications.

Being a pastor, a leader, and a theologian within the same church made me both an insider and an outsider. This stance had an advantage in this project because, unlike an outsider researcher who might not be familiar (or at least less familiar) with the social group or sociocultural and religious traditions under study, I knew the languages of communication and some ways of the people. This eased my entrance into the field as far as cultural ethics were concerned. The IR-VICOBA groups used Swahili, the national language, and sometimes the local language, *Nyakyusa*, which I also know very well. This allowed me to easily understand the communication among them, and I did not need an interpreter. Aguiler has argued that interaction is more natural for an insider researcher, and they are less likely to stereotype and pass judgment on the participants under study because they are familiar with the group and social setting; an insider researcher best knows how

---

[38] https://www.uio.no/english/for-employees/support/privacy-dataprotection/personal-data-in-research.html#toc5.

[39] Nina Hoel, "Embodying the Field: A Researcher's Reflections on Power Dynamics, Positionality and the Nature of Research Relationships," *Fieldwork in Religion* 8, no. 1 (2013), p. 30. Nina writes about women, but this can be applied to poor people too.

[40] Ibid.

to approach individuals.[41] The participants easily communicated in my presence and without hesitation because they presumed I understood them better as we shared the same faith, cultural identity, and philosophy. Moreover, being a partial insider helped me to converse with many people even outside the Bible study venue and talk with them about issues concerning their life, economy, politics, and daily struggles. This also assisted me in correlating with the IR-VICOBA Bible study interpretation because they share the same context and struggle.

Correspondingly, my insider position gave me easy access to contact gatekeepers and insights into my subject, which might not be very easy for an outsider. The advantage of being an insider is accessing the field 'more quickly and intimately' has been referred to as 'dependency of access.'[42] This notwithstanding, I also had the position of an outsider. What made me an outsider was that these people had their own experiences, including experiences of reading the Bible as poor people, which were unique to them and made me an outsider. I could only *imagine* what it meant to be a poor Christian, but I could not completely appreciate the reality of their situation. Moreover, not being a member of the group also made me more of an outsider regardless of the fact that I knew some of the people within those groups. This is why Hoel argues as follows:

> A researcher is never fully an 'insider,' nor never fully an 'outsider.' By moving like a pendulum along the insider/outsider continuum, a shifting interactional process in which the relationship between the researcher and the respondent is formed, there is an opportunity to explore the multiple subjectivities of both researcher and respondent.[43]

Nevertheless, being both an insider and an outsider helped me to do my research objectively. Moreover, being an insider/outsider helped me to visit them in their homes as I was received with a heartfelt welcome by their families, which helped me to correlate their discussed experience in the IR-VICOBA Bible study and microcredit session with their lives at their homes.

---

41 Donald A. Messerschmidt, *Anthropologists at Home in North America: Methods and Issues in the Study of One's Own Society* (Cambridge: Cambridge University Press, 1981), pp. 15–26.

42 Christina Chavez, "Conceptualizing from the Inside: Advantages, Complications, and Demands on Insider Positionality," *Qualitative Report* 13, no. 3 (2008), pp. 474–494 (here p. 482). http://www.nova.edu/sss/QR/QR13-3/Chavez.

43 Hoel, "Embodying the Field: A Researcher's Reflections on Power Dynamics, Positionality and the Nature of Research Relationships," p. 32.

2.7 Facilitation of the Participant-Centered Contextual Bible Study in IR-VICOBA Groups

Every IR-VICOBA group had gatekeepers who were the chairpersons, secretaries, and cashiers of those groups. Additionally, all groups had pastors, evangelists, and Christian education educators trained as theologians at different levels. For example, in the two groups I studied, the pastors were all trained at Tumaini Makumira University, the former Makumira Theological College. Lay members had enjoyed a simple education, and most of them were standard seven-leavers of primary education, with a few who held diplomas and degrees in different disciplines like nursing and education.

An appointed member facilitated the Bible study session, also facilitated by one pastor. Other pastors kept silent because the appointed pastor had been asked to facilitate beforehand and was the one who asked the generic questions. These generic questions served to stimulate the group to be active, and the facilitating pastor always improvised other questions to keep the discussion lively. The fun thing I learned was that members were also allowed to ask questions to the group during the Bible study. They did not ask the facilitators questions but posed questions to be answered by all members in the group.

During each season (6 months) of the Bible study, the leaders gather suggestions from members about themes and Bible texts, and then they determine the schedule of the Bible study and themes to be studied every week they meet. For my research, being investigative, I provided my selected texts from the Synoptic Gospels: Matt 5:1-12, the Matthean Beatitudes; Matt 25:31-46, on a range of poor people; Mark 10:17-22, the rich man; Luke 4:18-19, Jesus and the Kingdom of God to the poor; Luke 16:19-31, the rich man and poor Lazarus; and Luke 6:20-21, Luke's Beatitudes. The readings from the Synoptic Gospels were important to me, since they had been used to indicate how the members dealt with the religious, economic, and social aspects of life from their ordinary understanding, how they understood what Jesus said, and what they thought of the character of the texts and their contributions in the Gospels as recorded by the Evangelists. Moreover, I investigated how they related their own context to the texts after reading them concerning the Kingdom of God and the poor.

Therefore, the gatekeepers and pastors had the selected texts before them and continued using them as a source for one Bible study in a month I recorded. At other times when I did not record, they used the regular schedule of themes or Bible texts already arranged.

Moreover, the facilitators improvised additional probing questions according to the text so that the group would be warmed and stirred up. The objective of these probing questions was to ensure that every member participated fully in the Bible study. These are questions, to use Mligo's language, whose objective was "to awaken a community consciousness, a critical consciousness and to lead them toward a possible transformative action plan."[44] The questions, which the IR-VICOBA had adopted from the ELCT house-to-house Bible study, were both textual and contextual. The facilitator also asked almost every member about their opinions and gathered suggestions on the theme under discussion. The rationale of doing that was to ensure that people who dominate the group should hear the opinion of more introverted members and to ensure that everybody participated. The facilitator, in my observation, did not like to reduce the power of some who were more learned or more talkative than others.[45] Interestingly, some members, instead of contributing their opinions, asked questions to other members to reflect upon the topic. I was surprised to discover that the facilitator did not answer those questions, although they certainly had their own opinions on the questions. Instead, they left it to the group to assist one another.

There were times when I saw these people change a little bit in their participation style in Bible study. I saw this in Upendo (Agape) IR-VICOBA when they invited a person to teach them how to do simple bookkeeping for their simple business. Here I saw the 'banking method' used, as Paulo Freire called it. However, they complemented this with another session, where they discussed the same topic to ensure that they understood what the person had taught. Moreover, they shared among themselves how they do their simple bookkeeping. I wanted to see how they tried to correct everyone so that they correctly recorded. To me, as a trained accountant, it was very simple numbers, but I saw their intention to ensure everyone understood how to record correctly.

I was astonished by their slogans when they started their VICOBA sessions. The Amani IR-VICOBA start by saying "VICOBA," and everyone replies, "… eradicates poverty and builds the economy of the family." The Upendo Agape IR-VICOBA had a different slogan: The chairperson said "VICOBA" and the members replied "We want to be rich." I was astonished by those slogans, but it showed their objective was to fight poverty, so they used those slogans to show their vision as members to fight poverty until they changed their present situation.

---

44 Mligo, "Jesus and the Stigmatized: Reading the Gospel of John in a Context of HIV/AIDS-Related Stigmatization in Tanzania," p. 137.
45 As mentioned above, the group of the IR-VICOBA members have different levels of education. Therefore, if they are were left with no control, you might see the power of education make some of them refrain from talking and sharing their responses on what they know on the matter.

2.7.1 The Facilitator's Task During the Participant-Centered Bible Study

To observe the tasks of facilitators in IR-VICOBA groups, I wanted to check whether they follow the suggestions of the excellent facilitator, as indicated by Gerald West, who maintains there are five characteristics of Contextual Bible Study:

> The facilitator should use a method that encourages the whole group to participate; the facilitator should manage conflict and make the group a safe place for members contributions; the facilitator should train others to be facilitators; facilitator should clarify what is not clear and should summarize the discussion; and facilitator should enable the group to become aware of and involved in the needs of the community.[46]

The facilitators in the IR-VICOBA groups were responsible for creating a suitable environment for the group to participate fully in the Bible study. They were the ones who made sure that everyone's opinions were respected and could be contributed equally. Motivational facilitators encouraged using conventional and straightforward language among themselves and members. They were all encouraged to use pure Swahili, the national language.

The discipline personnel, assisted by the facilitator, had the obligation to make sure that the rules were being followed. For example, no one should talk when another person was contributing to the theme at hand. There were two ways to ensure that everyone talked: The facilitator would call out a person to contribute, or a person would raise a hand to be given the chance to contribute. The facilitator would read from the audience and decide to give to a person who had been silent for a long time the opportunity to talk. This ensured that everybody contributed to the theme under discussion.

The facilitator was the one who allowed these people to differ but made sure that they did not diverge from the texts. The differences in opinion were what made the Bible study lively. Sometimes it would become like a debate; a discussion arose as if two teams were opposing each other on the same theme. I remember one day in particular, when they were discussing the section of the Beatitudes about "blessed are the poor." The discussion was challenging and raised many questions. There were two teams, where some said Jesus was praising poverty, and some wanted to defend Jesus as being right that the poor were blessed. Sometimes when the issue concerned gender or culture, I saw a tug of war between women and men within

---

46 Gerald O. West, *Biblical Hermeneutics of Liberation: Modes of Reading the Bible in the South African Context*, vol. 1, Cluster Monograph Series (Pietermaritzburg: Cluster, 1991), p. 228.

the group, with everyone pulling for their side. That was the moment when the facilitator needed to control the group and let the discussion proceed accordingly.

The facilitator had a responsibility to ensure that they stayed within the time limits they had agreed on, since sometimes people wanted to continue with the discussion even when the time was up. The facilitator was obliged to ensure that all the general and probing questions were discussed within the allotted time. The facilitators would have to take the time to ask the others to contribute so that the extroverts did not dominate the conversation too much.

Overall, it was the facilitator's responsibility to ensure every theme raised on a specific topic was concluded. The facilitator did not do the summing up of the idea, which surprised me; rather, the facilitator asked someone from the group to sum up the theme or the idea under discussion. If the appointed person dropped some issues, other members could add to the summary. For example, in the first Bible study on the Beatitudes, after the issue was raised about whether Jesus wanted people to be poor in order to inherit the Kingdom of God, the facilitator in Amani IR-VICOBA asked a member to summarize what they had discussed on the issue of blessedness and inheriting the Kingdom of God.

This, to me, seemed like the right way to empower members to have confidence in whatever they had discussed. This attitude of the facilitator created an environment of trust between members and their pastors. If members had not been calling their pastors *Mchungaji*, no one would have known that they were pastors because they were at the same level as the other participants. I think that attitude ensued because both were members of the same group, and they were able to build that unity and loveliness between themselves.

2.8 The Problems Raised Within the IR-VICOBA Participant-Centered Contextual Bible Study

Some problems occurred during the Bible study. Here, I would like to highlight some weaknesses and problems that arose during the IR-VICOBA Bible study, according to my perspective.

The first problem was the balance of power and empowerment. In participant-centered Contextual Bible Studies, empowerment was an essential item since every participant came with what they had to contribute within the reading process. The learned theologians came with their expertise in Biblical studies and theological education, while the lay Christians came with their regular education and experiences from their own context. The lay Christians and learned theologians in the Contextual Bible Study also use their education to empower others, mainly when theological or everyday matters arose during the reading process, which sounded good. However, sometimes this did not become the case; some theologians or lay Christians wanted to dominate the Bible study. In the Agape-Upendo group, I overheard one of the pastors saying, "These issues we study in colleges for a long time." By making this comment, he was claiming power and authority. However, the facilitating pastor on duty then corrected the other pastors, saying it was a learning class where they needed all opinions from both sides.

Because of the difference in education among the groups, it appeared to me those who hold diplomas and degrees were more confident in what they were talking about, even if they were the minority in the group. The facilitators tried to ensure that every voice was heard during the Bible study; still, one could observe the nature of power differences. Furthermore, the learned theologians in the group had the power of knowledge, even though you would hear facilitators of the group saying, "Please, everyone should contribute, and we want to hear everyone's opinions." Because lay Christians were not knowledgeable in that area, any discussion of the historical backgrounds of the text depended on the theologians who were there. This was the case when the members would say, "Let's hear what our pastors say on this." In such cases, they wanted to hear the pastors' contribution to the historical background of the texts.

Often, one would hear lay participants saying, "Let's ask the pastors about this issue." Generally, this was a good thing since it showed they wanted to hear a theological reflection or background on the issue from members who were theologians. Nevertheless, on the other hand, it caused the theologians in the group to exercise their power in the Bible study. Describing this, Paulo Freire comments: "That the educator has a certain amount of power is undeniable. This power lies precisely in the power of his knowledge, which is sometimes assumed, but that does not matter. They know that they has a certain power that is rooted in the fact that they knows something."[47] I agree here with Freire; the only problem is when the theologians *want* to dominate instead of sharing and hearing from other members.

The second problem lay in rescheduling the Bible study because of social and religious challenges. In both groups, we had to reschedule sessions many times because the members lived a communal life. If a death happened in the neighborhood, we were forced to reschedule the Bible study because all members were supposed to attend the funeral. In rural Tanzania, attending burials is not a wish but a necessity. If you do not attend, the society members will not recognize you and might not attend to your problems. Therefore, people cancel all other activities to attend burial services. Moreover, if the scheduled time fell on a religious festival, like Passover, then the Bible study was rescheduled.

---

[47] Paulo Freire, *Pedagogy of Commitment*, Series in Critical Narrative (Boulder, CO: Paradigm Publ., 2014), p. 99.

Third, attendance was another problem. As stated elsewhere, these people were attempting to fight poverty to the best of their ability. Therefore, they engaged in many economic activities, making attendance during the cultivation season meager because many members were working in fields in different areas. Members who were involved in petty-cash business sometimes did not attend the Bible study because they needed to buy goods for sale in towns or in the city.

The fourth problem observed was the interpretation based on 'experience.' Even if this is a strength of the participant-centered Bible study, it can also be a problem since most members shared what they knew, which was their experience. One would expect more from learned theologians, but sometimes even they were much taken by the lay Christians putting so much emphasis on sharing their own experience with very little knowledge of the background of the text. They were afraid of seeming as if they were dominating the reading process.

In conclusion, this chapter is related to Chapter 3, where I further discuss the Bible study session of the IR-VICOBA members. Before analyzing their discussion, I begin Chapter 3 by explaining how I collected the data and how I did the transcription, coding, and data analysis. Moreover, I discuss the languages I used to collect, transcribe, and analyze my data in this pursuit.

Chapter 3: Presenting the IR-VICOBA Members' Reading of the Synoptic Gospel Texts and the Poor

3.1 Introduction

In the next three chapters (Chapters 3–5), I want to situate the analysis and interpretation of the IR-VICOBA members' Contextual Bible Study. These three chapters answer the first research question: How do the members of the IR-VICOBA groups relate the relationship between the Bible and social reality? In this chapter, I first present how the IR-VICOBA groups were reading the main selected pericopies in the Synoptic Gospels and the main topics of their interpretation. We will see that the IR-VICOBA members frequently read the text from the position of their social reality. I present this in the form of a more chronological reading of the three chosen pericopes. In Chapters 4 and 5, I return to this approach, albeit from a more analytical, organized perspective. The interpretation stems from the two selected groups, the Upendo Agape IR-VICOBA and the Amani IR-VICOBA.

I produced a transcription of the IR-VICOBA from Kiswahili to English from the two groups. Christina Davidson quotes Green and his colleagues, who define transcription as follows:

> What is represented in the transcript (e. g., talk, time, nonverbal actions, speaker/hearer relationships, physical orientation, multiple orientation, multiple languages, translations); who is representing whom, in what ways, for what purpose, and with what outcomes: and how analysts position themselves and their participants in their representations of form, content, and actions.[1]

Knowing both languages, I had the advantage of easily being able to transcribe from Kiswahili to Swahili first and then from Swahili to English. Davidson maintains there are two types of transcriptions, the idea taken from Bucholtz: naturalized and denaturalized. Naturalized transcription occurs when written features of discourse have primacy over oral features; written transcriptions of talk exhibit many features of written language that do not occur in spoken languages, such as commas, full stops (periods), and paragraphing. Denaturalized transcription preserves the features of the oral language such as any 'ums' and 'ers'.[2] Davidson also maintains

---

1 Christina Davidson, "Transcription: Imperatives for Qualitative Research," *International Journal of Qualitative Methods* 8, no. 2 (2009), pp. 36–52, here p. 37.
2 Ibid., p. 38.

that "Transcription that encompasses translation from one language to another present an especially complex and challenging situation. It might require the use of interpreters."[3] I used the naturalized method in my transcription, since it allowed me to work well from one language to another, i. e., from Kiswahili to English. Therefore, I did not face the complexity of the language differences or of hiring someone to translate and transcribe.

I chose this method to avoid obscuring the communication. Bucholtz, quoted by Davidson, highlights that, the more a transcript retains the features of spoken language, the less transparent it becomes for readers unaccustomed to encountering oral features.[4] Second, I did not need such transcriptions for my research because I intended to follow their interpretation of the Bible texts. However, by doing that, I might have missed some of those 'ums' and 'ers' of verbal communication which would be good indications of doubts or happiness. I therefore supplemented my research with nonverbal communication-like gestures that assisted me in my transcriptions.

I played and replayed the audio to develop good transcriptions after each research session while still in the field, usually the same day or the day after, depending on when I met with the IR-VICOBA group. Since the participant-centered Bible studies were conducted with two groups on different days, I waited until the other group had conducted its participant study so that I could order the themes in accordance with those that appeared after transcription. The themes presented in this chapter are taken from both groups.

After preparing my transcriptions, I read all the contents of the transcriptions and then started doing the so-called 'content analysis,' which I later did thematically to give me a meaning. It helped me observe their interpretation of the text and the move from the text to their context or context to the text as they were interpreting. Chad and Woods define content analysis as "a form of textual analysis used to describe and explain characteristics of messages embedded in texts."[5] Moreover, content analysis is defined as "research techniques for making replicable and valid inferences from texts (or other meaningful matter) to the context of their use. It includes any of several research techniques used to describe and systematically analyze the context of the written, spoken or pictorial communication."[6] They continue that "textual analysis is the method used to describe and interpret the characteristics of a recorded or visual message."[7] According to Sue Wilkinson, "Content analysis produces a relatively systematic and comprehensive summary

---

3 Ibid. 38.
4 Ibid., p. 39.
5 Stausberg and Engler, *The Routledge Handbook of Research Methods in the Study of Religion*, p. 109.
6 Ibid., p. 110.
7 Ibid., p. 110.

or overview of the data set as a whole, sometimes incorporating a quantitative element."[8] She further argues that "content analysis is based on examining data for recurrent instances of some kind; these instances are then systematically identified across the data set, and grouped together by means of coding system."[9] In this pursuit, I analyze the hermeneutics of the IR-VICOBA groups concerning the Kingdom of God and the poor, as described in the methodological chapter.

To enable a meaningful analysis based on their reading, I coded the transcription into themes and issues. According to Stake, "Coding is sorting all data sets according to topics, themes, and issues important to the study."[10] In this study, I thematically analyze the themes and issues, which the two groups of VICOBA raised in their Contextual Bible Study. Some themes appeared from both groups, and some were from either group. In these codes, I decided that the unit of my analysis was "the whole group and the individual participant utterances."[11] The center of the groups was a conclusion and agreement or disagreement drawn from the discussion. However, the center depended on the participants' utterances in the discussions. Direct utterances from some members have been of much use and are presented in this chapter. These are supplemented with nonverbal communication, with some members either nodding in support or shaking their heads in opposition. To make coherent arguments, I requoted some in the following chapters.

The layout of this chapter reflects the IR-VICOBA members' presentation of the hermeneutical interpretation of the Matthean Beatitudes (Matt 5:1-12), the parable of the rich man (Mark 10:17-31), and the rich man and poor Lazarus (Luke 16:19-31). In all of these texts, I present a subchapter containing; some of the themes from the the perspectives of the members' understanding of those passages. The IR-VICOBA members also read other Synoptic Gospel texts: Matt 25:31-46 (the sheep and goats), Luke 4:16-19 (ministry of Jesus to the poor), and Luke 6:20-21 (the Lukan Beatitudes). For the sake of presentation of their readings in this project, I present the first threelater texts are given only when required.

The generic questions the facilitators asked in every Contextual Bible Study session were as follows: 1. What are we reading about today? 2. Who are the specific characters in the text we are reading? Can you explain their role in the text? 3. What can we learn from the passage we have read today? Socially? Economically? Also, religiously? 4. How can we apply the text to the context we are living today? To our country or the world at large? 5. Is there any specific thing to avoid from

---

8 David Silverman, *Qualitative Research*, 4th ed. (Los Angeles, CA: Sage, 2016), p. 84.
9 Ibid., p. 85.
10 Robert E. Stake, *Qualitative Research: Studying How Things Work* (New York: Guilford, 2010), p. 151.
11 Silverman, *Qualitative Research*, p. 85. Here, Wilkinson explains the unity of analysis to be the whole group, the group's dynamics, the individual participant, or – most commonly the case – the participants' utterance.

the passage? What was interesting with these two groups was that members were free to ask questions during the discussion and answer the questions regardless of whether the facilitating pastors had posed those generic questions. Besides the generic questions, the facilitators improvised questions to stir up the discussion of the generic questions.

This chapter contains some themes that are repeated according to the pericope under discussion. Nevertheless, in the subsequent chapters, in which I incorporate more analysis and discussion, there are no repetitive themes.

3.2 Discussion of Matthew 5:1-12 by Two Groups of IR-VICOBA

The Text:

> 1 When Jesus saw the crowds, he went up the mountain; and after he sat down, his disciples came to him. 2 Then he began to speak, and taught them, saying:
> 3 "Blessed are the poor in spirit, for theirs is the Kingdom of Heaven.
> 4 "Blessed are those who mourn, for they will be comforted.
> 5 "Blessed are the meek, for they will inherit the Earth.
> 6 "Blessed are those who hunger and thirst for righteousness, for they will be filled.
> 7 "Blessed are the merciful, for they will receive mercy.
> 8 "Blessed are the pure in heart, for they will see God.
> 9 "Blessed are the peacemakers, for they will be called children of God.
> 10 "Blessed are those who are persecuted for righteousness' sake, for theirs is the Kingdom of Heaven.
> 11 "Blessed are you when people revile you and persecute you and utter all kinds of evil against you falsely on my account. 12 Rejoice and be glad, for your reward is great in heaven, for in the same way, they persecuted the prophets who were before you."
> (Matt 5:1-12)

3.2.1 Participants and Their Discussion on Texts

This section begins with the presentation of participants and how participants discussed the above-noted text. Each group discussed the text in one session over 2 hours. In the Agape Upendo IR-VICOBA discussion, there were 10 people: 5 females and 5 males. In the Amani IR-VICOBA group, there were 17 people: 10 females and 7 males. In both groups, there were already prepared generic questions that served to stimulate the discussion. Facilitators were also allowed to improvise questions during the discussion of those generic questions. Facilitators utilized the generic questions they were familiar with, which were part of the Bible study of the house-to-house cells; they modified them to fit the text they were reading.

The pastor gave the historical background of the text and then returned to them for the discussion. The first question for both groups was "What are we reading about today?" The members openly portrayed their attitude toward Jesus talking about how people should live their lives to be blessed in heaven. However, as the facilitator continued asking additional questions about the passage, they started to think more critically.

In the two groups, their interest centered around verse 3: "Blessed are the poor in spirit; for theirs is the Kingdom of Heaven." This verse led to a more extended discussion than before; it was a verse of special interest since the readers were also poor. An example of critical thinking in the Itete Agape-Upendo IR-VICOBA group may be seen in members asking some questions instead of responding to the question, "What have we read about today?" These included questions like: "Did Jesus want people to be poor so that they can be blessed? Why did Jesus differentiate the blessing?" Examples of the answers given include the poor having the Kingdom of Heaven, the meek will have land, those who mourn will be comforted, and those who hunger and thirst for righteousness will be filled; the pure in heart will see God, peacemakers will be called children of God, and those who are persecuted for righteousness' sake will have the Kingdom of Heaven. Therefore, as they continued with the discussion, it made them think more critically.

3.2.2 Characters Review within the Text

The groups responded to the questions, "Who are specific characters in the text we are reading? And "What is their role in the text?" from a very broad perspective. They went deeper than one might expect. For example, as well as describing Jesus, the disciples, and the crowd, they described the group in connection to each of the Beatitudes. Some members of the IR-VICOBA described the poor in spirit, people who mourn, the meek, those who are hungry and thirsty for righteousness, the merciful, the pure in heart, the peacemakers, and those who are persecuted for righteousness as characters in the text. Nevertheless, in the end, they concluded that the characters were Jesus, the disciples, and the crowd.

In this subsection, I present several themes expressed by the members of IR-VICOBA which were of great interest as they were continuing with the assessment of characters in their discussion. These themes were: Jesus and the downtrodden in the text, Jesus as a good teacher of the Kingdom of Heaven, the poor in spirit as the heralds of the Kingdom of Heaven, people who are persecuted and mourn for righteousness' sake and servanthood to other people. The character assessment made the members of IR-VICOBA reflect more on the role of those characters and go deeper into their understanding of the text.

Jesus as a Good Teacher of the Kingdom of Heaven

The group viewed Jesus as a good teacher of the Kingdom of Heaven. They reflected their teaching in catechism class that "Jesus was a true God and was a true human being. Therefore, he was teaching people good teachings about the Kingdom of God." One member of the group commented that "Jesus was teaching how people could inherit the Kingdom of God here on Earth and in heaven, and Jesus in the Beatitudes gave all the descriptions on how to live on Earth and in heaven." This participant said this because Jesus' teaching reflected both the indication of heaven and Earth. For example, they indicated that "Peace is needed on Earth, while righteousness is needed for entering into heaven." For the VICOBA members, Jesus was a teacher of the Kingdom of Heaven on Earth and in heaven. Reflecting theologically on this discussion of IR-VICOBA groups, one can say he was teaching the present and future Kingdom of Heaven, while the former is the decisive case for the latter.

The Poor in spirit as inheritors of the Kingdom of Heaven

The poor in spirit was also an important issue in the discussions. However, the IR-VICOBA members denied that Jesus meant the material poor; they emphasized that "Jesus meant the 'poor in spirit,' those people who were in the situation of needing God's presence, anointing, blessing, and who seek him in their daily lives." One member said, "Some groups of fellowships (charismatic groups) think being poor means being near to God; we [in the] VICOBA group do not agree with this notion but fight poverty with all our means." This understanding was the motive in those groups regardless of their poor economic status. In conversation with a leader, I asked her why they took this position. She said, "One of the motives of VICOBA, regardless of teaching the Word of God, is to empower us to fight poverty; and this is what we try to do in the VICOBA session to empower each other." For people like them, believing that Jesus thought the 'blessed poor' were the 'material poor' would not have been the case.

To make the above assertion clear, one member said, "I think that the disciples of Jesus, in this case, were not poor because they trusted Jesus to be the Messiah." Even if this notion made other members laugh, he thought that these people were spiritually rich even if materially poor. Others laughed because the facilitator told them that "some of the Jews were 'materially poor' since they were under the colonial regime and possessed less land. The facilitator claimed that these Jews were poor regardless of the blessing they got from the Torah (Deuteronomy 28:11)." Still, some IR-VICOBA group members denied connecting spiritual poverty with material poverty.

The interesting note from the IR-VICOBA groups was their conception that "Spiritual poverty can be the cause of material poverty." They meant that there is 'material poverty' that is rooted in being 'spiritually poor.' They said that Jesus regarded some people as spiritually poor, which was why they were materially poor. According to the IR-VICOBA groups, to be the inheritor of the Kingdom of God (both present and future) depends on how you solve your spiritual poverty. Then, to be blessed by Jesus in the manner intended, they were supposed to solve their spiritual poverty and become the inheritor of the Kingdom of God in the present time.

The IR-VICOBA groups thought one becomes empowered spiritually, and then, automatically, one becomes empowered economically. This argument brought tension among them, but later they agreed that even inadequate economic systems were there because of spiritual problems of human beings, such as being egocentric and not trusting God to be the source of blessing to the human race. For example, they discussed that, "if people in the text were in trouble, the problem lay in the powers that dominated and exploited them. That is a spiritual problem that affected people materially." The IR-VICOBA groups thought that, if no one exploited anyone in the text they were reading, they would have empowered themselves, would have had a good life economically as well as spiritually, and they would have the right relationship with their God. Therefore, people in the text were in that problematic predicament because they were affected in both ways, whereby the spiritual problem was causing the economic problem.

Those Who Are Persecuted and Mourn for Righteousness' Sake

The IR-VICOBA groups discussed characters Jesus said were persecuted and mourned. One member said, "These people were persecuted because of their faith in God, and that caused them to mourn. Possibly, they were people who stood against the colonial regime and wanted freedom, which is why they were persecuted even if they did not do anything evil." The IR-VICOBA members thought like that because they were reflecting upon what the facilitator had said about the background of people under the colonial regime, which reminded them of when Tanzania was under a colonial regime. They remembered how people were sent to prison even when they had done nothing evil or were forced to pay the head tax.

The members of the VICOBA groups continued to reflect that being persecuted for righteousness was possible. One member said that this is because of "people trying to fight for their freedom against the colonial regime and the religious suppression, and then Jesus was giving a message of consolation that, if they believe in the Kingdom of Heaven, which he was preaching, they will get freedom and see God." They reflected with a similar knowledge of being under the colonial regime that exploits and dominates people in their whole sphere of life. They mentioned themselves as examples, when they were under German and British colonial rule. Many people were persecuted and sent to prison, and some people were also killed.

They continued discussing, and one member said, "We see in this context people who are mourning and being persecuted. Possibly there are rich people who use their money to send people to jail or court and use their financial status to change the rights of people by paying bribes to the people judging the case." They continued arguing that there may have been people in jail because of tricks and forced confessions from authorities because they were telling the truth on behalf of people oppressed by the rich or political authorities. They gave examples of wives and children of people sent to jail because of evil and corrupt judicial institutions. They would mourn for their relatives who were persecuted for righteousness' sake. Therefore, according to members of the VICOBA groups, social interaction within the text reflected the exploitative nature of people and caused people to mourn and be persecuted.

The VICOBA groups discussed the issue of mourning, and one member said, "Possibly there were many things which caused people to mourn; therefore, Jesus wanted to console them and encourage them." Moreover, "Jesus as God, knew them from their hearts and saw their hearts troubled and their problems because of the colonial regime, religious organizations, rich people, and powerful people." They discussed the issue of people being forced to pledge much money to their churches and were left impoverished. Another member said, "I visited one church where members had been asked to give much money so that God could bless them, and the members were giving a lot of money and properties. But I also met some members from the same church complaining that they were becoming poor." According to this person, these people were mourning that church leaders had caused problems for members to such an extent that they had started mourning. This member encouraged other members to reflect on the issue, which the facilitator, while talking about the background of the passage, said that religious organizations emphasized offerings like tithes, seed offerings, and first fruit offerings, which became a burden to members and caused them to mourn because they were being exploited in many ways. Therefore, according to the IR-VICOBA members, people were being persecuted for righteousness' sake, and those who were mourning did so because of the harsh colonial regime, social injustice, and harmful practices of religious institutions.

Servanthood to Other People

The theme of interest among the VICOBA group was that of servanthood to other people, which Jesus mentioned in the Beatitudes. They discussed the issue of merciful people (v. 7), people who hunger and thirst for righteousness (v. 6), and people who are peacemakers (v. 9). In the course of the discussion, one member said, "Jesus wanted these people to serve other people without discrimination and without fearing any situation so that they could inherit the Kingdom of Heaven." During their discussion, they even reflected on world peace, peace in particular countries, and righteousness, which sometimes cost other people their lives. They indicated that Jesus wanted his audience to serve other people regardless of their situation, which is why Jesus said, "Blessed are you when people revile you and persecute you and utter all kinds of evil against you falsely on my account. Rejoice and be glad, for your reward is great in heaven, for in the same way, they persecuted the prophets who were before you" (v. 11). This was a move that motivated them to serve one another as a reflection on the Matthean Beatitudes. Therefore, for the IR-VICOBA groups, serving others, even if costly, was the motive Jesus wanted the disciples and the crowd to follow up so that they could inherit the Kingdom of Heaven.

Jesus and the Blessed

The blessedness of the downtrodden was another issue the groups discussed with some difficulties. They saw Jesus as someone who encouraged the downtrodden with the assurance of their being blessed. However, most of them were astonished at the irony of Jesus' statement; for example, that someone could be both poor and blessed. In the course of the discussion, most members of the IR-VICOBA group centered the discussion on the assurance of Jesus' teaching that most downtrodden were assured of being blessed in the present and future promise of the Kingdom of Heaven. One IR-VICOBA member commented, "Jesus saw people in hardship in their daily lives and thought God had forsaken them; therefore, he taught them that they are blessed if they depended on and trusted in him." The IR-VICOBA members reflected on their situation but went further, saying that this blessedness was from God. They trusted that, if they believed in God and worked hard, they would regain their blessedness and their dignity. Therefore, for them to work hard to fight poverty to regain their blessedness from God was Jesus' message for the downtrodden from his Father, who blessed people abundantly in his Kingdom, now and then.

Another issue discussed related to blessedness was that of "spiritual blessedness" (v. 3). One of them said, "There are some people in some groups who think being poor is a sign of being spiritually rich, and they teach their members to be against material richness." The IR-VICOBA was strongly against that notion. They said they believed that Jesus did not want them to be poor as the criterion to inherit the Kingdom of Heaven but rather was making a consolation to all downtrodden. Otherwise, he would not have encouraged them to work hard if being poor was the criterion to entering heaven. They also commented on Matt 6:33, where Jesus said, "But strive first for the Kingdom of God and his righteousness, and all these things will be given to you as well." The IR-VICOBA members, in making this intertextual comparison, saw that Jesus aimed at the same notion of people trusting God in everything; from this, other things like blessing would follow if they worked hard.

3.2.3   The Context Assessment

In their discussion and interpretation of the characters in the text and their roles, the IR-VICOBA members reflected on their context compared with the text. This is an area where the IR-VICOBA members used their experience and managed well because they were discussing something they knew more than anything, namely, their context, the issue that caused them to reflect on many situations. The themes raised from reflecting on their context were exploitation and injustice as causes of poverty, disrespect among believers because of their differences in faith, and socioeconomic status causing people to be persecuted, defiled, and disrespected. In addition, they discussed the theme of gender differences as the cause of disrespect and injustice within families.

The Issue of Exploitation and Injustice in Society

The issue of exploitation and injustice came up as they discussed the background of the text given by the facilitating pastor, namely, that characters in the text were under the regime of the Roman Empire and had no autonomy in many aspects of life. They were also astonished to hear that church leaders were also exploiting them. Using the improvised question, "What made the people poor in their context?" the IR-VICOBA members further discussed injustice and exploitation. Retrospectively, they remembered when Tanganyika (Tanzania Mainland) was under the control of a colonial regime and their own struggle as poor people. The IR-VICOBA members mentioned the Roman Empire, reflecting after the pastor mentioned that the crowd and the disciples whom Jesus was teaching were under the Romans. In this case, the people were under the Roman colonial regime, which made IR-VICOBA members reflect more generally on the meaning of being under a colonial regime. It meant being colonialized, exploited, having no autonomy, and consuming what you do not produce and producing what you do not consume.

Nevertheless, they discussed the lives they are living as poor people in relation to the lives of rich people. One member said, "Even now we are made poor every day by the government. Some people exploit the poor like us in our country. They buy our crops for a low price and go to the towns or cities and neighboring countries where they sell those crops for a higher price." One of the members elaborated on the scenario in this way:

I have an example, which a wealthy person told me from Dodoma. I went to Dodoma for mission visitation and stayed with a wealthy family. During dinner, we had a conversation, and I wanted to know what he was doing to earn his living because he was wealthy. He told me he was doing business, buying crops from farmers, and bringing them to sell in Dodoma. I buy bananas and potatoes from Rungwe district, he said. His richness is from this business.

That member was astonished to see how wealthy the man was, since he had not seen anyone in such a good place in rural places like the Rungwe District, where they produce bananas and potatoes. This rich man had a nice car, a good house, and a very promising and significant business. Then members thought that these were the people – fellow Christians – who exploited the peasants and made them miserable everyday. Reflecting upon the poor people in the crowd whom Jesus was teaching (v. 3), the IR-VICOBA members discussed that these people were poor in the text, possibly like them, and were being similarly exploited.

The IR-VICOBA groups critically weighed in on their situation after hearing about the businessperson from Dodoma, who was buying crops in their area. Another group member added, "Besides that, we grow cash crops like coffee, tea, and cocoa, but we are still poor. We grow crops but do not set the price for them. The company from afar buys our crops, but we do not set the price at all. Business companies come with new prices every year, which makes us poorer, and the government does not care for this at all." By complaining like that, they indicated that there were injustices in businesses, even though they did not know that such business practices were global. The IR-VICOBA members just complained about their government not intervening.[12] Members of IR-VICOBA thought that business people from within the nation who buy cereal crops and horticultural produce like bananas, maize, beans, and potatoes and do business within the country were not acting fairly or justly at all. The business people thought only about making a profit and did not consider the situation of the poor peasants and their production costs. Members of IR-VICOBA discussed how their products benefitted other people more than themselves; they mentioned an example of how bananas were being sold to consumers in big cities and neighboring countries. One member indicated how this unjust business went on:

There is a supply chain for any crop, and in every stage, business people benefit more than the peasants. For example, a businessman in Dar es Salaam gives money to the middlemen

---

12 The intervention of the government in businesses was done during *Ujamaa* (Tanzania socialism), and now Tanzania is practicing trade liberalization, where the government does not interfere in business according to the World Bank and the IMF.

in Dar es Salaam, who give the money to other intermediaries in Mbeya. And those in Mbeya pay the intermediaries in our district. For example, if the businessman in Dar buys a bunch of bananas for Tshs 10,000, then the intermediaries take Tshs 3,000; in Mbeya, they take Tshs 2000, then we poor farmers get the remaining Tshs 5,000 or less, while we labor for those bananas almost the entire year. This is exploitation since I am sure if Jesus were here, he would say, "Blessed are you poor" since we are being exploited a lot. We need to be liberated and redeemed.

The example above portrays how businesspeople in big cities and towns exploited peasants and the peasants became more miserable every day. Therefore, according to the IR-VICOBA members, the poor people whom Jesus taught in the Beatitudes also experienced a similar situation, which hindered them from fighting poverty every day without success.

Interestingly, while discussing the matter of being exploited, the IR-VICOBA members also discussed the issue of how some politicians exploit people. They mentioned a politician who had bought many motorcycles and sold them to young men on credit, who were supposed to pay extra profit to this politician. A member spoke up and said,

> Our leaders are using their political power to exploit peasants ... There is a political leader in our village who asked young ones to borrow money from him and buy motorcycles. They had to pay back a total of Tshs 3,500,000 after 2 years, while the price of a motorcycle was only Tshs 2,000,000.

This politician gave the young peasants the loan under cover of 'helping them' to have a job, while making a profit of Tsh 1,500,000, which is a super profit of 75% and unfair. If he would make a lesser profit, let us say 25%, asking them to pay 2,500, 000, that would have been fair. Therefore, in this matter, the politician, who was a leader of those people, was not helping them but was making them more miserable and making himself richer.

Disrespect Among Believers Because of Differences in Faith and Social Status

The IR-VICOBA members, in response to the issue of disrespect among the people of faith communities, responded to the question of people being despised (Matt 5:11). Members reflected upon some groups that despised others they considered not having good faith within the church. They mentioned other groups that despised other Christians as lesser believers because they were not attending their groups. In her own words, one member said,

We Christians fight among ourselves now and despise other people, e. g., fellowship members, counting others as not good believers or people of some other denomination – despising people of other denominations by segregation and some counting themselves righteous more than others. If Jesus were here, he would say, "Blessed are you when people revile you and persecute you and utter all the kinds of evil against you falsely on my account. Rejoice and be glad, for your reward is great in heaven, for in the same way, they persecuted the prophets who were before you." (Vv. 11-12)

The IR-VICOBA members thought these people were like the Pharisees, who did not respect tax collectors and other government officials because they considered themselves as righteous and others as sinners. "There are charismatic groups and Pentecostal churches that do not consider other Christians as faithful as them; the act of which does not comply with the grace of God since that is a self-justification." The IR-VICOBA members recalled that, if Jesus were here, he would say their reward was high in heaven. Therefore, Pentecostalism and charismatic movements were revealed as rivals of non-Pentecostals and non-Charismatic churches within a society where the VICOBA members lived.

The Issue of Gender as the Cause of Disrespect

Discussing the matter of revilement and persecution, IR-VICOBA members introduced the issue of gender inequalities in families in which men controlled and abused women because of their thinking that women are second-grade people. In the discussion, a member of IR-VICOBA said, "There are some traditions that make women in the African context like property. For example, women are not allowed to possess wealth, only men; or inherit land and cattle, which is still occurs in some rural areas." The IR-VICOBA members discussed that revilement and persecution according to gender is another evil system where Jesus would have said, "Blessed are you poor women even if men revile you and persecute you." The IR-VICOBA members pondered this situation and came up with the following thought, as stated by one of them: "There are changes in the world we are living in today compared to the traditional African world, for example. Today, there is a little bit of justice. Even women can stand up before men to preach the Word of God and can also possess wealth, which didn't used to be like that in some areas: Men did everything." However, this is not for all people. In some families, where whatever the women earn belongs to their husbands; for instance, if they earned money or any other form of wealth, it would be taken from them and controlled by their husbands, regardless of their efforts.

In some families, women are beaten and treated by men as animals or inanimate things. Sometimes they are treated that way because they are Christian women and are married to non-Christian men; or they are newly converted women who are married to nonbelieving men, who persecute them because of their faith. In the discussion process, one of the IR-VICOBA members argued:

> There are still some traditions that make women tools for work and not creations of God with men in the family. There are women who are beaten by their husbands. This happens because they say women are bought since men pay a bride price (dowry) for their wives.

Thus, when Jesus says, "Blessed are the ones who are persecuted because of their faith," to the people of IR-VICOBA, it seemed to be something that enlightened their neighborhood and reflected a fight over these practices that reviled women and other downtrodden. The IR-VICOBA members reflected on what they should avoid. One member said, "We should continue helping people to fight for justice, and we should love one another." The IR-VICOBA members meant that if they wanted to follow Christ, they should help women and other downtrodden live in peace and help them fight for justice – regardless of what the social injustice was, which still prevailed secretly and sometimes openly in their neighborhood.

3.2.4 Response of the IR-VICOBA Group Based on the Reading of the Beatitudes

Reading texts encouraged the members of IR-VICOBA to respond to some issues, which was the outcome of their reading process. They reflected on some social, economic, and religious issues in their context.

Social Response to the Beatitudes

Socially, the IR-VICOBA members responded that they were supposed to be dangerous to others in terms of different issues, like fighting for justice regardless of what they were themselves, e. g., deprived and powerless. One of them argued, "If we want to be blessed by Jesus now and inherit the Kingdom of God, we are supposed to continue to lead people justly in different perspectives in our lives. We should not oppress anyone in our society but advocate for others if they are persecuted." Socially, they emphasized continuing to do justice within their community. To reflect on this issue of injustice, one woman among the group members said, "I remember advocating persecution of my sister-in-law who had been asked to leave the premises of our elder brother (her husband) after his death. Knowing what I now have learned, I would not advocate that as a woman because I know I was promoting persecution of other people, especially my fellow women." Although other members laughed at her, it was a lesson for reflection in the Bible study, since the Beatitudes instructed them to hunger and thirst for righteousness' sake and advocated for peace as peacemakers. Therefore, the Beatitudes made them respond positively, namely, that they were not supposed to act against peace and be the cause of persecution to other people.

The IR-VICOBA people also responded to some social injustices that took place in their social situation, like men beating women. One man argued, "I think, in the world we are living in today, there is no need for men to use their wives as objects or as a means for production. Men should stop beating their wives and use their masculinity to spend wealth at home the way they like and stop their wives and children from suffering." They argued like that because of some reflections about people who mourn and are persecuted within society by their spouses or people from their families.

Another group of IR-VICOBA members emphasised caring for orphans and the needy within society. One member responded, "To be Christ-like, we need to continue to assist the needy people who are poor, assist the church when it starts the orphanage centers." This was a move toward change after reflecting on the text in their context. They said that, even if there were some pretenders, it was their obligation to help others who were poorer than they were. Therefore, the Beatitudes made the IR-VICOBA group more responsive to the needy. As one member said, "We are required to assist one another as a body of Christ."

Economic Response to the Beatitudes

The response from IR-VICOBA included many economic aspects, even though the members were poor. One member said, "We should continue to empower each other regardless of our being poor, and we should learn to work hard to become economically capable." Moreover, another member said, "We should also learn more about how to empower each other to emerge from this situation we are facing as poor people. The Word of God should continue to illuminate us to know to be empowered economically." These IR-VICOBA people responded like that because they put more emphasis on fighting against poverty. Then, for the IR-VICOBA members, continuing to empower themselves and others was their response to the Matthean Beatitudes.

On the issue of being exploited, the VICOBA members responded that they wished to make personal changes. One member said, "We are supposed to unite together and make our market system work so that we can avoid other middlemen exploiting us. So, we can ask our local government to interfere on this issue." In their discussion on this issue, this member responded like that because intermediaries were exploiting them. The member wanted others to work together so that they could start to sell directly to people who bought bananas and potatoes in the cities, towns, and, if possible, in the neighboring countries. Therefore, the Beatitudes made them think critically about the poor in the Bible and rethink why they were poor, i. e., they reflected on their poverty.

They also responded that they wanted to ask their Members of Parliament to intervene with their business when they sold their cash crops. One member said, "We want our Members of Parliament to assist us in these businesses where they are cheating us." However, the Beatitudes helped them to think more critically about these businesses and how they were exploited and finding themselves miserable every day, regardless of the effort they were making.

Religious Response to Beatitudes

The IR-VICOBA responded positively to the issue of caring for the needy, although their response seemed very social. But they wanted to respond in a way that made them think about religion. They wanted their pastors to emphasize that caring for orphans and widows ought to be more prominent, not only at the personal level but also at the parish and diocesan levels. One member suggested that "the church should do more than what it is doing at present, for example, by establishing connections between rich people and orphans in rural areas, who would care for them and make themselves parents to these children from well-off parishes in town." He added that "the ELCT-Konde Diocese has one orphanage center, but this is just a drop in the bucket. The diocese has many more orphans than those who are being cared for in the orphanage center." Another member also commented that "the advocacy plans which the ELCT-Konde Diocese has in its function and performance are not enough. It would be better if they employed lawyers instead of depending on volunteers. The lawyers should be caring for all judicial issues in a court of law for people being oppressed by bad traditions and injustice in the rural areas – and women in particular." The IR-VICOBA members thought that, by doing that, the diocese would be fighting for peace and justice for all people, which was the mission Jesus had when pronouncing the Beatitudes.

3.3 The IR-VICOBA Members' Reading Intellectual Activity: Mark 10:17-22

3.3.1 Introduction

The Text:

> 17 As he was setting out on a journey, a man ran up and knelt before him, and asked him, "Good Teacher, what must I do to inherit eternal life?" 18 Jesus said to him, "Why do you call me good? No one is good, but God alone. 19 You know the commandments: 'You

shall not murder; You shall not commit adultery; You shall not steal; You shall not bear false witness; You shall not defraud; Honor your father and mother.'" 20 He said to him, "Teacher, I have kept all these since my youth." 21 Jesus, looking at him, loved him and said, "You lack one thing; go, sell what you own, and give the money to the poor, and you will have treasure in heaven; then come, follow me." 22 When he heard this, he was shocked and went away grieving, for he had many possessions. (Mark 10:17-22)

3.3.2   Character Assessment during the Reading Process

During the readings, the members contemplated different themes that occurred as they continued their Bible study. The themes were Jesus, the poor, and the rich; Jesus and the Commandments; and Jesus as a good teacher of the Kingdom of God. Hereafter, I touch on those themes that reflect the character assessment.

Jesus, the Poor, and the Rich

The IR-VICOBA members discussed the text of the rich man who followed Jesus and asked how he could inherit eternal life (v. 17). In one group, the question whether Jesus wanted his followers to become miserable because he asked the rich man to sell everything and follow him. One member asked some questions: "Why did Jesus ask the rich man to sell everything he had? Does it mean he wanted this person to go to ground zero and become poor? Does this mean that having wealth is a sin? Does it mean that when someone wants to inherit the Kingdom of God they *should* be poor?" In their discussion, the IR-VICOBA members denied that Jesus wanted the rich man to be poor, but their emphasis was that Jesus wanted to test this young man to see if he loved God or loved wealth more, as one of them asserted:

> The answer Jesus gave to the rich man was not to require him to sell everything. Otherwise, this young man would become a poor person and beggar. Rather, Jesus was testing the man's faith. It is like when God tested Abraham to sacrifice his son, but when he agreed, God gave the sheep instead of sacrificing the child. In addition, he would not have allowed this rich man to become poor, since we know being poor is a bad situation. Jesus knew that this man depended much on his wealth regardless of saying that he knew all the Commandments.

In their discussion, they denied that Jesus aimed to make people poor in this world. Nevertheless, they continued discussing that Jesus wanted them to depend more on God than on wealth, as the rich man did in the text. To emphasize their understanding, they referred to Zacchaeus, who was rich. When Zacchaeus met with Jesus, he said he would take half of his possessions and give them to the poor. Jesus made no comment but continued praising Zacchaeus by saying that salvation had entered his household (Luke 19:1-10; cf. Luke 12:20-21). According to one of them, "Jesus was not against the wealth; he was against the bad character of the rich people of not caring for the needy people, the poor among their societies. Jesus wanted people who had been blessed to care for the people who were poor in society." Therefore, for the IR-VICOBA members, Jesus wanted this rich man to put the Commandments – which he knew from his childhood – into actions rather than only memorizing them. Thus, Jesus wanted the rich man to walk the walk, not just talk the talk.

Jesus and the Commandments

Another issue that arose during the discussion was Jesus asking the rich man if he knew the Commandments (v. 19). It seemed that the Commandments were essential for people to live in the world and with their neighbors. According to the IR-VICOBA members, when Jesus asked the young rich man if he knew the Commandments, he wanted to know whether he was putting the Commandments into loving his neighbors – not stealing, not murdering, not bearing false witness, not defrauding, and honoring parents. The part of the Decalogue Jesus gave to the rich man was the part that touches on the human being in relation to another human being. The IR-VICOBA members went on discussing, and one member said,

> This person had everything, and then Jesus asked him if he knew the Commandments. Possibly this man was stealing and squandering money from any organization. Possibly the person had enriched himself from evil sources and did not care for the poor and needy people in society. Jesus was not against wealth but [was against] the rich man's attitude of selfishness, which is why Jesus asked if he knew the Commandments.

The IR-VICOBA members reflected like that because it was their reading that the rich man was so rich (v. 22) that he wanted to get more of what he had. He wanted to inherit the Kingdom of God after having possessed much wealth in this world. The testing requirement Jesus applied asked him to sell his possessions and give them to the poor to inherit the Kingdom of God or to follow Jesus. This served to prove he had understood the Commandments in their real meaning. The IR-VICOBA members affiliated him more with a person getting wealth through evil ways rather than the usual honest ways.

Jesus as an Excellent Teacher of the Kingdom of God

In their discussion, the IR-VICOBA members found that the rich man knew that Jesus was an excellent teacher even though he had denied it and said only God was good (v. 17). Regardless of his wealth, the rich man wanted to inherit the Kingdom of God, and he knew that the person who could assist him with entering into the Kingdom was Jesus. According to the IR-VICOBA members, Jesus' answer was very difficult for the rich man to swallow: "Jesus was teaching people to be humble, trust God, and help people in their neighborhood. The test he gave to the rich man seemed difficult, but Jesus had already delivered the lesson. He was a good teacher, according to the rich man." The IR-VICOBA members continued to discuss that Jesus was an excellent teacher who favored no one like the scribes in the Bible. When he tested the rich man – whether he would put the commandment into reality – it proved that the man understood the Commandments only in his mind and not in his heart. Therefore, the IR-VICOBA members emphasized that Jesus was an excellent teacher who taught people to serve and help one another in society. The rich and the poor share the blessing of God in the present Kingdom of God before the future Kingdom of God comes.

3.3.3   The Contextual Assessment

The IR-VICOBA members reflected on different themes from the text in their Bible study process which related to their own context. They came up with the following contextual assessment themes: people who exploit others and get rich, wealthy people who do not care for their families, and wealth becoming a god to some rich people. Moreover, they discussed rich people who did not care for the needy and who even overpowered justice in the court of law, churches, and religious groups, making their members more miserable.

People Who Exploit Others and Get Rich

When the IR-VICOBA members reflected on the improvised generic question about how the rich man became rich, they came up with different perceptions. Some said that possibly the rich man was a very diligent person who worked extremely hard to utilize his resources and got rich through that endeavor. However, other members of IR-VICOBA who reflected on their own experience thought this person would be like many people in their society who exploited them by cheating. They commented that he was possibly using his position as an officer who squandered money from the government or a businessperson who exploited peasants. One person said, "Take, for example, business people who buy our coffee, tea, or cocoa by cheating us, giving low prices so that they get more profit in the place they sell called 'world market.' People like these must be rich by exploiting peasants like us."

Another group reflected on the issue of people who had resources like land, money, or food and rented to the poor people, in return asking them to pay them much. Therefore, they used them to enrich themselves. They thought that even the rich man in the text was possibly like that. One of them said,

> There is another example of people exploiting other people in our society because they do not have land. They exploit them by providing land and asking them to pay with rice from the harvest. Nevertheless, in a real sense, they are exploiting those peasants without land by lending the land to them and asking them to pay back with crops, which sometimes is more than what they are required to pay back.

The people who lend resources are plentiful, which is why the IR-VICOBA members were making such a reflection comparing their own situations with that of the rich man. Therefore, the IR-VICOBA members were very reflective in their discussion that the rich man in the text was almost the same as the rich people in their own surroundings who became wealthy through evil ways, accumulating wealth by cheating, exploiting others, and doing tricky business.

Rich People Who Do Not Take Care of Their Families

The members further discussed the issue of rich people and their characters. They brought up the issue of the rich man who was told to sell everything he had and give it all to the poor. They indicated that, today, there are rich people who do not care for their families, but lavish their richness on their friends and sometimes even forsake their wives and look for concubines and prostitutes, like the prodigal son in the Bible did (cf. Luke 15:11-32). As they were discussing, one member said,

> There is a tendency among rich people to love wealth more than anything and to misuse that wealth; even they do not want to give or show their wives what they have because they love their wealth more than God and their families. Some use the wealth with the concubines and friends in big hotels, pubs, and bars but not for caring for their own families.

Another member added, "There are rich people who have many cattle but do not send their children to school because they revere their richness more than educating their kids." This is another example of the wild nature of some men, which some rich people follow, thinking their wealth is to be used not only for serving home affairs but also as an 'ornament' for their pride and status, while not caring for their families. For the IR-VICOBA members, a person's wealth is supposed to be used to care for the family and not to be misused by one family member or used as an ornament.

Wealth Has Become a God to Some Rich People

When discussing why the rich man became unhappy upon being told to sell everything he had and give it to the poor, they reflected on the first commandment, as it states:

> I am the Lord your God, who brought you out of the land of Egypt, out of the house of slavery, you shall have no other God besides me. You shall not make for yourself an idol, whether in the form of anything that is in heaven above, or that is on the Earth beneath, or that is in the water under the Earth. You shall not bow to them or worship them for I am the Lord your God am a jealous God. (Exod 20:2-5; cf. Deut 5:6-8)

These words of the first commandment made them think about the rich man who knew that commandment but loved wealth more than he loved God, to the extent that he did not think of God at all in his actionsonly in his words. In their Bible study, one member continued to say that in their society

> Wealth has become god, and some rich people torment other poor people because of their wealth. Even in our midst, there are rich people who have affairs with poor people's wives because they are plentiful. That is going against God's commandment and worshipping wealth; as a result, they spread HIV-AIDS. We should not trust wealth but believe in God, the creator of every creature.

Therefore, the wealth of some rich people has been wrongly used to mistreat poor people, so richness has become a source of spreading HIV-AIDS, a leading fatal disease in Tanzania and Africa in general.

Rich People Who Do Not Take Care of the Needy

The whole issue with the rich man was his possessions, which Jesus told him to sell and give to the poor. The IR-VICOBA groups discussed the case where Jesus asked the rich man to sell everything and give the money to the poor, consequently making the rich man miserable. They said that that was not the intention, but that Jesus aimed to test the person because he was not caring for the needy, even though he claimed to know the commandment. One member commented:

Having wealth is not a sin; rather, the only problem is that rich people fail to share their wealth with others. That is here where sin starts. However, God provides everything to human beings, but he also wants others to get a share of that possession, and sometimes rich people despise and degrade others because of their poorness.

Some rich people do not care for the poor and needy people in their surroundings. Another factor was that these rich people despise and degrade others only because they are poor. Jesus tested the rich man to see if he knew this in his heart rather than merely memorising it.

Another person from the IR-VICOBA group gave another example of wealthy people who use their material power to undermine the downtrodden in society. She said, "We have the Chinese who are constructing the road near our area, and these Chinese mistreat poor workers, pay little money, and use their money to seduce young ladies only because they are rich and have money in this village and nearby villages." One member added another ethical issue regarding Chinese constructors seducing young women for sexual fulfillment, since these constructors do not come with their wives. Therefore, they buy cheap customers – the young, poor women who need money from these unethical Chinese constructors.

Another issue raised during the Contextual Bible Study was that of rich people taking advantage of the poor because they would not do anything to them. A member in one group said, "There are rich people who have an affair with poor people's wives. It is not just that they are taking the poor people's right; the poor people cannot send them to court because they do not have money or [because they are] afraid of those rich people. The result is divorce among those married and children living in difficulties." In the discussion, they indicated that this injustice, committed by many rich people in society, is inhuman, and that the rich do it because they have money they can use to override the law by paying a bribe to court lawyers and officials.

The Rich People Even Overpower Justice in the Court of Law

The IR-VICOBA members, when discussing the issue of the commandment of not bearing false witness, had the idea that there were rich people who override justice in courts of law, as one of them claimed: "Even in the courts, rich people subvert justice by bribing lawyers. The poor go to jail without justice in the courts." According to the IR-VICOBA members, the poor in society have no money to bribe lawyers or hire advocates. As a result, some poor people end up in prison or have to pay fines, even if they are not guilty, which causes more poverty to their families. Some poor people decide they had better stay without asking about their rights being subverted by influential rich people. They just keep a calm attitude.

Churches and Religious Groups That Make Their Members Poor

The IR-VICOBA members discussed the issue of this rich man knowing the commandment in his head and thought that maybe it was that way, too, among church leaders who confiscated wealth from their believers. They referred to the day when Jesus struck people outside the temple who were doing business and told them: "It is written, my house is a house of prayer and not business" (Mark 11:15-17). One of the members said, "Today, in our areas, there are people with spiritual gifts, and some who become rich because they force people to give much money, but they take all of the offerings, especially in charismatic and Pentecostal churches." Another member, commenting further on this issue, indicated that

> These people preach to their members to give much to the church, but all the offerings they get they use for their personal purposes while making those poor people more miserable than before. They are tricking them when they teach about offerings. They tell them that they will be blessed and will get more from God. There are people in rural areas who even give their land and cows while failing to send their children to hospitals or schools.

In another group, one of the members described how the church leaders make people offer a lot, and this was very alarming – more a business than a church . He demonstrated the way they did so as follows:

> Some people cheat believers and want believers to offer more money, for example, by telling them that those who have Tshs 10,000 will get more blessings from God, and those who have Tshs 5,000 should go to the following line. Those preachers also say that they will start praying for those with Tshs 10,000 and then following those who have little, like having Tshs 5,000, and some give other material things more than they have. This is selling the gift of God, and these preachers make themselves richer than ever and cause others to be poor.

3.3.4 The Response of the IR-VICOBA Based on the Reading Intellectual Activity

The IR-VICOBA members, after they had discussed the reading process of the text, made the following responses: avoid loving wealth more than loving God; loving one's needy neighbor is a required responsibility to Christians; avoid Christian traditions that make people more miserable.

Love of Wealth More Than Loving God

The IR-VICOBA members responded to the reading process by saying they were supposed to work hard and make themselves prosper. However, they thought they were not supposed to love wealth as the rich man did. One of them retorted, "There are people who respect their wealth more than God or who do not want to go to church because they are busy with other activities or possessions." They discussed that loving wealth more than God was a dangerous attitude, since God wanted them to believe and trust in him. They insisted on going to church as a sign of believing in him and trusting in him to take control of everything. In the discussion, one member indicated that

> In the world we are living today, people have many possessions, but God wants us to believe in him and not believe in possessions. We remember Job, Abraham, King David, and Solomon, who were plentiful but still trusted God. We must find the Kingdom of God first; other things will be added to us.

Therefore, to the IR-VICOBA members, believing in God was a number one priority, and for other things, they trusted God to take control, even though they were putting more emphasis on working hard. They did not want to be like the rich man who enriched himself.

Loving Needy Neighbors as a Required Responsibility to Christians

The IR-VICOBA groups continued contemplating on the issue of the rich man going without happiness since he had a lot of possessions (v. 6). They came up with the idea that the rich man did not care for the poor who were his neighbors, so Jesus tested him by telling him to sell everything and give it to the people with who he was currently not sharing. A member responded that "We have to love God and our neighbors by sharing what we have. We are required not only to care for the needy because we are rich, but Jesus wants us to share even the little we have with the needy." The IR-VICOBA members pondered such issues because, for Christians, sharing involves sharing even the little one has with their needy neighbors. Therefore, the reading process led them to think they were required to share what they had as followers of Christ.

Avoidance of the Christian Traditions That Make People Poor

The IR-VICOBA members responded to the improvised question: "Why was this man rich while other people remained impoverished?" They came up with the issue of the Christian tradition, which makes people miserable. In the discussion, one of the members asserted:

> Some people say they are content with the life they are passing through, even if they are poor, because the Bible tells them to do so. If you tell them to work hard or be productive, they refuse, and they say God has ordained them to be like that. In fact, these people are inviting poverty into their lives.

According to the IR-VICOBA members, people who hold such a stance lack the incentive to know that even the Bible preaches about people's development. Therefore, IR-VICOBA members hold that people should avoid these teachings.

3.4 Discussion on the Reading Intellectual Activity: Luke 16:19-31

3.4.1 Introduction

The Text

> 19 There was a rich man who was dressed in purple and fine linen and who feasted sumptuously every day. 20 and at his gate lay a poor man named Lazarus, covered with sores, 21 who longed to satisfy his hunger with what fell from the rich man's table; even the dogs would come and lick his sores. 22 The poor man died and was carried away by the angels to be with Abraham. The rich man also died and was buried. 23 In Hades, where he was being tormented, he looked up and saw Abraham far away with Lazarus by his side. 24 He called out, 'Father Abraham, have mercy on me, and send Lazarus to dip the tip of his finger in water and cool my tongue; for I am in agony in these flames.' 25 But Abraham said, 'Child, remember that during your lifetime you received your good things, and Lazarus in like manner evil things; but now he is comforted here, and you are in agony. 26 Besides all this, between you and us a great chasm has been fixed, so that those who might want to pass from here to you cannot do so, and no one can cross from there to us.' 27 He said, 'Then, father, I beg you to send him to my father's house – 28 for I have five brothers – that he may warn them, so that they will not also come into this place of torment.' 29 Abraham replied, 'They have Moses and the prophets; they should listen to them.' 30 He said, 'No, father Abraham; but if someone goes to them from the dead, they will repent.' 31 He said to him, 'If they do not listen to Moses and the prophets, neither will they be convinced even if someone rises from the dead.' (Luke 16:19-31)

The two IR-VICOBA groups discussed this pericope in their participant-centered Contextual Bible Study. They continued with their usual generic questions, and the facilitator asked them some improvised questions to stimulate the discussion.

3.4.2 Character Assessment

The IR-VICOBA members discussed the characters and their role in the text and came up with different themes presented in the subsections below. Briefly, these themes are: Jesus with the rich and poor in his context; richness, poverty, and heaven; Jesus and selfish attitude; and the Pharisees as lovers of money and the disciples as Lazarus.

Jesus with the Rich and the Poor in His Context

The IR-VICOBA people contemplated much on the issue of Jesus' parable about the rich man and poor Lazarus. They also wondered why he did not mention the name of the rich man but just said a 'rich man' and poor Lazarus. The IR-VICOBA members thought that Jesus was giving an example of two groups, which represented the context of Jesus' contemporary Israelites at that time. Reflecting on the question, "What have we read today?", one member said,

> We have read about the parable of Jesus and the poor people and the rich people who are exemplified by the rich man and Lazarus. The rich man was wealthy, and he used that richness selfishly and egocentrically, while the poor were so extremely poor, such that he wished to feed himself from scraps from the rich man's table. He had bruises and was possibly dirty.

For the IR-VICOBA members, it seemed that Jesus wanted to tell the disciples that, in that world, there were two types of people, represented by the rich man and poor Lazarus. Jesus wanted them to learn that that relationship was not good since one used what he had without thinking of the other person who had nothing. The discussion indicated that "The rich man was very brutal, and his spirit did not care for the needy. He thought he would even go to heaven by being just a rich person in this world." One member said, "The role of Lazarus in this lesson portrays the character of people who have nothing in that society, in need of help, and the rich people who use their richness in a manner that shows they do not care for other people who are poor and sick like Lazarus." Through these reflections, the IR-VICOBA members gave examples of groups of people living within the society in Palestine during the time of Jesus. Lazarus represented the poor, and the rich man represented rich people in the text. Therefore, according to the IR-VICOBA members, Lazarus and the rich man are figuratively perceived to represent the whole of society.

Richness, Poverty, and Heaven

One of the exciting subjects within the reading process about the characters in the text was Jesus' attitude toward richness. The IR-VICOBA groups thought Jesus was not against wealth per se but wanted people to share more. Contemplating on the improvised question of whether Jesus connected richness with Hades, the IR-VICOBA members thought that Jesus did not mean that all rich people would go to Hades. The attitude of not caring for the needy and being selfish and boastful can make someone go to Hades regardless of being rich or poor. One member commented, "The rich man did not know that he was supposed to become rich in his heart and spirit by caring for the poor people like Lazarus to, in the end, inherit the Kingdom of God."

The rich man's character puzzled the IR-VICOBA members since they went as far as to think that this man was very evil and therefore might have got the richness through evil ways. One of them indicated:

> The rich man was wealthy and used that richness selfishly and egocentrically. Possibly, he had gotten the richness in evil ways, like stealing, cheating, or doing evil and illegal business. Maybe he inherited that richness from his parents, and that is why he used it in that way and did not fear even God.

To the IR-VICOBA members, a person who is blessed by God knows that God would instruct him that he was blessed to serve even those who had no such blessing, referring to the Lazaruses in society. They were sure that his brutal way of acting showed his inner manner, which he revealed to poor people like Lazarus. Therefore, this attitude hindered him from going to heaven, not his richness as such.

Lazarus was poor, but according to the IR-VICOBA members, this was not a guarantee to enter heaven. Lazarus was someone who had trust in God and believed in God always, unlike the rich man, who was afraid of nobody. The IR-VICOBA members did not want to justify poverty with entering heaven, but they were sure that going to heaven was connected to a person's belief in God, revealed by how that person lives with other people. One member indicated, "It is not his poverty that made Lazarus go to heaven. It seems that, despite being poor, he was worshipping God and depended on him, and that was what made him enter heaven." Poverty, then, is not a ticket to heaven but a person's faith and good relationship with God and fellow human beings are what counts, whereas the character of the rich man had none.

Jesus and Selfishness Attitude

The IR-VICOBA members discussed that the rich man was very selfish, which is why he missed entering heaven. It was not his wealth that sent him to Hades. It was stated in the discussion, "The rich man was very selfish and used that richness very selfishly and egocentrically." Therefore, according to the IR-VICOBA members, the sumptuous use of his resources without caring for the needy showed his attitude of not caring and of being afraid of nobody. Jesus was against this attitude.

Pharisees Were Lovers of Money, and the Disciples Were Lazaruses

Referring to verse 14, a member came to understand that Pharisees were among the characters there. She said,

> Jesus was indirectly sending the message to the Pharisees, who were lovers of money, as we see in verse 14. It is possible that 'the rich man' represented the Pharisees who were there, and that Jesus wanted to warn them that they were supposed to care for the 'Lazaruses' of this world, although these people were rich and although they did not acquire their richness justly.

The IR-VICOBA members made the connection that Jesus may have been giving the message to the Pharisees because he had had confrontations with them in many ways. These people, being religious leaders, did not show good examples in their society. They loved money more than God, even though they purported to serve and love God.[13] Another member commented:

---

13 The issue of the Pharisees as lovers of money has spawned many controversies. Scholars have argued more against it than for it. See Halvor Moxnes, *The Economy of the Kingdom: Social Conflict and Economic Relations in Luke's Gospel*, Overtures to Biblical Theology (Philadelphia: Fortress Press, 1988), pp. 2–3, where he quotes T.W Manson, who emphasizes that the description would fit the Sadducees more than the Pharisees. He gives five reasons for this: 1. The Sadducees were more abundant and more visibly 'lovers of money' than the Pharisees. 2. The Sadducees were more likely to scoff at Jesus' teaching about heavenly treasures. 3. In the Aramaic, the form 'Saddiq' in16:14 would make a play of words together with 'justify' Sdq in 16:15. 4. The Sadducees were wealthy and proud and considered themselves righteous people. 5. The parable of a rich man and Lazarus would fit a Sadducean audience. Moxnes quotes many scholars who go with the frequent descriptions of avarice among the Pharisees, which goes along with the attitude of IR-VICOBA members. Nevertheless, this should not be taken to be their general character since we have good Pharisees like Nicodemus and St. Paul to mention two in the New Testament. Moreover, this shows the misunderstanding Jesus had with Pharisees in his ministry in Palestine.

If the Pharisees who were there were lovers of money and were rich, then the disciples were poor Lazaruses who loved Jesus and the Kingdom of God he was preaching. He used Heaven here symbolically to show that they had entered into the Kingdom of God.

Therefore, the IR-VICOBA members saw Jesus' symbolic representation as being separated into two groups, the poor and the rich, and how the rich people used their wealth in sumptuous living while the poor had no food, no shelter, no clothes, and other necessary materials, which would have allowed them to live comfortably in society. These Lazaruses were also sick with sores and had no one to pay for medicine to heal them.

The Pharisees, as teachers of the law, knew only the law in their mind and not in their heart, which is why they did not put it into action. They knew they were supposed to care for the poor according to the law, but they failed in this respect since they were lovers of money.

3.4.3 The Contextual Assessment

The IR-VICOBA members reflected more on their context by comparing their own context with that of the text. They came up with different themes, as discussed below. These are the themes under discussion: people who exploit others and become rich; wealthy people who do not care for others; poverty resulting poor government regulations and policies; belief in witchcraft; and false preachers as sources of poverty.

People Who Exploit Others and Rich

In reflecting on why Lazarus was poor, the IR-VICOBA members discussed in detail some of the factors that made people like Lazarus poor. They argued that some people exploited others in their businesses. As one of them directly put it, "There were rich people who exploited other people; for instance, when they give poor people a temporary job by paying them a meager salary or just giving them food. Payment like these makes people poorer, and they may end up like the Lazarus we read about in our passage." One such factor discussed was that those poor people were underpaid compared to the work they performed.

Another issue discussed here was the influence of the government of being on the side of the rich people more than the side of the poor. The members discussed that "The government systems create a lot of Lazaruses. For example, the government takes large fertile lands that belong to the people and give it to settlers who turn peasants into laborers. The settlers pay only a minimal salary that does not satisfy the daily needs of workers, causing families to turn to begging in villages." Therefore, according to IR-VICOBA members, this government attitude has engendered more poor people than before.

The IR-VICOBA members discussed another issue that was a problem for people who drank too much. One of them pointed out that,

> Outsiders own most of the beer companies, which sell beer to other people, including peasants. Peasants with little income have developed a drinking attitude such that they care for drinking more than for the family and finally end up being the Lazaruses of the day – poor with no clothes, food, and shelter.

As they continued, one of them said, "The rich people go into businesses that kill the youth and cause them to be poor, while they become richer every day. If you meet with addicts in the streets, you pity them because they have become beggars in the streets and villages." Therefore, for the IR-VICOBA members, the outsiders who do business within the country are the ones who create richness by causing poverty to many peasants. Moreover, the government does not support the peasants.

Rich People Who Do Not Care for Others

The issue of caring for needy people like Lazarus arose in the discussion concerning the improvised question "How do rich people live with poor people?" One participant said, "The rich people who do not care for the poor people despise them in such a way that they dehumanise them to be very little or nothing, like how the rich man did in the passage we have read today." The member said this in a thoughtful way, that the rich man showing that attitude was extremely inhuman and should be avoided. The IR-VICOBA member was comparing how poor Lazarus was treated in the story. Another member added another example, "There are rich people who despise even their relatives; for example, I know a person who is relatively rich but does not want to visit even his relatives – only because they are poor." This can be the case because rich people think their poor relatives will ask them for assistance.

However, it arose within the Bible study process the issue of those who were cared for misusing the assistance that relatively wealthy relatives gave to them. In their discussion, one of the IR-VICOBA members stated:

> There are many Lazaruses who pick food in pits, dumps, and some beg from good Samaritans. However, there are Lazaruses who ask for help but misuse the given aid, for example, a person who asks for money to buy food but after getting the money goes and drinks liquor or beer. Moreover, some people are brought to the street by relatives to beg money from people (good Samaritans), and then the family uses the money for family purposes. The poor beggars do not use the money in the streets.

This issue of misusing assistance given to them kindled much controversy in the discussion, and many members started giving examples of people who had cheated in churches or families that used people who were poor and sent them to beg in streets, market places, and houses. One member gave an example from a parish that she served, saying:

> When I was in Vwawa parish, one person came to church to ask for help as a poor person, and we assisted this person because we as Christians we wanted to assist him since he was in need. After the collection, the person left and went to the bar nearby to drink beer while boasting: "I have got money from the poor Christians, and now I am enjoying myself." People who heard him rebuked him not for speaking like that, but because he was drunk, he continued, and the news reached the parish, and people were furious.

In the discussion, they indicated that situations like that happened every day in societies and towns because people were poor. Sometimes they did not know any other means of living than begging or pretending they were sick, paralyzed, or disabled.

Corrupt Government Regulations and Policies as a Cause of Poverty

Another reflection of the IR-VICOBA groups on the reading process was the issue of the bad government's regulations and policies. They discussed that the government had put much emphasis on the rich and far fewer efforts on assisting the peasants to become enriched with the scarce resources in their surroundings.

The government also made people become poor despite the efforts of those people when they served the nation. In their discussion, people gave examples of people who had played a significant role in the nation's history, but the government did not establish good policies for their future. As one member put it:

> The government did not create a system that would make people respectful; instead, it created more Lazaruses in this society. I want to share examples that go well with my idea here: the person who drew our national emblem or soldiers who fought the Ugandan war. These people were significant to our country. However, when you look at them, their lives are like those of Lazarus in our eyes, and the nation does not care for them.

Another issue regarding the wrong policies of the government was the issue of privatising the land to the ownership of a few wealthy people. The group members thought that the government was supposed to have good policies to benefit its citizens on the land rather than siding with wealthy people who took more land from its citizens. Therefore, for the IR-VICOBA members, the government siding with rich people and giving them much land was a bad policy, which in the end tended to produce more Lazaruses who became street beggars.

In addition, the members discussed the issue of taxes, which sometimes did not help poor people and caused them to suffer more. One of them put it this way:

> There are more taxes, which affect peasants more than wealthy people who have industries or who deal in minerals. These pay relatively little taxes, for example, in Kiwila, where people sell bananas. For a bunch of bananas, poor peasants pay a duty to enter the market. Other people who buy the bananas also pay some duties for transporting it, especially when they travel to another district. The government thus takes sales duty three times from one bunch of bananas. It would be better if the person who buys the banana bunch pay that duty.

They continued their discussion during their Bible study, touching on many issues where the government did not establish reasonable policies and regulations to empower the poor peasants.

Another concern was the issue of bad policies and regulations, with which the IR-VICOBA members were concerned, namely, in the educational system. One of them indicated: "The educational system our nation maintains is not good for students. For example, Tanzanians are unprepared to be creative after leaving their universities and colleges. They depend on being employed and not being self-employed, which would enable them to create their own wealth." Therefore, according to the IR-VICOBA members, the educational policies and regulations produce many Lazaruses, especially when they have finished their studies and find no employment and thus become poor beggars like Lazarus.

Belief in Witchcraft and False Preachers as a Source of Poverty

In the area, the practice of witchcraft is still prevalent as a source of blessing. One member during the IR-VICOBA Bible study session said,

> Some people engage in witchcraft to become rich. They visit witchdoctors so that they can pray *juju* for them to become rich. They pay money to these witchdoctors and finally find themselves in trouble as they become poor. We must depend on God to bless us, be rich, and not on poor witchdoctors who cheat people.

Another issue raised by the IR-VICOBA discussion was the issue of fake pastors who make people believe they can make them rich if they donate money in return for prayers. In the discussion, one member of the IR-VICOBA scrutinised that, "There are pastors who cheat believers that they have to offer much so that they can pray for them to get blessings. However, unfortunately, these people do not become rich, but the pastors are the ones who become rich." Therefore, many Christians in cities, towns, and villages find themselves at ground zero and find themselves begging like Lazarus in the text read by the VICOBA members.

3.4.4 The Response of the IR-VICOBA Based on the Bible Study Reading Intellectual Activity

The IR-VICOBA members made different responses to the Bible study reading process. They talked about the following themes: love of richness was against the love of God and neighbors; advocacy for the poor and other downtrodden; the Gospel of prosperity against the true Gospel; avoiding selfishness; and empowering the poor and needy.

Love of Richness Against Love of God and Our Neighbors

The IR-VICOBA group members responded to the reading process by concentrating on many things that arose from the discussion. The first response regarded the love of richness more than the love of God. The IR-VICOBA members saw that the love of richness of the rich man was not something to rely on because the best desire of a human being was not richness but the love of God and the love of neighbors. To justify this, one member said, "Our relationship with God is shown by how we relate with our neighbors. The vertical relationship with God was of much meaning to a human being, a relationship with our creator, and a horizontal relationship with our neighbor manifests this first relationship." Therefore, the participants agreed that both poor and rich people depend on each other according to scripture. To them, the rich man lacked this relationship because he failed to care for poor Lazarus who was near his gate wishing to have only scraps from his table.

The above note made them think of themselves as Christians who wanted to fight poverty, which would mean that they would increase economic power and would take up the responsibility of helping the Lazaruses in the societies in which they were living. They responded, "We should continue to work hard, so we do not remain poor. When we have many things, we should be humble; we should treat poor people more fairly and help them accordingly, because God is the one who enables us to build that economy." In reflecting more on the issue of love for one's neighbor, the thoughts of the IR-VICOBA groups may be summed up in a statement of one member: "Whatever economic move we are doing is connected to our God whom we trust to be our source of blessing, and therefore we should not despise the downtrodden but serve them as a means of serving our God." For this participant, the economic power someone attains makes one responsible for serving the needy.

Another issue raised as they were discussing the issue of love of money was the teaching of pastors. The IR-VICOBA saw that pastors, as church leaders, would teach and preach more on the relationship between the rich, the relatively wealthy people, and the poor people. One member said, "You pastors who are here – you are our spiritual guides. We ask you to teach parish members about the good relationship between the poor and the rich so that you build parishes that care for others." Therefore, the IR-VICOBA members thought to deliver the message to pastors and urge them not to be afraid to tell the truth to the rich people because of worries that they would not give as much support to the church. When one member said that, the others laughed and nodded to show that pastors sometimes did not want to offend rich people by telling them the truth because they were funders of those parishes – and yet they treated poor people the same way the rich man did in the text.

In this matter of love of richness against the love of God and neighbor, the IR-VICOBA members were very much concerned about being more humane by caring for the needy. Moreover, they were not against working hard to strengthen their economy and become rich or to live a better life.

Advocacy to the Poor and Other Downtrodden

In response to how other people became rich in today's world, the IR-VICOBA members noted that, even though they are among the poor, they have been illuminated with light and the Word of God. In this case, they encouraged each other to serve and become advocates of their fellow poor people in society. They concentrated on the issue of using their church leaders to advocate where there was injustice, which was taking place from people who exploited them and other poor people, mainly when they sold their goods. One of them put it this way:

> We poor people are treated like toys who have no voice. However, now we want our voices to be listened to by everybody. You pastors tell the bishops, and we will tell the political leaders to fight for us so that those rich people do not take advantage of us, who think we do not know the market. They have to work for us in this regard. These wealthy businesspeople despise us like the rich man did poor Lazarus, and we are tired of them. They buy our bananas, tea, coffee, etc., and pay us very little. They pass us with their gorgeous cars they get from cheating us; it is the same attitude the rich man had who gave no food to poor Lazarus.

The IR-VICOBA members thought that even the rich man in the Bible was the same type as the rich men and women who did business with them in their streets, buying bananas, coffee, tea, and cereals. Now they wanted the church to hear their voice. The IR-VICOBA members were raising their voice to be heard and were promoting a matter of their pastors becoming advocates for other poor people, who were being exploited or despised by the rich.

Prosperity Gospel Against True Gospel

The IR-VICOBA members reflected on the Prosperity gospel pastors who preach to their followers to give more money to the church so that God could give them much money in return. Their concern in this regard was that their churches should try to teach parish members the right way of blessing. One of them stated vehemently:

> Some fake pastors use witchcraft to teach the Word of God so that people can give more to them, and these pastors are wealthy compared to other pastors who teach the true Gospel of Jesus Christ. These pastors exploit their members, and the members remain poor. We ask the government and other church leaders to be vigilant of these pastors and not to imitate them in their teaching.

The IR-VICOBA members thought like that to urge their members not to join those churches and pastors because those pastors implicitly make peasants miserable to the same extent as Lazarus' situation. They said some people join those churches because of the promise of becoming extremely rich, which was cheating. Then, to the IR-VICOBA members, working hard and strategically was the means to fight poverty – not by using fake miracles, which those pastors promised people. The IR-VICOBA members wanted the pastors of their churches to fight those teachings in their church sermons, giving well-balanced ethical teachings on how to prosper through hard work.

The IR-VICOBA group also knew that fighting poverty was a matter of depending on God but not on fake miracles. One member said:

> These pastors are witches because they attract people, especially those who have money to go to their parishes. My brother, who had a shop and cows in our village, was asked to give his cows and money on the promise of being productive. However, now he has no shop, and the cows are gone. The problem is that my brother is still hoping to get more from them and be richer than before and is still attending the same church. He does not understand when we tell him to come back to the church that raised us.

Their response to this was to ensure that everybody understands that the aims of these 'prosperity' pastors are to make them people poor instead of rich, and the irony is that the pastors are the ones who become extremely rich.

Empowering the Poor

In response to their being exploited by the rich people, the IR-VICOBA members went further, discussing the wish Lazarus also had to feed on scraps that fell from the rich man's table. One member said:

> We Lazaruses of today should not wish to have 'scraps' or the whole 'fish' but should look for 'nets.' We should be empowered to get our food. That would be good news for us. We are supposed to continue to work hard and empower one another by together learning how to fight poverty and come up with our strategy for self-empowerment.

Although the IR-VICOBA members were relatively poor, their aim and intention were always to fight poverty. They recognised that poverty was their big enemy, and that they needed to fight it. In every meeting, they talked about how to fight poverty, which was why they looked at the texts more seriously in a socioeconomic way than from any other perspective.

Regarding empowering, the IR-VICOBA members thought they should empower themselves, and that empowering other poor people by providing education to them was also needed. One member said:

> We were taught by people from the Christian Council of Churches (CCT); now we bear the same responsibility of empowering others in our villages. Do you remember that teachers from CCT said that education is a way of empowering one another to fight poverty? Therefore, we have to continue to establish other IR-VICOBA groups in order to reduce the number of Lazaruses in our societies.

That was an attitude most IR-VICOBA members had: They wanted people to gain an economic voice by being empowered economically. That was why one of them came up with the idea that "We should avoid poverty by all our means and power." Therefore, the cry for empowering Lazaruses in the societies was one of their main motives.

Avoiding Selfishness

Another thing the IR-VICOBA groups responded to was the attitude of selfishness. They concentrated on the issue of the rich man not giving food to a needy person like Lazarus. The group response was to avoid such an attitude, which dehumanised the poor people, reducing them to very little or nothing. They concentrated on this issue, and one member came up with the idea that, "Selfishness is a sin like other sins, we as IR-VICOBA people should avoid that because being so is going against the will and love of God who blesses us. That is why the rich man did not enter into heaven but went to a tormenting place." People laughed at him because he said that was why the rich man went to a tormenting place. Another fellow continued saying that, "It is not a matter of going to heaven, people do not like even rich people who are here and who are selfish, and if you are not liked, then it is like being tormented. Heaven is with us here before we go to the real heaven which Lazarus entered." Therefore, for the IR-VICOBA members, heaven and a good life begin here on Earth; one does not wait until one enters heaven. They thought about the Kingdom of God as not only relating to the future Kingdom of God; they thought of the Kingdom that starts here on Earth and then continues later in heaven. However, because they connected it with caring for needy people like Lazarus, then it is symbolised that being a religious person means taking responsibility in showing the love of God (diaconia), which arises from a vertical relationship and caring for the needy, a horizontal relationship (sharing is caring). Therefore, this response of the IR-VICOBA groups showed that working hard to discourage selfishness was a way to perform diaconia work.

The members wanted to be like the rich, who were responsible for caring for the needy. As one member contributed, "There are rich people who care for the poor. We want to continue to be like them because, by doing that, we serve God. We do not want to be like the rich man who did not care about anybody. He thought that, by having everything, he would acquire even heaven, which was wrong." For the IR-VICOBA members, the rich man portrayed a terrible habit and attitude, which should not be imitated by anybody in this world. It was like experiencing hell while still in this world. In their discussion, they nearly thought such a selfish habit was a devilish attitude, suitable only for hell. In this case, the IR-VICOBA members fought against selfishness and encouraged diaconal work.

3.5   Conclusion

In this chapter, I have presented various interpretations from the reading processes of the IR-VICOBA groups in their participant-centered Contextual Bible Studies. These presentations are based on the reading process of the characters, the context of texts, and how the IR-VICOBA members approach the texts from their own contexts and responses. The three different Bible texts commented on show that the IR-VICOBA groups approach the texts with often-parallel comments, even if the texts are chosen from Matthew, Mark, or Luke. In the context of this work, however, it was important to present comments on all texts, even if they are parallel. In Chapters 4 and 5, I present a more interpretive analysis of the topics. The overall project question concerns the relationship between text and context in the IR-VICOBA Contextual Bible Study groups. In my view, that the same questions pop up no matter what kind of text is being discussed is of high significance. It impacts how the text and the context are related.

In the first selected Bible study (Matt 5:1-12), the IR-VICOBA members developed many themes, such as Jesus as a good teacher of the Kingdom of Heaven and the poor in spirit as the heralds of the Kingdom of Heaven. However, they noted that those who are poor in spirit are supposed to solve their spiritual poverty. Moreover, they discussed other themes: being persecuted for righteousness' sake and people who suffered because of the colonial regime and religious captivity. These themes also encouraged them to reflect on their fathers and mothers under the colonial regime. On this issue, they moved further, implicitly discussing their new colonial regime in globalisation, which, to some extent, caused them to mourn their poverty.

Reflecting on their context, they found that they were living in a similar context regardless of the difference in time. They saw many similarities in the texts with their own lives, for example, the issues of exploitation and injustice, of disrespect among believers (people) because of differences in faith, and of social status or economic status, which also seemed to prevail during the time of Jesus and Matthew. They reflected on people like the Pharisees, who despised tax collectors, and they compared the situation that Christians do similar things because of differences in denominations, traditions, and customs. Further, the issue of defilement also involved the issue of gender as the cause of disrespect in society.

In their responses to the text, the IR-VICOBA members emphasized the issue of self-empowering and empowering the neediest people in society. They thought that would be a way of fighting poverty, the exploitation of nature by the rich people, and inadequate socioeconomic systems, which produce more poor people. Although they emphasize gaining their voice by self-empowering, the IR-VICOBA members decided to use politicians and religious leaders as their megaphones when encountering the government and the international world.

In the second selected participant-centered Contextual Bible Study reading of Mark 10:17-22, the IR-VICOBA members discussed various issues. In their character assessment, they viewed Jesus and considered how he dealt with the poor and the rich. They observed what Jesus meant regarding the Commandments. To them, Jesus was an excellent teacher of the Kingdom of God on Earth.

They also contemplated their own context concerning the text and thought that some people exploit others and become rich. These rich people sometimes do not care for their own families and neighbors; to them, wealth becomes their God. Moreover, the rich people overpower justice even in the court of law, which made other people weep, suffer from persecution, and become more miserable. In their discussion, they also reflected that some religious groups make their members more miserable by instructing their followers that poverty is part of being a Christian.

Nevertheless, some made their members give many offerings so that God could bless them, which made those pastors richer and left the members more miserable.

In their response to the text, the IR-VICOBA members thought about loving God and loving their needy neighbors more than loving the wealthy. Moreover, they responded that they were supposed to avoid Christian traditions that made people miserable because God created wealth to be used by human beings like them.

Discussing the third selected Contextual Bible Study on Luke 16:19-31, the IR-VICOBA groups contemplated characters within the text and saw the relationship between Jesus and the poor and the rich, where Jesus was firmly against selfishness. They included the Pharisees as lovers of money, while the disciples were like the Lazaruses of those days.

The IR-VICOBA members assessed their own context in relation to the textual context and came up with different themes related to people who exploited others and failed to care for the poor. They also contemplated the cause of some people living in precarious situations, such as poor government policies and regulations and false preachers. The IR-VICOBA members do not show any differences when they read Synoptic Gospels; to them, all are the Word of God: Differences in those Gospels are not their concern.

In their responses to their Contextual Bible Study, the participants thought that the love of God and neighbors was better than the love of richness, being Christians in their context. They also responded that they continued to serve as good advocates for the poor and other oppressed people by empowering and caring for them although they themselves are poor. To reach that measure, they promised to ensure that they educated people differently in economic and social matters, e. g., being self-reliant and not following preachers who taught the prosperity gospel. Such people cheated others in order to enrich themselves.

Chapter 4: Analytical/Thematic Interpretation of the Reading of the Synoptic Gospels About the Poor by the IR-VICOBA Groups

4.1　Introduction

The previous chapter presented the reading of the IR-VICOBA groups in their Contextual Bible Study. It presented the Bible Study, following the development during their regular Bible study meetings. In this chapter, and in Chapter 5, I analyze, interpret, and discuss those themes that came up during their reading. This time, I do not present the topics as they were addressed during the meetings but in a more analytical, synthesized, and organized way. This analysis shows us more clearly that the IR-VICOBA members interpret texts based on their experience. Their socioeconomic reality informs the interpretation of the texts. Robert Stake writes:

> Much qualitative research is based on the collection and interpretation of episodes. Episodes are held as personal knowledge more than aggregate knowledge. An episode has activities, sequence, place, people, and context. Some of the more useful-appearing episodes, the ones we think of as 'patches,' need to be studied, analysed, their parts seen and more seen. We observe them and seek other interpretation. We observe them and record other people's observation. We interpret them to seek other interpretation.[1]

In this chapter and the following, I look at the content of the coded data from IR-VICOBA members in their Contextual Bible Study and systematically describe and explain their interpretation. Finally, I give my interpretation of their discussion. Accordingly, I interpret those themes without following the Biblical texts the IR-VICOBA members were reading. Rather, I present them in the way I coded them from Chapter 3. Some themes appear in both texts, and some appear in either one or two texts. Nevertheless, I do not interpret and discuss all of the themes here except those reflected in this study.

In this chapter, I first look at how the IR-VICOBA members use their context to interpret the texts. In Chapter 5, I do it the opposite, asking "How do the IR-VICOBA groups use the Bible texts to interpret their practice?" With that approach, my intention is to discover how the participants let the pericope inform and support existing practices.

---

1 Stake, *Qualitative Research: Studying How Things Work*, p. 133.

My argument in both chapters is that Contextual Bible reading of the IR-VICOBA members engenders many liberation themes among poor people in Tanzania and other Third-World countries. In most cases, their socioeconomic reality helps them to interpret the texts because they are very knowledgeable and experienced about their own context. Their means of reflection, action, and commitment in their daily lives are well-hearkened as one hears them. They also reflect on what is happening in their midst, whether good or bad. This can be easily elucidated from the IR-VICOBA members' Contextual Bible Study in their reading intellectual activity. There are a few incidences, especially as a way of response, where the texts interpret their context. This is the situation Musimbi Kanyoro writes about: "I have noticed that popular Bible readers do not care what scholars think. They read the Bible with the eyes of their context, and they apply a mirror-image reading. Sometimes the Bible helps to read their context; sometimes, their context gives meaning to the texts of the Bible."[2] The words of Kanyoro show that, many times, the interpretation of the Bible in the local community is quite different from scholarly interpretation. However, their interpretation is still varied and meaningful.

The following chapter consists of two sections: first, the character assessment of the IR-VICOBA groups' Bible study reading. By this, I mean the interpretation given by the IR-VICOBA members to the most important characters in the Biblical pericopes, with Jesus as the absolutely most-commented-upon character. In this subsection, I analyze and discuss the reading of the IR-VICOBA members' views on those themes. I discuss how these people read and look behind the text to the historical background, as assisted by the facilitators. In most cases, the IR-VICOBA members mostly interpreted these texts by using their reflection on experience, commitment, and practises in their context.

In the second section, I analyze and discuss some of the main topics the IR-VICOBA members regarded when interpreting the selected main topics from their context. In the rest of this chapter and the next one, I analyze and discuss their understanding and reflection of their context within the Bible study.

4.2 Assessment of Characters by the IR-VICOBA Members in Their Contextual Bible Study

The themes selected for discussion are as follows: Jesus, the poor, and the rich; the downtrodden; the blessings; Jesus, the giver of sight; Jesus, the announcer of freedom to captives; Jesus, the teacher of knowledge; the good news; Jesus and the

---

2 Musimbi Kanyoro, "Reading the Bible from an African Perspective," *Ecumenical Review* 51, no. 1 (1999), pp. 18–24 (here p. 19).

Commandments. I chose those themes because they relate to the Kingdom of God, the poor, and injustice in one way or another.

4.2.1 Jesus, the Poor, and the Rich

The IR-VICOBA members, as part of the intellectual reading activity of their participant-centered Contextual Bible Study, discussed the relationship between Jesus, the poor, and the rich in the text. The most challenging question during the discussion was: "Did Jesus intend to justify poverty as a guarantee to enter heaven?" The IR-VICOBA members asked many rhetorical questions, which, in my opinion, aimed to provoke discussion. For example, concerning Mark 10:17-22, cf. Luke 18:18-25, they asked: "Why did Jesus ask the rich man to sell everything he had? Does it mean he truly wanted this person to go to ground zero and become poor? Does it mean that to have wealth is a sin? Does it mean that if someone wants to inherit the Kingdom of God they should be poor?" These questions received different answers within the group during the Bible study. Nevertheless, the attitude of questioning the texts informs how these people, very experienced in their socioeconomic reality, engage with the text. Their socioeconomic reality leads them to question the text they are engaging with in their Bible reading.

As I presented in Chapter 3, the members responded to the questions by saying that Jesus had no specific preference for the poor and was not justifying poverty as the means to enter the Kingdom of God. Rather, he used this as a yardstick to see how much individuals wanted, loved, and sought to enter the Kingdom. The main argument was that Jesus would not justify poverty because he is the Creator[3] of everything and would not deprive anybody of having anything. To justify that, the IR-VICOBA members used the examples of Zacchaeus (Luke 19:1-10), who was rich but was nevertheless received by Jesus after his confession; or (in the Old Testament) Abraham offering his son, Isaac, and God providing the sheep instead (22:1-19).

The intertextuality of the IR-VICOBA members referring to the Old Testament meant that God would not cause somebody to start from scratch. They indicated that God, who is full of love, would not let somebody return to poverty. It is true that God is on the side of the poor, but not that he likes poverty. The IR-VICOBA members do not believe being poor is a guarantee to inheriting the Kingdom of God. To them, poverty cannot be praised, uplifted, or guided toward obtaining the Kingdom of God. However, they are very keen on other issues of the poor. They

---

3 The IR-VICOBA members reflected on Jesus as a Creator. I think they were cross-referencing with the prologue of the Gospel according to John about the Word (John 1:1-5).

reflected in this way because they are still experiencing the same life, and their socioeconomic reality readily informs the situation.

For example, in the narrative of the rich man who was told to sell everything and give to the poor (Mark 10:17-22), the IR-VICOBA members seem to presume what was in Jesus' mind, and that he did not want the rich person to become poor. Rather, he wanted him not to trust in his wealth but instead trust God in everything. Moreover, in the parable of the rich man and Lazarus (Luke 16:19-31), Jesus aimed to tell the disciples that they are supposed to care for the needy like Lazarus. Their reference to the Old Testament was a way of justifying that in the past God had liberated people. Therefore, Jesus was testing the rich man as God tested Abraham to sacrifice his only son Isaac (Gen 22:1-19). That is why, in their discussion, they added the example of Zacchaeus (Luke 19:1-10), who was not asked by Jesus to sell everything but was instead praised that salvation was in his house. In this case, one person said, "Jesus was not against the wealth; he was against the bad character of the rich people of not caring for needy people, the poor. Jesus wanted people who had been blessed to care for the people who were poor in society." For the IR-VICOBA members, Jesus was encouraging the care of the poor within the society.

As discussed in the Introduction, the IR-VICOBA members are Christians who fight poverty with all of their ability, making them believe that Jesus would not favor poverty. As Christians, the IR-VICOBA members know that Jesus, as the Savior of the world, also holds their blessings and would not ordain poverty as a guarantee of entering heaven. In addition, as good readers of the Bible, they emphasised both the Old and the New Testaments. For the IR-VICOBA members, there is no difference between the Old Testament and the New Testament, since they both have messages from God. They know most of the phrases that describe blessings from God, the Creator, and other verses from the Bible that describe caring for the poor.

However, Sobrino seems to be saying that God's mission was primarily for the poor when he argues:

> Since the poor are those to whom Jesus' mission was primarily directed, they ask the fundamental questions of faith and so with power to move and activate the whole community in the process of learning what Christ is. Because they are God's preferred, and because of the difference between their faith and the faith of the non-poor, the poor, within the faith community, question Christological faith and give it its fundamental direction.[4]

---

4 Sobrino, *Jesus the Liberator: A Historical-Theological Reading of Jesus of Nazareth*, p. 30. See also, Gutiérrez, *A Theology of Liberation: History, Politics, and Salvation*, pp. 162–165.

This stance held by Jon Sobrino and other liberation theologians differs from that of the IR-VICOBA members. Both liberation theologians and the IR-VICOBA groups emphasize the materially poor and the downtrodden and only reference other types of poor people, like the spiritually poor, which I call in totality "the holistic meaning of the poor."[5] However, the IR-VICOBA members do not emphasize more Jesus' preference for poverty in their lives and making the Kingdom of God available only to the poor.

When listening to the IR-VICOBA members' Bible reading, one finds that they have reasons to argue for the holistic meaning of the poor, as I mentioned in Chapter 3. Their reason for placing more emphasis on *all poor people* (the holistic picture of the poor) is that Jesus came to save all people from their needs, which qualifies them to be "poor in a holistic meaning." In addition, the Bible gives examples that disqualify the preference for only the materially poor, like the issue of Zacchaeus, a tax collector (Luke 19:1-10), and Nicodemus (John 3:1-21), who was still a religious leader and a Pharisee. When he visited Jesus at night, he was instructed on how to achieve salvation, and the instruction was not to become poor. In their understanding, Jesus was for the poor in the sense of the holistic meaning; otherwise, he would be one-sided as a Savior of the world. Whoever is deprived of anything, whether material things, spiritual things, or material things, Jesus came to save that person from their predicament.

Their arguments for having this stance on poverty and the poor are as follows: First, Jesus is the son of God, and according to Christian theology and tradition, Jesus is 'Son of God' and he is 'God-God, the Son.' He is a Creator of good creation and would therefore not want people to be poor; Jesus would want people to receive his blessings, created by him, and shared without discrimination. However, since there are less privileged people – the 'have-nots'[6] – the issue here is to make all people share what they have, a matter that is very difficult in the present world. As we have seen in Chapter 3, being well informed with her context, a member said, "We should continue to empower each other regardless of our being poor, and we should learn to work hard so that we become capable economically."

Their second argument on this stance is that poverty is closely connected only with material poverty; however, the IR-VICOBA members looked mostly at material poverty in their discussion while implicitly indicating that, according to Jesus, poverty meant both physical and spiritual poverty. Jesus was also thinking of people like Zacchaeus and Nicodemus, who were socially and spiritually poor

---

5 I have used this term elsewhere to indicate all types of downtrodden persons within society, including, for instance, being socially, politically, or religiously downtrodden Someone who is materially rich can be socially poor, like Zacchaeus, who was rich financially but very poor religiously and socially.
6 Pam Peters, *The Cambridge Dictionary of English Grammar* (CUP, 2013). The term "have-nots" refers to poor people.

but materially rich and would be willing to voluntarily share what they had after meeting Jesus. On the other hand, some disciples, one can say, were spiritually rich and willing to share what they had while being materially deprived. This way of viewing the relationship between Jesus, the poor, and the rich includes everyone and makes them all responsible in the Kingdom of God.

Their third argument was that Jesus was there for all poor people, addressing the materially poor and the poor in spirit. This can be another way of making other people responsible. Those poor in material wealth, who are sometimes rich socially, can help the material rich to socialize and can relate positively with them. Doing so becomes a blessing to the entire world. On the other hand, the materially rich can be a blessing to those who are materially poor by sharing their wealth when they consider their wealth as a gift from God to share. Jesus wanted the entire world to be blessed by whatever someone has, so that the world can be in harmony, as we need each other in this world. Therefore, being rich or poor is a situation that calls upon everyone to help one another. In this sense, then, the IR-VICOBA members thought Jesus was for both the poor and the rich. This position on poverty clearly reflects the lived reality of the IR-VICOBA members in the community, namely, that all people are summoned – not only the material poor.

4.2.2 The Downtrodden and the Blessings (Gifts)

The IR-VICOBA members dealt with texts reflecting many issues arising as they continued with the discussion and as the facilitators continued to ask generic questions. The common generic question was, "Who were the characters in the texts we are reading and what was their roles?" Since most of the selected texts dealt with Jesus and the downtrodden, the IR-VICOBA members, themselves poor people, discussed many issues relating to characters and their roles. The two VICOBA groups' members saw the characters as much in need, which is why Jesus encouraged them by giving them hope. For instance, in reading Matt 5:1-12, the IR-VICOBA members saw that some people were promised the Kingdom of Heaven, some to be fulfilled, some to inherit the land, some to receive mercy, and, lastly, the great reward in heaven is the Kingdom.

The IR-VICOBA members reflected on the poor, the mourning, the hungry, the thirsty, and those persecuted for the sake of righteousness. This theme of 'Jesus and the downtrodden' was reflected in all Bible studies, to the greatest extent, however, when they discussed people in the text having difficulties and leading perilous, miserable lives: the Beatitudes (Matt 5:1-12), the sheep and goats (Matt 25:31-46), the rich man (Mark 10:17-22), the Lukan Beatitudes (Luke 6:20-26), and the rich man and poor Lazarus in Luke (16:19-31). The IR-VICOBA members' interest was their relationship with Jesus; they then reflected on their reflection and response, as I present in Chapter 5.

They reflected more on those serving others within the Beatitudes, like the merciful, the pure in heart, and the peacemakers. In their reflection on the needy and the servants in the Beatitudes, they thought Jesus aimed to assist the poor and needy. However, regarding people blessed because they are poor, the IR-VICOBA members seemed not to bless poverty in connection with the Kingdom of God. Being knowledgeable and aware of their own fight against poverty, they thought that Jesus said these words (e. g., in the Beatitudes and other texts) as words of encouragement, to give hope and empower them. They were assured of a blessing if they believed in him and the Kingdom of God. Taking an example from the Beatitudes, their argument was that Jesus gave different promises to these people, e. g., having the Kingdom of Heaven, inheriting the land, being comforted, being fulfilled, all of which showed that Jesus sought to liberate them in different capacities according to their needs. Therefore, Jesus was not indicating that the situation these people were experiencing was right or a privilege; Jesus aimed to liberate them from hardship, not trade it for the Kingdom of God.

The IR-VICOBA members asked all of these questions because they were themselves poor people who knew the meaning of being poor. Their aim was to liberate themselves from such a precarious situation of poverty, mourning, and hardship within their failure scenarios These failures included the failure to procure bread daily for the family, to pay school fees for their children, and other necessities. On the other hand, they also endeavored in their faith as committed Christians to receive the Kingdom of Heaven now and in the future. However, they thought about how Jesus dealt with the poor, the mourning, and the persecuted and wondered whether Jesus was set against being rich, fulfilled, and satisfied. The question was: "Why would Jesus, the Son of God, want them to be poor, while all the richness belonged to his father who created the world?" In their discussion, they came up with the idea that Jesus might have an intention greater than just saying that the poor, the mourning, and the persecuted were blessed or happy. In the words of one member (see Chapter 3):

> I think Jesus was giving encouragement and hope to the poor and the mourning because being poor, as we are, it is not a good thing and sounds like a curse. I think Jesus aimed at telling them that, because they believed in him, they had entered the kingdom of the assured, where they would be happy, fulfilled, and empowered. To be in a situation like the one we are experiencing here, you cannot tell someone that they are blessed or happy.

This language of the IR-VICOBA members somehow reflected their context compared to the context of the poor to whom Jesus showed a predilection in the text. The words of Jesus seemed like words from someone who was not serious about the situation. If the Beatitudes were stand-alone scriptures, they would not believe in Jesus' words and think Jesus was mocking the poor, the mourning, and the persecuted. Therefore, the IR-VICOBA members, all Christians who believed in Jesus as their Savior, thought Jesus was in fact encouraging and giving hope to the downtrodden in the text. They did not discuss much about the characters; however, they delved into their understanding of that message as poor people in a global economy who face many difficulties and challenges economically, socially, politically, and sometimes religiously. This situation justifies how experienced they are with their context, and the context interprets the text.

Possibly, this is what Holladay means when he writes about the Beatitudes having been interpreted according to the context throughout Christianity:

> Employing utterly realistic, concrete images that connect with everyday experiences, including weeping, hungering, thirsting and suffering unjustly, but also embracing the hard work of peacemaking, and extending to the higher reaches of spiritual ecstasy that takes the form of seeing God and becoming children of God, the Beatitudes have connected with Christians in every time and place.[7]

I find that Holladay's words agree with those of the IR-VICOBA members, that Jesus said these were words of encouragement, hope, and empowerment. This stance regarding the downtrodden also goes hand in hand with their attitude toward fighting poverty. In the Bible study, one said, "One of the motives of VICOBA, besides teaching the Word of God, is to empower us to fight poverty. This is the case when we include the VICOBA contributions session to empower each other." Moreover, Jesus did not embrace poverty as a good thing, according to the IR-VICOBA groups; rather, Jesus thought 'not caring for the poor people' was a serious and significant problem in the world since there were many downtrodden.

The IR-VICOBA groups discussed the preference of Jesus for the downtrodden with care. According to them, it sounds as if some people think being in a precarious predicament is a ticket to heaven and is preferred by Jesus (cf. Chapter 3). Reflecting on the Matthean Beatitudes, one member said, "There are groups of fellowships (charismatic groups) who think being poor means being near to God. We at the VICOBA group do not agree with this notion: We fight poverty with all our means." On the Lukan Beatitudes, a member from the other group came up with a similar notion when they said,

> In some groups and churches, they practise poverty so that they can inherit the Kingdom of God. This is self-deceit. Some members of those groups follow all those writings so that they can be on the side of Jesus, being poor. But they cheat themselves; they suffer

---

7 Carl R. Holladay, *The Beatitudes: Happiness and the Kingdom of God* (2013), p. 168.

from many aspects of life while they somehow live longer in the world. They say Jesus did not use cars, shoes, or other clothes, and they avoid buying those luxurious goods.

In the Beatitudes, according to the IR-VICOBA members, Jesus was talking to people from different economic statuses who followed him, among them poor people, rich people, and middle-class people. The IR-VICOBA thought that peacemakers, merciful, and good-hearted people could also be wealthy or middle-class people.

In Sobrino's language, the downtrodden in these selected texts are the 'crucified people,' people who continually live miserable lives. Describing the preferential option for the poor, Sobrino says, "God is God of the poor, as well as an epistemological break 'God is known through the poor.'"[8] Here, Sobrino's thought runs parallel to that of the IR-VICOBA members, who were perplexed that the preference of God (here, Jesus, God the Son) is the poor people. However, they differ in how they answer the questions because the IR-VICOBA members agreed that Jesus is for the poor, whereas the IR-VICOBA members went further: God is also God of the rich who believe in him and serve him like the peacemakers, the kind-hearted, and the merciful people in the Matthean Beatitudes. I understand this stance from what they argued about God not being against wealth and being the provider, as one of them said:

> Having wealth is not sin. Rather, the only problem is that rich people fail to share the richness they have with others – and that is where sin starts. But God is the one who provides everything to human beings, though he does want others also to get a share of that possession, and sometimes the rich people despise and degrade others because of their richness.

This indicated that they are against poverty and not propoverty in any way. Their emphasis lies in helping one another regardless of the economic status of being rich or poor. Therefore, the IR-VICOBA members significantly differ from Sobrino here, as I discussed above, because, to them, God is the God of all, whether poor or rich, while Sobrino seems to be only on one side – that God is for the poor.

Jesus said, "Blessed are the poor." The IR-VICOBA members did not take the interpretation that God had preference only for the poor literally. For them, in many places, the Bible shows that God works with people who believe and serve him on Earth. Many passages in the Bible describe how God requires the rich to care for the poor and the downtrodden, for example, Isaiah 42:5-8 and 1 Tim 6:17-19. These passages require the rich to care for the poor people and not to be selfish. If they

---

8 Sobrino, *No Salvation Outside the Poor: Prophetic-Utopian Essays*, p. 23.

care for the needy in this way, then they align with God, the Creator of Heaven and Earth to whom the downtrodden belong.

First, according to the IR-VICOBA members, saying that 'God is the God of the Poor' makes God too small if he deals only with the poor and the downtrodden; God is the God of *all*. Second, God is the creator of all the richness in the world and heaven; therefore, he cannot be *against* something he has created. Third, the relationship with other people exemplified in the Bible, like Job, Abraham, David, and Solomon, shows that God is the one who gives the blessing of richness to those people who believe in God; therefore, God cannot go against it. The problem here is how one behaves as a believer in God and Christ when dealing with the poor. According to the IR-VICOBA members, the problem here (cf. Chapter 3.3.2 and elsewhere) is not being rich as such but acting responsibly toward the downtrodden. This is why, when responding to the narrative of Lazarus and the rich man, one of them said, "There are rich people who care for the poor people. We want to continue to be like them because by doing that, we serve God. We do not want to be like the rich man who did not care about anybody. He thought, by having everything, he would acquire even heaven, which was wrong." Such a comment shows that they were referring to occasions occurring within their society, where some rich men care for poor people.

Furthermore, the example given by the merciful people mentioned by Jesus in the Matthean Beatitudes about the peacemakers (people who fight for the peace of other people who may be wealthy or destitute) and their response to those who are persecuted for righteousness' sake, gives the right relationship with the downtrodden in this world.

4.2.3 Classes of People Within the Context: The Last Judgment and Serving God Now

In the Contextual Bible Study about characters within the text, the IR-VICOBA members summed up these characters as 'the poor and the rich.' They easily recognized this class of people in the text when discussing the parable of the sheep and goats in the last judgment (Matt 25:31-46). Interestingly, they divided the poor and the rich into four groups: "Rich people who took care of needy people, rich people who did not care for people, poor people but who took care of the neediest people, and poor people who did not care for the needy people." This demonstrates how they approach the text with their own experiences from their socioeconomic context. Therefore, according to the members, some rich and poor people cared for the poor, and some rich and poor people did not care for the poor.

I think the IR-VICOBA members were concerned with reflecting on their own context alongside the text in scrutiny. The picture given by IR-VICOBA members above portrays the context in which they are living since one can see how it is represented. There are rich people in their context who care for poor people in many ways; there are also poor people, like the IR-VICOBA members themselves, who emphasize helping those who are poorer than them to extract themselves from their extreme poverty. On the other hand, some poor and rich people do not bother caring for other people. Therefore, there is a direct relationship between their interpretation of the text and their own context. Their context informs how they interpret the text since they use their experiences to also interpret their practices, their perception of society, and their commitment to their faith.

Moreover, the groups of people discussed above are invited to think of the other issue of characters, as discussed by the IR-VICOBA members. Those who care for the needy, whether rich or poor, serve Jesus. Therefore, they can be termed 'sheep,' and those who do not care for the needy can be termed 'goats.' The animal keepers know why Jesus used these two animals symbolically. In Africa, especially in rural areas where animals are kept, people know that sheep are cool, calm, and manageable, especially if they are kept in free-range grazing areas, whereas goats are troublesome, tireless, and unmanageable. If one is looking after these animals near somebody's field, one has to be careful with the goats, as otherwise they will rush and go into the field to eat the crops instead of eating grasses. This depicts those who do not care about the needy; they are like goats who do not care for their keeper and cause them trouble. Moreover, they can even destroy crops, which are not for their benefit. Therefore, those who take advantage of their understanding and knowledge, ignoring other people, are like goats from our environment. Nevertheless, those who are calm, relaxed, and contented with what they have and who like to share what they have with others are like sheep.

4.2.4 Jesus, the Giver of Sight to the Blind

Another theme the IR-VICOBA members discussed during their reading process, particularly as they were dealing with character assessment, was "Jesus the giver of sight to the blind," as we have seen in Chapter 3. One member said, "The message was one of liberation from poverty, empowering people with new knowledge and making them exercise freedom, especially people who were under the colonial regime." The meaning of giving sight, according to the IR-VICOBA members, is that, in those texts, Jesus came to teach people how to use their resources to become free human beings. The VICOBA members thought that these people were blind since they did not see opportunities on how to make use of those opportunities, which is why they were in that precarious predicament. They were so poor that they urgently needed a savior, a liberator from their condition. During Contextual Bible Study, one member said,

When Jesus said that he announced the accepted year to these people, he opened them to utilise the opportunity they have to the maximum so that they would manage their environment and manage their economy. This would mean empowering them spiritually and materially, so they would be free in whatever they were planning to do.

The IR-VICOBA members went into more depth in discussing Jesus or the Word of God giving sight. Another member came up with these words:

> In this country, people and the government are under captivity and are blind. For example, this country has many resources like minerals, but her people are poor because outside people get much of her richness and take it to their respective countries. Business people from outside this country exploit this country and get the richness of our resources. This country would get divine knowledge, which we need more to enlighten us so that we can get enlightened and enriched starting from our mind, and we can treat our environment for the betterment of the family and society and the entire country we are living in. If Jesus were physically here, he would tell the whole nation the Good News and make people not blind in all spheres of our lives.

These members interpreted the text in these ways because they saw that the characters Jesus was talking to – and his disciples – seemed to be in difficulties. He came to release them, give them sight, empower them, and show them the way to the new Kingdom of God, so that they may see the various obstacles that hindered them from moving forward. Then, according to the IR-VICOBA members, Jesus came with such power that made them see their surroundings and educated them to see different opportunities. The IR-VICOBA members thought that Jesus had a broader sense of the poor and blind than just their physical impairments. Rather, his teachings are instead related to being poor or blind economically, socially, and religiously.

The IR-VICOBA members discussed this after reflecting on their own environment, where many people were living precariously. These members were needy and among the poorest people in their surroundings. In their midst, they live with the blind, the lame, the mentally ill, the sick, beggars, paralytics, and the like. It was easy for them to visualize the sort of situation Jesus was mentioning concerning the captives and the blind. Moreover, the IR-VICOBA members were also thinking of other physically fit people who were beggars, which made them think these people were blind to the opportunities to have at least daily bread. These members had nothing against people who were disabled and needed care. For the IR-VICOBA members, then, Jesus came to open the eyes of beggars who did not see the opportunities God had set before them.

Moreover, on the issue of blindness in their context, the IR-VICOBA members reflected on how Jesus, through the word of God, is helping them. They also came to recognise that, when Jesus said that "he announced the accepted year" (Luke 4:18-19) to these people, he opened their minds to utilizing the opportunities they had in abundance. They could manage their environment and manage their economy, meaning they would be empowered spiritually and materially and be free in what they were planning to do. The IR-VICOBA members discussed this in this way because they knew the meaning of being exploited and what it means to use one's opportunities. From their Contextual Bible Studies, they learned how to efficiently use any opportunity to fight for their dignity as well as economic and social relationships, among other things. That is why, in the discussion, one member said, "There were a few people with the knowledge of how things were done who dominated and exploited the downtrodden, so Jesus came to save people like them to become free from the economic, social, and spiritual exploiters." The IR-VICOBA members knew that there were people who had knowledge and information about something but did not reveal their knowledge to anybody so that they could continue to exploit and dominate others. They gave as an example of such knowledge the marketing of their products. Business people who dominated and exploited the peasants did not reveal the facts of the market, remaining as they were and selling very cheaply so that the intermediaries and business people gained much profit from those products. The IR-VICOBA members looked on the characters in the texts they were reading and interpreted them using their own experience of the socioeconomic reality of Tanzania. What happened in their midst and their context is what informed their interpretation.

4.2.5 Jesus, the Announcer of Freedom to Captives

Jesus announced freedom to captives and the accepted year of the Lord (Luke 4:18-19). The IR-VICOBA groups pondered on these verses, where Jesus announced that he had come to free the captives, whereby the term "captive" meant a multifaceted meaning of captives. In their discussion, one member indicated, "When your mind is opened, then you become illuminated and have that ability to produce. The people in the texts were poor because, in their mind, they were still dominated, so Jesus wanted them to be more productive in every sphere of life." They discussed people in the text who were under the Roman colonial regime, and that they were not free. They also mentioned a lack of knowledge, which Jesus gave them so they could be emancipated from the domination and exploitation that controlled them from their innermost mind. They said that Jesus wanted them to fight poverty and not become under the control of ignorance, which was another captivity for many people in this world.

Positive thinking is an idea of the IR-VICOBA members, implying that Jesus wanted people to be emancipated from all powers that holistically dominated them politically, economically, socially, and religiously. The dominators do not allow the dominated to be free since they dominate them for their own interests; however, by having the power of knowledge, especially having divine knowledge from Jesus, the poor can learn how to fight for their emancipation. This was what Jesus meant when he said that he was proclaiming release to the captives (cf. Luke 4:18). By reading the Word of God, the poor become illuminated and liberated from all economic, social, and political forces – if not entirely, then at least by entering into the fight to liberate themselves.

Religiously, according to the IR-VICOBA groups, the Jews would not continue to be cheated by the synagogue leaders, since they would have acquired the divine knowledge that would empower them to fight a good fight in faith and make them completely free. Therefore, in this case, Jesus announces freedom to the poor of the world – and still does to today's poor, which also applies to the IR-VICOBA members. Nevertheless, the poor continue this fight, especially when one sees some church leaders who are part of the problem. Some preachers create many of the poor in society through their teachings. An example of these un-Christ-like teachings includes the promotion of the 'Prosperity Gospel,' implicitly mentioned by the IR-VICOBA members, which effectively makes poor people more miserable. This is seen as another trap for poor people. Poor people offer their money and other assets to these religious groups and make their leaders extremely rich while impoverishing themselves. I think the IR-VICOBA members' perception of blessing in that way was because of the understanding that God has no partiality. God is God for all, Christians and non-Christians. That is why the blessing is extended not only to Christians but to all people created by him.

One sees many religious leaders in the world today who use the Bible as a tool of enslavement rather than liberation; who use Jesus' word to benefit themselves at the expense of the poor. In churches in which many preachers preach like that, the intent is to make themselves – the preachers – richer.

4.2.6 Jesus, the Teacher of Knowledge (Good News)

The IR-VICOBA members viewed Jesus as a teacher of good news to the poor. They thought that, in the whole pericope of Luke 4:16-19, Jesus was identifying himself as a person who came to teach and empower others. On this issue, one member said, "Jesus was a teacher teaching them the Word of God as we read in v.18 when he says the Holy Spirit is upon me to preach good news to the poor."

All members in both groups agreed that, when Jesus said "to proclaim good news to the poor," he intended to empower them by educating them that they would know that he was there to teach them so they would become free. The exciting idea was that most members were very positive that Jesus wanted the poor to be self-sufficient economically; that would increase their dignity in society. The IR-VICOBA members were also very positive that Jesus taught the good news since they all believed in empowerment and self-reliance. Otherwise, they would think that Jesus came to teach about salvation only, as some people perceived, which would be a half-conception. According to them, Jesus came to save a human being in a holistic manner, where a human being is saved economically, religiously, politically, socially, and psychologically.

The IR-VICOBA members thought this way because they intended to fight all of the wrong Bible interpretations in their society which undermine the poor and downtrodden in society. The IR-VICOBA members emphasized the liberation of the downtrodden, themselves being miserable in their society.

Good news is significant to someone who receives such news, especially if they make them change or receive an advantage from that news. Thus, the IR-VICOBA members understand the good news to the poor to mean any restoration of the person to a good life here on earth; anything which enhances life is good news. For example, one member said, "The message was one of liberation from poverty, empowering new knowledge and making them exercise freedom, especially people under the colonial regime." Therefore, the IR-VICOBA members thought of good news as something holistic, referring to liberation from all forms of injustice and oppression by providing good news, which is new knowledge.

4.2.7 Jesus and the Commandments

Another theme discussed by the IR-VICOBA groups in their teachings was that of the Commandments. While discussing the rich man's story in Mark 10:17-22, the IR-VICOBA members reflected on the importance of the Commandments because Jesus asked the rich man if he knew them. The story of the rich man is the only passage of all the selected passages in this study, which mentions the Commandments. This produced interesting perceptions. According to the IR-VICOBA members, the rich man did not understand how great the question of Jesus was until he was asked to sell everything he had and give the revenue to the poor. According to the IR-VICOBA members, Jesus wanted to know whether the rich man put the Commandments into practice by loving his neighbors and loving God. The IR-VICOBA members thought that, because this person did *not* understand Jesus, he thought only about memorizing the Decalogue.

The IR-VICOBA members, content on how people are enriched in their context, thought this rich man possibly became wealthy from evil ways, which is why he left when told to sell everything. One member said,

This person had everything, and then Jesus asked him if he knew the Commandments. Possibly this man was stealing and squandering money from any organization. Possibly the person had enriched himself from evil sources and did not care for *the poor and needy people in society. Jesus was not against wealth but the rich man's* attitude of selfishness, and that is why Jesus asked if he knew the Commandments.

According to the IR-VICOBA members, Jesus was not against wealth but wanted a person to be responsible. Second, the Commandments should not be memorised but should be put into orthopraxy and not remain an orthodoxy for people to memorize. It is possible that the IR-VICOBA, being mostly Lutherans,[9] were referring to the catechism. Many members of the IR-VICOBA groups know about the catechism because they have passed through the catechist class, where the pastors and evangelists teach using the larger catechism. As I have argued elsewhere in this thesis, the IR-VICOBA members use their faith. All being members of the same church, they attend confirmation class, and in that catechism class, the Decalogue is part of the teachings. Using their knowledge from the catechism class, they interpret that the rich man did not understand the question of Jesus about the law. In their understanding, the Decalogue must be practiced, not merely memorised. Luther, in the Large Catechism, maintains:

> It is a fact that anyone familiar with the ten Commandments is, in consequences, familiar with the scriptures as a whole. He is able in all affairs and emergencies to counsel, to help, to comfort and to come to an understanding and decision, whether the subject is temporal or spiritual. He is qualified to sit in judgment on all doctrines, estates, spirits, and laws and everything else in the world.[10]

The words of Martin Luther in the Large Catechism quoted above, which most Lutherans in Tanzanian Christianity follow, might be the source of the IR-VICOBA members' reflection on the rich man's attitude toward wealth in connection with that part of Decalogue. Jesus gave him a practical test – go and sell what you own, give the money to the poor, and you will have treasure in heaven, then come, follow me (Mark 10:21).

---

9 Njinga, *The Shift from Ujamaa to Globalization as a Challenge to Evangelical Lutheran Church in Tanzania*, p. 47. The IR-VICOBA members are members of the ELCT-KoD, which I presented in Chapter 1. Nevertheless, the ELCT-KoD is a Lutheran diocese, a product of the mission of the Berlin Mission Society, which originated from the low-church revivals of the early century in Eastern Germany. Its background was that of the Prussian United Church.

10 Martin Luther and John Nicholas Lenker, *Luther's Large Catechism: God's Call to Repentence, Faith and Prayer, the Bible Plan of Salvation Explained* (Minneapolis, MN: The Luther Press, 1908), p. 39.

Therefore, like Martin Luther, the IR-VICOBA members think that the Decalogue serves to assist us; it is not just to be memorized but to be lived. Many people know the 10 Commandments by heart and yet do not put them into their daily practices. To put them only into memory is hypocrisy and does not assist the person who does so, as they become like the rich man (Mark 10:17-22) or the Priest and Levites in the parable of the Good Samaritan (Luke 10:25-28). In this case, according to the IR-VICOBA members, the Commandments are a form of spiritual guidance to help people live in peace, harmony, and with good relationships with their God and their neighbors.

4.3 Contextual Assessment of the IR-VICOBA Members in their Participatory Bible Study

After having interpreted and discussed the IR-VICOBA members' interpretation of the selected texts, I now analyze their interpretation of the contextual assessment, that is, how they move from the text to their own context. In some cases, as indicated earlier, the context more openly informs the text. This subsection contains several themes that reflect their context, taking advantage of the fact that they used much time discussing many aspects of their own experience, context, and environment to inform the text's interpretation. The IR-VICOBA members have a rich experience compared to the assessment of the character discussed above. Many things happen in their lives which reflect what happens in the text. The text becomes like a mirror through which they can reflect on their own life experience, knowledge, and practices.

Here, I analytically interpret and discuss selected themes taken from the IR-VICOBA members' interpretation. These are the themes I discuss in this section: the issue of exploitation and injustice in society and the world at large; the rich and the use of the power of money and overriding of justice; disrespect among the believers because of differences in faith and social status; the issue of gender as the cause of disrespect. In addition, I also discuss the best use of resources empowered by teaching, poor socioeconomic systems as the world's new enslavement environment degradation and poverty, the gap between the rich and the poor and injustice in business, and lack of knowledge as a new type of blindness in the world today.

4.3.1 The Issue of Exploitation and Injustice in Society and the World at Large

Another theme of interest during the discussion of IR-VICOBA members was the exploitation of peasants, as noted in the previous chapter. Reflecting on texts from Matt 5:1-12, Mark 10:17-22, and Luke 16:19-31, the issue of how the characters in the texts became poor and how people are made miserable in their society raised the issue of exploitation and injustice. The issue of exploitation of people who were under the Roman colonial regime triggered the IR-VICOBA members' knowledge of Tanzania's own history, which was once under a colonial regime that exploited them for whatever they could: Everything went to their masters in Europe. The members contemplated the issues of why people were poor in the Matthean Beatitudes, why Lazarus was poor in Luke, and why the rich man was so rich in Mark. The IR-VICOBA members, since they interpret and give meaning to texts using their own experiences and socioeconomic reality, were also more concerned with their own present experiences of exploitation taking place in their midst. One member during the Bible study said, "Even today we are made poorer every day by the government and people who exploit the poor like us in our country. They buy our crops for a low price and go to other towns, cities, and neighboring countries where they sell those crops at a high price." To justify their discussion on the issue of exploitation, they gave different examples (portrayed in Chapter 3) of how the rich get richer and the poor become more miserable. This shows that, for the time being at least, the IR-VICOBA members know how people become rich because of the exploitation of land products and other natural resources, especially from people who live in rural areas, like the IR-VICOBA members. The wealthy business people who know how to market crops in different areas cheat the peasants and buy their products at such low prices that the peasants do not receive any profit at all, while the rich make themselves extremely wealthy, like the people in the quotation above.

Furthermore, the IR-VICOBA members argued that, through the use of technology and other knowledge, business people exploit them because they set the price, which makes rich people have more and peasants have little. As a result, they become even more miserable. The significant problem here might be a lack of communication among themselves and other peasants, since such rich people act like that because they have a good network with other business people in other countries. They communicate easily from one market to another without any problems. They enrich themselves at the expense of the peasants, which is why they have good cars, houses, many assets, and excellent promising businesses.

Moreover, by using technology like emails, smartphones, computers, and good transportation, which peasants cannot access, business people can cheat and exploit peasants. These business people have many facilities that assist them in doing business, like cars and proper storage facilities as well as other means that assist them in buying goods with no problem. Nevertheless, the cost of those facilities does not justify this exploitation of the peasants. One main problem here is the business objectives, such as making a 'superprofit' at any cost – even by cheating.

To cement this idea, Osberg and Bandara write: "The problem is found in the fact that the farmers cannot control the price at which they sell their crops."[11]

Osberd and Bandara argued more economically; but, in a real sense, regardless of the force of demand and supply, the IR-VICOBA members argue that business people in their country and abroad find other ways to make their businesses work in their favor, not only because of the application of the laws of demand and supply. The market of peasants applies not only to local markets but reaches far beyond to international markets, too. There, poor peasants are even further disadvantaged because they do not know the power of that market and have fewer communication skills and facilities.

The situation mentioned above makes poor peasants, like the IR-VICOBA members, complain about the business being done in their area since there are no barriers. People from both within and outside the country take advantage of them since they know very little about the market in a globalized economy. Moreover, when the government abolishes agricultural subsidies, these business people take advantage of the peasants by making them their market for products from big industries from abroad. I learned this when I stayed in Itete (one of the places of my fieldwork). During my research, I saw peasants take out loans for fertilizers, and the money was then deducted monthly after they had sold their fresh tea leaves. Therefore, the factory took advantage by giving out fertilizer loans, where peasants would end up paying more than what was required. I found this exploitative, although the peasants were happy to get the fertilizer for their tea fields.

The world economy has made Transnational Corporations (TNCs) richer than ever before. As mentioned earlier, some TNCs buy crops from peasants around Itete, the Rungwe District, where members of IR-VICOBA live. These TNCs buy products at low prices, which is why these IR-VICOBA members mentioned being exploited in their discussion. However, when one visits a country like Tanzania, one finds many TNCs working with peasants to grow cash crops like cocoa, tea, and coffee. These TNCs do not pay these peasants reasonable prices, and the government does not interfere. The government not interfering is a requirement by the IMF and the World Bank on free trade.[12] Therefore, the IR-VICOBA members are right in saying that the global economy has indeed caused peasants to become more impoverished. They experience much exploitation and injustices in business – and it is planned to be like that.

Thus, the IR-VICOBA members implicitly perceived that, in many cases, problems of global injustice can be solved only if the victims of business, like the peasants,

---

11 Lars Osberg and Amarakoon Bandara, "Why Poverty Reamins High in Tanzania: And What to Do About It?", *REPOA Special Paper*, January 2011–2012, p. 15.
12 Joseph E. Stiglitz, *Globalization and Its Discontents* (New York: W.W. Norton & Co., 2002), pp. 6–7.

can reach 'the light.' The IR-VICOBA members have started to gain the light that illuminates their understanding of society and implicitly the world's problems and challenges. Other poor people follow because the victims have already gained that light and already received that insight, which is the power of illumination and liberation. The way might not be more comfortable in a well-structured and fabricated phenomenon like global economic injustice, but, still, they will make the way – they have the light. Therefore, the poor people like the IR-VICOBA members, who know very little about the global economy, can still be a source of that liberation if they come together in one way or another to learn and teach others about many aspects of their precarious lives in rural areas and how to fight for their betterment.

4.3.2 The Rich People, the Use of the Power of Money, and the Overriding of Justice

Another theme that came up during the Bible study discussion of the IR-VICOBA members was that of people using their wealth poorly and treating others as objects by paying bribes to lawyers. In their discussion about Matt 5:11 and Mark 16:16-31 on the narrative of the rich man and poor Lazarus, the IR-VICOBA members responded to the improvised question, "What causes people to be poor in our present context?" In the Bible study, they indicated that the poor are sometimes imprisoned even when they do not commit any wrongs. Quoting directly, one of them said, "We see in this context people who are mourning and persecuted; possibly there are rich people who use their money to send people to jail or to court and use their financial status to change the right of people by paying bribes to people who were judging the case." According to them, the poor have no money to fight for their justice; they cannot afford to hire a lawyer in their case. Therefore, in many cases, they find themselves mistreated like Lazarus, going to prison even when they are not guilty.

Another member in Agape IR-VICOBA said, "We have the Chinese, who are constructing the road near our area. These Chinese mistreat poor workers, pay little money, and use their money to seduce young women only because they are rich and have money in this village and nearby villages." These people did that because they had the power of money the poor want. Therefore, they used this weakness of the downtrodden to treat them however they wanted. Prostitution in Tanzania is illegal, but poor young women have no money. To them, having sex and receiving money in return does not bother them. They do not know how much it affects their own life. To them, having sex with Chinese contractors is a lucrative business, and they do not think of the legality of what they are doing. The local government does not interfere; prostitution is done secretly, unless the outcome of that business results in giving birth to a colored child. Then people start to gossip, but without reporting it to the government.

The Chinese contractors do all of these things because they can exploit the weak knowledge of people in the area, who do not know their regulations. These people come from a country with stringent regulations regarding sexual intercourse, but here they treat people that way. Moreover, they know that these poor women cannot go far in a court of law because they do not have the money to pay for lawyers, while they themselves can pay.

Theologically, this is sin, the sin of misusing other human beings like objects to give themselves pleasure. It is a humiliation of human beings, which produces more poor people. To give an example: A woman gets pregnant when the Chinese contractor has already gone back to China. The woman becomes a burden to her parents, who must care for her and her baby.

Writing on this issue, Teresa Okure states:

> Traditionally Africa had high moral values, especially in regulating sexual relationship and in inculcating truth and honesty in human relationships and the respect of the land. Globalization has introduced and sustained sex commerce. Western tourists have penetrated even into remotest villages to attract young girls with cheap money, thus sustaining the spread of HIV/AIDS throughout the continent.[13]

Okure is writing about the tourists in villages, in an era of globalization, when foreign companies bring workers in from other countries (not only from the West, as Okure writes). I agree with her that in this time of globalization, people have no limits, and in a country like Tanzania, where regulations are not well disseminated to all citizens, people enter into illegal businesses, knowingly or unknowingly, as in the example given above of IR-VICOBA members of the Upendo Agape group in Itete. This attitude allows people with money – the rich – to use poor people for their pleasures while violating human rights and entering into global sins.

The rich men and the Chinese workers in the above example behave like the rich man in the narrative in Luke, acting selfishly without considering their neighbors and the impacts of their deeds. One member of the Upendo Group IR-VICOBA said if you asked why they acted this way and whether they know the effects of such sexual business, such as the danger of contracting HIV/AIDS, the poor women who indulge in that business say that it is "better to contract HIV/AIDS, which will kill me slowly, than dying of hunger and poverty. These men give me money to sustain my children's life, who will at least live on after my death." Therefore, the young women are not afraid of HIV/AIDS, compared to how they are afraid of hunger and poverty. However, one sees that now, because the world has become smaller, it is

---

13 Felix Wilfred and Jon Sobrino, *Globalization and Its Victims*, vol. 2001/5, Concilium (London: SCM Press, 2001), p. 72.

easier for people to travel, for wealthy people from within and outside the country to spread the killing disease of HIV and AIDS across the world, unknowingly or knowingly. The real problem is the power of richness, which rich people use to self-satisfy themselves via these poor women. The IR-VICOBA members thought that, if the women had a good economy, they would not indulge in such illegal business. To them, poverty leads women to work in that business.

4.3.3 Disrespect Among Believers Because of Differences in Faith and Social Status

The disrespect among believers because of their differences in faith and social status was another matter the IR-VICOBA members discussed. As they reflected on the issue of poor people being despised, they noted the people who despise others (Matt 5:11-12) because they are of other denominations with traditions different from theirs. One member said,

> We Christians are now fighting among ourselves and despising other people, e. g., fellowship members, counting others as poor believers or people of one denomination despising people of the other denominations by segregation, and some counting themselves more righteous than others. If Jesus were here, he would say, "Blessed are you when people revile you and persecute you and utter all the kinds of evil against you falsely on my account. Rejoice and be glad, for your reward is great in heaven, for in the same say way they persecuted the prophets who were before you." (Verses 11-12)

Another member added, "There are charismatic groups and Pentecostal churches that do not count other Christians as faithful like them. This does not comply with the grace of God since that is a self-justification."

I believe these members gave these comments because many denominations in Tanzania make people laugh at and despise each other because of their different denominational traditions. There are mainline churches like the Roman Catholic Church and Protestant churches like the Anglicans, the Lutherans, the Moravians, Presbyterians, Seventh Day Adventists, and several Pentecostal churches. These members despise one another because of different doctrines on baptism, teachings, renunciation of sins, and traditions. For instance, the Pentecostals consider members from other denominations not to be Christians because of being baptised with little water, while they believe in baptism by immersion. The Seventh Day Adventists consider others poor Christians only because they do not observe the Sabbath. These attitudes are worldwide because these churches receive their traditions from their sister churches abroad – and sometimes they contextualize them to their local setups. Therefore, the IR-VICOBA members thought that this issue of people despising other members is a problem since it causes people to fight and let other people down, especially from Pentecostal churches, which attempt to re-evangelize people from other denominations and re-baptize them.

There is a severe and challenging idea here, that of the "prosperity gospel." Most Pentecostal churches believe in the prosperity gospel, while other mainline churches do not place much emphasis on it. One member explained, "I visited one church where members were asked to give a lot of money so that God could bless them, and the members gave a lot of money and properties. But I also met some members from the same church complaining that they were becoming poor." In the Bible study, members nodded their heads as others told the story – a sign that a teaching among churches within the area of Tukuyu was causing members to mourn. Another member illustrated how these preachers go about their teachings:

> Some people cheat believers and want the believers who offer more money, for example, by telling them that those who have 10,000 will get more blessings from God than those who have 5,000 should get to the following line. Those preachers also say that I should start praying for those with 10,000 and then following those who have little, like those with 5,000 and some give other material things – more than they have. This is a selling of the Gift of God, and these preachers make themselves more abundant than ever and cause others to be poor.

The IR-VICOBA members continued to discuss the issue of some pastors acting shrewdly, such that their members gave more. A member of the group gave an example of her brother:

> These pastors are witches because they attract people, especially those who have money, to go to their parishes. My brother had a shop in our village and had cows. After going to them, he was asked to give cows and much money on the promise of being rich. However, now he has no shop, and the cows are gone. The problem is that my brother still hopes to get more from them, be richer than before, and still attend the same church. He does not understand when he is told to come back to the church that raised us.

One may ask why people go to these charismatic groups and Pentecostal churches. But in the real sense, they preach in conjunction with a healing ministry. The latter makes many poor people run to those preachers, even though they act very shrewdly for their own benefit.

Therefore, according to the IR-VICOBA members, the prosperity gospel is not proper Christian teaching because it makes believers view God as a God of partiality. Furthermore, the attitude of preachers to cheat people by using the prosperity gospel is not the right way of doing a mission for God. People who despise others because of those teachings do not know that what they are doing is just a self-justification and does not hold 'the' truth.

In their Bible study, the IR-VICOBA members brought up another matter concerning the status of the poor, despised only because they are poor. They scrutinized this because Jesus said, "Blessed are you when people revile you and persecute you and utter all kinds of evil against you falsely on my account. Rejoice and be glad, for your reward is great in heaven, for in the same way, they persecuted the prophets who were before you" (Matt. 5:11-12). Defilement of the poor was an important matter to them since the IR-VICOBA members were poor people whom some rich people had defiled and treated poorly. In their Bible study, the IR-VICOBA members indicated that there are people who even have affairs with the wives of poor people only because they are poor people and give money to the wives of those poor men. One member said,

> Some rich people have an affair with poor people's wives. This is not just taking the poor people's rights; the poor people cannot send them to court because they do not have money or [they are] afraid of those rich people. The result is divorce in those marriages and children living in difficulties.

This perception reveals why the IR-VICOBA members indicated that poverty is a horrible thing: Sometimes, these wives of poor men have secret affairs with rich people so that they get enough money to feed their children and their own upkeeping. They can use those means as the only way of earning income for their families. They are not doing it for the sake of pleasure. The consequence of those affairs is acquiring many diseases like gonorrhea, HIV/AIDS,[14] syphilis, and other diseases caused by sexual intercourse, and finally, family dislocation, and divorces. These wives of poor men do not *like* to have secret sex with the wealthy, but they

---

14 AVERT, "HIV and AIDS in Tanzania," in *Global Information and Education on HIV and AIDS* (2017), https://www.avert.org/professionals/hiv-around-world/sub-saharan-africa/tanzania, writes that women are heavily burdened by HIV in Tanzania, where 780,000 women aged 15 and over are living with HIV. In 2016, UNAIDS reported HIV prevalence for women at 5.8%, compared to 3.6% for men. In 2012, women aged 23–24 were also twice as likely to be living with HIV than men of the same age. HIV prevalence among women ranged from 1% among those aged 15–19 to 10% among women aged 45–49. In 2016, more than 25,000 women aged 15–24 became infected with HIV, compared to around 20,000 men of the same age. Women tend to become infected earlier because they have older partners and get married earlier. They also experience great difficulty negotiating safer sex because of gender inequality. The 'sugar daddy' culture is widespread in Tanzania. Women will often accept the sexual advances of older men for a variety of reasons, including money, affection, and social advancement. Intimate partner violence is also an issue, with more than 30% of married or partnered women aged 15–24 experiencing physical or sexual violence from a male partner in the previous 12 months.

need their money since these wives need to feed the family. Therefore, when rich people use their richness in such a way, it is both not good and risky. Furthermore, they do that on the backs of the poor people, by taking the little that the poor have for their own pleasure. This is a 'social sin' and an injustice.

This subsection has dealt with the issue of disrespect because of faith and social status, reflecting on the reading of the Synoptic Gospels. It has discussed one of the most challenging issues among people in the society in which the IR-VICOBA members live. It is a bad practice for people to be despised because of differences in traditions and because they are poor, to the extent that rich people even defile the marriage of poor people by having affairs with them. Moreover, it is dehumanizing, unethical, and a moral sin.

4.3.4 The Issue of Gender as the Cause of Disrespect

The IR-VICOBA members discussed the issue of women being treated as second-class people in their response to Matt 5:11. They also discussed that there were men who beat their wives. In such cases, their husbands despise these women. To make this more vivid, I want to repeat the words of one member:

> Some traditions still reduce women to tools for work and not cocreated by God with men in the family. In our neighborhood, some women are beaten by their husbands, and this happens because they say the women were bought since men pay the bride price (dowry) for their wives, and they have no say in anything within the family.

Furthermore, men think that whatever their wives produce belongs to them as husbands. Sometimes some women support the persecution of other women in their society. In Chapter 3, I discussed one woman, a member of the IR-VICOBA group, who was advocating that the family confiscate all her sister-in-law's assets after her brother's death. There were many incidences like that in rural Tanzania, and people think it is right to do so.

These people treat their women in that manner for various reasons. First, because of the tradition of paying a dowry: If they pay a dowry, they can treat their wives any way they like. Second, some of them behave this way from ignorance: They do not even know about human rights and laws. Third, some treat their spouses like this because of their own emotional character: They behave this way because they cannot tolerate it when their wives make mistakes.

The IR-VICOBA members asserted these things because they had been illuminated by the Word of God, which wanted to treat each other in godly love. However, a few Christians act like unbelievers and become shameful to the Church of Christ. In their Bible studies, the IR-VICOBA members also learned of other matters concerning home and family matters. Therefore, the IR-VICOBA members were knowledgeable about respecting each other in the family regardless of gender, and that everybody within the family owns together, i. e., what they get from their production or farming. This is why they do not like people who maltreat their spouses. A few men are treated that way in the community by their wives. Their wives are physically, and sometimes financially, powerful women.

In addition to that we find the issue of men beating their wives, which results in women being treated like animals without rights in their own homes. This act of beating women and treating them as objects goes against God's righteousness – or we may say it goes against God's justice and human rights. In their Bible study, the members emphasize that such practices are no longer fit to be carried out in the modern world since it is unjust and illogical. On the issue of injustice, Groody writes, "God's justice, in other words, is not principally about vengeance or retribution but about restoring people to right relationship with God, themselves, others, and the environment."[15] The arguments of the IR-VICOBA members, although viewed more locally, likely match Groody's more global thoughts that, in the globalized world, traditions like those of mistreating women are not condoned since they are outdated, and people should seek equality, love, and peace in their families. They should strive to produce more such that everybody has equal ownership or right to own what they earn regardless of their gender. In addition, such traditions are not life-enhancing but destroy life. Therefore, they should be abolished. In the African context, however, many people are traditionalists with a closed mind and treat others with inequity.

4.3.5 Environmental Degradation and Poverty

The environment is another theme that emerged when the IR-VICOBA members described the improvised question: "What makes people suffer and find themselves in hospitals and needing to be cared for by other people?" (Matt 25:31-46). The IR-VICOBA members indicated that some people were not attending to their living environment, so they contracted diseases like cholera, bilharzia, malaria, and dysentery, finding themselves in the hospital and asking for assistance from good Samaritans.

There is another cause of disease in rural areas, which is industrial air and water pollution. People suffer from diseases like cancer, skin diseases, TB, and the like. One IR-VICOBA member said:

---

15 Daniel G. Groody, *Globalization, Spirituality, and Justice: Navigating the Path to Peace*, Theology in Global Perspective Series (Maryknoll, NY: Orbis Books, 2007), p. 28.

This is the case in the area near Tukuyu; coal extraction has polluted the water, making it unsuitable for use from that area, and the river passing through it pours into Lake Nyasa. There is not much research done on whether the fish are affected by the coal, but people are using the water and consuming the fish from the lake and river.

The above example given by the member of IR-VICOBA is not as severe as it is mentioned here. There are other rural areas like Geita, Mara, and Mwadui, where people living near gold and diamond mines complain of water pollution causing cancer. They complain about the effects of chemicals used to purify gold, like mercury, which is known to cause cancer in the neighboring villages, especially among those who use the river and stream water passing through the mines. I think this is why the member spoke about a lack of evidence of any data because there are no complaints about coal causing cancer in fish and humans in the surrounding area and near Lake Nyasa. Nevertheless, their point needs much research from the government. Coal might indeed have effects no one has yet discovered, since the water is colored by coal from the mines onward, and no one knows how safe that water is. This notion is supported by Groody, who maintains that "care for the Earth is also a concern for the poor, not only because the Earth is 'mother' but also because the poor, in the places [they are] forced to live, more often suffer the effects of contaminations, toxic wastes, and even ecological disasters."[16]

Crispin Kinabo notes some of the consequences of using low-level technologies to process minerals as well as rudimentary tools, which have a greater effect on the environments and people:

- Wastage of minerals because of poor ore and mineral recovery during mining and mineral processing respectively;
- Direct discharge of process waters and tailing into rivers;
- Spillage of tailing dams during heavy rains;
- Erosion and desertification;
- Damage to river banks in alluvial mining regions;
- Scattering of mine waste products and
- Mercury pollutions[17]

Some of the above-given consequences are reflected in the doubts of the IR-VICOBA members in their connection between poverty and the mining sector.

---

16 Ibid., p. 117.
17 Crispin Kinabo, A Social-Economic Study of Small-Scale Mining in Tanzania in the Social-economic impacts of artisanal and Small Scale Mining in Developing Countries, Charles Birch, "Christian Obligation for the Liberation of Nature," in *Liberating Life: Contemporary Approaches to Ecological Theology* (Maryknoll, NY: Orbis Books, 1990), p. 277.

In their discussion on the cause of the predicament, as mentioned in the Lukan Beatitudes and the pericope of the rich man, the IR-VICOBA members came up with another issue concerned with environmental degradation which had a connection with poverty. The IR-VICOBA members indicated that the environmental condition was not conducive to supporting the situation they were going through. They indicated that in most parts of Tanzania drought caused people to live miserable and precarious lives, although they were hard workers. However, they showed concern that most people are the cause of such situations that reciprocally affected them. For instance, as mentioned during the Bible study discussion, people in rural Tanzania cut trees for energy consumption (i. e., for firewood and making charcoal), and some overgraze the land, causing the soil to erode. Thus, people in rural areas destroy nature, resulting in its failing to sustain them in their economic activities. In turn, they become more impoverished. Quoting directly from their own words, one member said, "In our neighboring village, there are people who sell charcoal, and the government does not take any steps to forbid them. We see in the same area draught increasing year after year, which is not a good sign."

Moreover, the IR-VICOBA members were concerned with the government continuing to give permits or remaining silent, while acknowledging that the consequences of such activities occur at the cost to all citizens. This was a fascinating theme that came up during the discussion. I was trying to think how they connected their situation with the Beatitudes, the rich man, and poverty, especially on the issue of poor people and environmental conservation being 'part and parcel' of the cause. This was a reflection their situation, where many people worked hard but remained poor. Some IR-VICOBA members lived in Ilima, between the Kyela and Rungwe Districts, where the area is dry, but where people nevertheless still cut down trees for charcoal.

Their discussion shows it is true that environmental degradation is among the many problems facing people in rural Tanzania, Rungwe being one of the most wettest areas in Tanzania. In the Lukan Beatitudes or the parable of the rich man, however, people in the text might have been impoverished because of the desert. The IR-VICOBA members did not think of the landscape of Palestine; they used their own experiences to look at some causes of poverty, hunger, and mourning and found that, in their experience, environmental degradation was one of them.

The situation of environmental degradation, which was described by the IR-VICOBA member above, can be supported by the research done by Gilarowski in Tanzania, who indicated that forests surrounding the villages were disappearing because people cut down trees for firewood and charcoal production (which covers 90% of the energy needs among Tanzanians) as well as to obtain arable land and pastures for herds.[18] Gilarowski's research refers to focussed several regions, in particular, Dodoma, Kagera, Kigoma, Lindi, Manyara, Mbeya, Morogoro, Mtwara, Shinyanga, Singida, and Tabora. Tanzania has 31 regions, and among the regions mentioned by Gilarowski, only Dodoma and Singida lie in the semiarid regions, while the remaining regions are very wet. The regions mentioned are only examples to justify how the environment is being destroyed in Tanzania. Among these areas, Mbeya is where the Rungwe and Kyela Districts are and where the IR-VICOBA members live. This confirms that energy consumption has caused poverty. The picture given by Gilarowski justifies the idea that environmental degradation is one cause of people living precarious lives in the areas.

Another issue is the regulation of climate in the area and global warming, something the IR-VICOBA members do not know much about. In areas like Busale and Ilima, there is an increase in temperature over previous years when there were good forests around the area. Now the area is experiencing long dry seasons. The destruction of trees affects the global climate because there is a relationship between air movement and weather regulation; trees planted in Africa, Europe, or elsewhere affect the global climate. The desert, which is growing in Africa, thus causes global warming. That is why the issue of environmental conservation is a global problem. Gilarowski writes:

> According to Intergovernmental Panel on Climate Change (2007), the temperature in Africa within XX century rose by 1.0°C according to the same source, in the period between 1970 and 2004, in the eastern, central and northern part of Tanzania the increase in temperature was 0.2–1.0°C and in western, Southwestern and southern Tanzania between 1.0 and 2.0°C. The projection for 2030 indicates that the region will get more rain but become drier as the temperature rises. For Tanzania, the predicted increase in temperature is 2.5–4.0°C.[19]

As I mentioned above, the areas of Ilima and Busale, near the coal-mining industry at the middle of the Rungwe and Kyela Districts, have been affected because of the inhabitants destroying the environment. The area lies in the midst of mountains, which one would expect to have much rainfall, but this hasn't been the case because people are destroying the environment and causing the area to become semidesert. In this case, environmental degradation has caused people in the area to be poorer and face hunger year after year. There are few efforts by the government to protect the area from tree cutting, and there are no plans to plant trees to rescue the area

---

18 Bandara, "Why Poverty Reamins High in Tanzania: And What to Do About It?", p. 100.
19 Ibid., pp. 105–106.

from becoming semidesert. People are still cutting the trees there. This environmental degradation vividly affects people, and people do not know the problem causing their poverty as they themselves are cutting most of the trees down on that mountain.

4.3.6 The Gap Between the Rich and the Poor and Business Injustice

Another theme the IR-VICOBA members discussed was the gap between the rich and the poor, where the rich take advantage of the poor people, as shown in Chapter 3. They reflected on the gap between the rich and the poor in their society while discussing the pericopes of the rich man and poor Lazarus (Luke 16:19-31) and the rich man (Mark 10:17-22), and both the Matthean and Lukan Beatitudes (Matt 5:1-12; Luke 6:20-26). During the Bible study, the IR-VICOBA members complained about wealthy business people taking advantage of them and making themselves extremely rich. One IR-VICOBA member gave an example:

> I am a small grower of avocados, and we sell our avocados to settlers, who then sell our avocados abroad, where I think he gets much profit. We sell one kilogram of avocados for Tsh 1,000, and this is a new price. I am sure when they sell to Europe, they get much more money, which is not fair. They are cheating us in that business, and they make us cheap laborers and get all of the profit.

As they continued with the discussion, another member gave another example of this unjust business:

> I have another example, I sell milk to a prosperous business company called ASAS, which owns a big dairy farm, but when he comes to buy milk, he pays only Tshs. 600, which is very little while he makes a super profit. Our fellows from Mbeya sell milk for Tshs. 1,000 per liter – at least a reasonable price. This is how rich people exploit us poor people.

From the examples they gave, the settler who was buying avocados by paying Tshs. 500, approximately $0.21 per kilogram, is a white settler from Zimbabwe. Milk was sold to one rich company called ASAS for Tshs. 600 (approximately $0.27) per liter. The company is a prosperous one that produces many milk products like yogurt, chocolate, sweets, and drinking milk. Regarding this and commenting on the parable of the rich man and poor Lazarus (Luke 16:19-31), Karen M. Hatcher writes, "The parable presents a disturbing critique of today's global money economy, which creates an ever-widening chasm between the poor and the prosperous."[20] By using these immoral methods, business people make much profit. Therefore, the profit that makes them richer also creates a large gap between the peasants and the wealthy companies and business people.

The above businesses and others have given Tanzania an increase in economic growth but have not positively affected rural Tanzania, such as the areas where the IR-VICOBA members live. Mashindano and Shepherd commented on this situation: "In Tanzania, liberalisation and de-agrarianisation have led to unequal growth; stagnating and some places increasing poverty; fragmented landholdings; and rise of the cost of essentials."[21] The above-mentioned complaint from the IR-VICOBA members is directly supported by this argument made by Mashindano and Shepherd regarding unequal growth, meaning only a few people gain significantly in this era of globalization. The people who buy avocados and milk are not Tanzanians. For example, ASAS is Asian by origin, and the buyer of avocados is a British person from Zimbabwe. They can increase the nation's per capita income but do not increase the peasant' income growth in rural Tanzania like the IR-VICOBA members. Likewise, an increase in national income does not reduce poverty in rural Tanzania. Instead, a few people gain more profit, like ASAS and the avocado buyers who sell them abroad. The gap between rich people and poor people increases daily.

This gap still describes the situation that prevailed at the time of Jesus (as we read in the Beatitudes and the parables of the rich man and the rich man and Lazarus) and the range of needy people (as we read in Matt 25:31-46). This gap compels the world and society, as the IR-VICOBA members suggested, to take action. Jesus suggested in Matt 25:35-36, Luke 6:27, and Luke 4:18-19 that we have to care for the needy and poor people among us the same way he did and taught. We can reduce the concomitants of that gap if this is done seriously and with good intentions.

4.3.7   Lack of Knowledge as a New Blindness in the World Today

The lack of knowledge was another issue that emerged during the reading process of the IR-VICOBA people. The good news that Jesus proclaimed was discussed mainly with the improvised question: "What is good news to the poor today?"

> In today's world, some people exploit others economically and do not want to reveal the source of their being empowered economically, politically, and socially. They cheat and exploit us because of our ignorance about the market and lack of communication

---

20 Karen M. Hatcher, "In Gold We Trust: The Parable of the Rich Man and Lazarus (Luke 16:19–31)," *Review & Expositor* 109, no. 2 (2012), p. 281.
21 Bandara, "Why Poverty Reamins High in Tanzania: And What to Do About It ?," p. 5.

technology. If Jesus were here today, he would tell the truth to the peasants and even to people who exploit others, which would be good news to all of them, instead of keeping it a secret. Nevertheless, today, the Word of God as good news has the power to free people from this captivity, from this blindness, and from poverty in general.

Peasants in rural areas lack communication, which is the power of any business. Peasants are like the characters in the text, who had very little knowledge of how to liberate themselves and remain poor, blind captives because only a few have the power of knowledge. 'Knowledge is power' when doing anything in this world. Knowledge makes things happen quickly. If peasants knew about the world market and had this knowledge, it would be like salvation to them, and they would not complain. Now, only few people know how to do business and thus control that 'power' so that they can continue exploiting others by buying their products cheaply. It is hard for marketers to empower peasants with knowledge unless these peasants do so for themselves. That is why Paulo Freire argues as follows:

> In order for [the] oppressed to be able to wage the struggle for their liberation, they must perceive the reality of oppression not as a closed world from which there is no exit, but as a limiting situation which they can transform. This perception is necessary but not sufficient condition for liberation; it must become the motivating force for liberation action.[22]

The argument Freire makes holds much water for the situation, as the IR-VICOBA member stated. The IR-VICOBA members claim that the Word of God empowers them and illuminates them. However, I think they have a long fight ahead of them with this significant oppressor – neocolonization. Their reading intellectual activity plays a significant role, but I find the war to be tense in third-world countries, Tanzania in particular. For example, Sobrino, writing on economic globalization, says: "A globalization without truth – worse, contrary to truth – cannot humanize and, furtherance, cannot 'globalize' but can only 'exclude.'"[23] He continues, "Lies and deceit also produce division and antagonism."[24]

Knowledge/good news, which is power, may still be a determining factor, which is why Jesus said in the text that it is good news to the poor (Luke 4.18). However, in the world economy, knowledge is kept such that it remains a "hidden transcript"[25]

---

22 Freire, *Pedagogy of the Oppressed*, p. 31.
23 Wilfred and Sobrino, *Globalization and Its Victims*, 2001/5, p. 109.
24 Ibid.
25 James C. Scott, *Domination and the Arts of Resistance: Hidden Transcripts* (New Haven: Yale University Press, 1990), p. 14.

of the oppressor, exploiting peasants by cheaply buying their products to gain more profit. According to Scott (and also the members of IR-VICOBA), complaining about the market and being cheated is a type of 'hidden transcript'.[26] The profit and wealth maximization of the rich has been the 'hidden transcript' of most people doing business today. They do whatever it takes to get that profit; profit is their number one priority: "The end justifies the means." This attitude causes much suffering among poor people. It does not affect the rich, even if they know that they cheat or plunder. You have to get the profit! Sobrino writes, "This suffering is on a massive scale, unjust and cruel; it battens on innocent, defenceless people, and is the product of the world power (economic, military, political, media, sometimes even church and university)."[27]

Moreover, peasants like the IR-VICOBA members have no communication facilities like computers of high capacity. A few have mobile phones, which they utilize not so much that they can communicate using emails to people who are doing business or with other peasants within their own country or abroad. If we take the IR-VICOBA members and their fellows in rural areas as an example, they grow coffee, tea, and cocoa, but they cannot communicate with other people who grow the same cash crops in Brazil, India, or Indonesia. The buyers of those crops communicate among themselves and buy crops according to the stability of the country they are buying the crop from. Nevertheless, some information you cannot get through the internet – secrets or something has been somehow covered up so that you cannot get to the real meaning or the truth. Lack of knowledge and technology has robbed peasants of the power of development.

4.4 Conclusion

This chapter analyzes and discusses various issues from the IR-VICOBA participant-centred Bible study. The study found that, during their Contextual Bible Study, the IR-VICOBA members use much of the experiences, commitment, and actions from their own lives to interpret the texts. The analysis reflects on the 'see, judge, act' they are doing in their lives and using the same experience they interpret the Bible. The socioeconomic reality they experience informs their interpretation. The issues of wealth and the preference of Jesus for the poor were among the issues they reflected on in their Bible study. Their stance was that, while they were themselves poor, they were against poverty. They thought that, even though Jesus did not want people to be poor, he was against the richness that made others miserable and the

---

26 Ibid., p. 82.
27 Wilfred and Sobrino, *Globalization and Its Victims*, 2001/5, p. 110.

fact that some of the rich did not care for the needy. Their justification was that Jesus wanted everyone to enjoy God's creation. According to their faith, Jesus took part in that creation. The only problem is people's greed and egocentrism.

Chapter 5: The Analytical Interpretation of the Reading of the IR-VICOBA Groups: Their Responses Based on Their Contextual Bible Study

5.1 Introduction

Many reflections and responses of the IR-VICOBA members from the Contextual Bible reading process reflect on the texts in the study. We've seen some significant aspects of this interpretation in the previous chapter in the discussion of the characters in the text and their role. It also puts other selected topics into their context.

My main perspective in this chapter is different from Chapter 4. There, I was looking at how the context influenced the text interpretation; in Chapter 5, I am interested to see how the text interpretation is used to understand, improve, and correct their practice. I am looking for text interpretations the IR-VICOBA members use to ensure a better practical life. It seems that the participant-centered Contextual Bible Study makes readers contemplate the text by using their own context as a yardstick of their interpretation of and response to the text. They judge their actions and reflections based on their context, and the Bible is used as a liberating justification and continuation of those actions. The Bible reading assists them in continuing with their actions and formulating new ideas that allow them to become more liberated.

The IR-VICOBA members responded to many themes that arose as they tried to tackle the challenges in the texts by referring to them in their daily praxis, meaning reflection and practises. In most cases, they responded with how they could continue to do, or to avoid, doing or avoiding such activity. For those practices, they continue to do them well, and the Bible study has helped them to solidify and cement their praxis.

The following reproduces the interpretation and discussion of the themes the IR-VICOBA members responded to during their participant-centered Bible study: self-reliance and the empowerment of the poor, the blind, and the captives; the dominating and exploitative nature of rich business people is not fit for society and the world. In addition, the following topics were also discussed: caring for the needy: the power of social capital; true love means serving the needy; loving wealth more than loving God and one's neighbor is sin.

5.1.1 Self-Reliance and Empowerment

The issue of being self-reliant and the empowerment of other poor people garnered much interest during the Bible study. In their response to the Bible study on Luke 16:19, the members showed much concern about how to be self-reliant. A member said, "We should continue to empower each other, although we are poor, and we should learn to work hard so that we become capable economically." This attitude of the IR-VICOBA groups goes well with their objectives: fighting poverty by being self-empowered in all they do in their lives. They advocate working hard regardless of other factors that might make them fail in their efforts. Therefore, for the IR-VICOBA members, self-empowerment is the number one objective so that they can be free in life. Saying "we should continue" means that the Contextual Bible Study has made them continue with the good practices they are already doing in their daily lives. The practice is justified and is good in light of the Word of God.

The IR-VICOBA members work hard in farming and small businesses and want to be examples within society. One member argued, "We should also learn how to empower each other to get out of this situation we are facing as poor people. The Word of God should illuminate us to know how to be empowered economically and spiritually." This IR-VICOBA member argued in this way because, when this group of people meets, they teach others many new ideas, especially social and economic ideas, so that whoever wants to can put this new knowledge into praxis to continue to be liberated in that area. Chapter 7 provides more discussion, where I discuss the theology of the VICOBA members as they undertake participant-centered Contextual Bible Study. Self-empowerment is a practice that gives them more liberty than being dependent upon any organisation or others. Self-empowerment is also a good sign that they are in the present Kingdom of God.

Another issue in their Bible study was that rich people exploited them and profited from their produce. One member from the IR-VICOBA said, "We should unite together and make our own market system work so that we can avoid other middlemen exploiting us. Then, we can ask our local government to interfere on this issue." This is the wish to be empowered, and this person called on everyone to control the market. All the members agreed with her since the intermediaries in business cheat them and make a profit on their shoulders. This is the situation in which the context now informs the text for more justice to take place in the context: The IR-VICOBA members want to concretely transform the ways of doing business. They want to flee the intermediary business people who exploit them. The only way to not be cheated is to unite and sell their products to the market by themselves, not through intermediaries. That is a challenge. Do they have the capital to do so? They need major capital to establish such businesses. Yet, these people have no means of fundraising and mobilizing people on this issue to take control of the world market. Maybe there were indicating only their local market.

They can perhaps control the local market, but for international business, they have a long way to go. However, beginning to control the local market can pave the way to controlling the international marketing of their produce.

This issue of empowerment and self-reliance goes hand in hand since no one can understand the experiences of the poor better than the poor themselves. This encourages the poor to adopt an attitude of self-liberation. The members of IR-VICOBA have such an attitude as downtrodden people. Brown writes, "The poor are discovering that they can organize, that they can have the right to think and speak and that the more united they are, the more they will be heard. No longer are [they] waiting for someone to speak out for them, or to empower them; they are speaking themselves and creating their own empowerment."[1]

The downtrodden confront many challenges because they are on the receiving end. For example, the peasants or 'have-nots' are in a global economy where the 'haves' are in total control, including control of the prices of their (the peasants') products. Nevertheless, the irony is that such a situation can be used as an experience to solve many challenges in other societies. Self-empowerment enables them to at least move from one stage to another, even if they may not reach the position of rich people. The express intent of the IR-VICOBA members is that they are not prepared to fight with rich people but rather fight with their own situation, the poverty, and injustice in business – and then improve their living standard to the best of their ability.

Moreover, the IR-VICOBA groups not only have an objective of self-empowerment but also want to empower other people; they believe in liberating others by teaching good ways of combating poverty and other financial enemies. They also want to emancipate others by teaching them a good way of self-liberation, e. g., doing agribusiness, running small businesses, repaying simple and low-interest loans. One member of the group commented on this: "To be Christ-like we need to continue to assist the needy people who are poor like us, or poorer, and assist the church when it starts the orphanage centers." This IR-VICOBA member said this because members always have opportunities to organize other poor people into groups and teach them how to start an IR-VICOBA group of their own in other areas. This interpretation uses the texts as a confirmation and theologizes about their continuation of praxis in their daily lives. Empowering others was their other objective, although they themselves were poor. The issue of Bible study occurs here because, in these studies, they learn more than just reading the Bible, as I indicated earlier. However, for the IR-VICOBA groups, economic injustice made them think that fighting back brings them dignity within society and the world at

---

1 Brown, *Gustavo Gutiérrez: An Introduction to Liberation Theology*, p. 69.

large. To them, social and economic injustices cause their indignity within society. For example, one member said in the Bible study:

> We poor people are treated like toys who have no voice. But now we want our voice to be listened to by everybody. You pastors tell the bishops, and we will tell the political leaders to fight for us so that those rich people do not take advantage of us. We do not know the market, but they have to work for us on this regard. These rich business people despise us like the rich man did poor Lazarus – and we are tired of it. They buy our bananas, tea, coffee, etc., and pay us very little. They drive by in their gorgeous cars, which they get from cheating us. It is the same attitude when the rich man gave poor Lazarus no food.

Therefore, to fight for their dignity, they attempt to liberate themselves from socioeconomic injustice, e. g., taking control of the market and setting good prices for their cash crops and businesses. If they can control business at their local level and fight injustice in business, then their lives will be improved, and they will automatically increase their participation in the decision-making processes within their society.

In the Contextual Bible Study, the IR-VICOBA members, besides solidifying and cementing their praxis in light of the Word of God, come up with new practices reflected from other societies, which need more training in their own discipline (like simple economics, bookkeeping, livestock keeping). Therefore, they add other types of training within the IR-VICOBA Bible-reading sessions. They find trainers of simple project management, simple accounting, and simple homemade industries, like making local soaps, fabrics, foodstuffs, and the like. They put into praxis whatever they learn from both the Contextual Bible Study and VICOBA sessions. For instance, if they learn how to keep livestock, produce cash crops, make local soap, cook donuts, make fabrics, and other handmade things, this ensures that they can put the skills into practice to make profit from those items. Moreover, from that standpoint, they go on to teach other IR-VICOBA groups so that they can understand these skills as well. These Bible students use money from their VICOBA fund to buy ingredients for whatever they want to learn to make before they go to the personal level, starting practising in their homes. Those who learn for the first time become 'Trainers of Trainees' (T.O.T.) to other IR-VICOBA groups.

Moreover, the poor also place more emphasis on backing up other poor individuals who are hoping to uplift themselves to a better standard of living. The IR-VICOBA members passed more reflection on Luke 16:19-31 as they were responding to the improvised question, "What makes poor people in society have the life that they have?" The IR-VICOBA members believe more in giving fishing nets to the poor than giving fish to the hungry. As one member said during their Contextual Bible Study session,

> We, the Lazaruses of today, should not wish to have 'scraps' or the whole 'fish' but should look for 'nets.' We should be empowered to get our own food; that will be good news to us. We are supposed to work hard and empower one another by together learning how to fight poverty and come up with our own strategies for self-empowerment.

Another assertion of the IR-VICOBA members on empowerment is to work hard. They believe in working hard since God promises to bless the work of every person who believes in Him in the world (cf. Deut. 28:12). During the Contextual Bible Study, one member said,

> We are needy people. We are poor, and we need to get rid of this situation. As VICOBA people, we continue to fight this situation of poverty, of being needy by working hard and coming together for the teaching that helps us to come up with some economic ideas and economic projects that help us to do other things.

The IR-VICOBA members believe that working hard is a source of development for any person. They engage in different activities such as agriculture, petty cash business, and animal husbandry. Sometimes, to safeguard their efforts, they diversify their economic activities so they can profit from several economic activities. If they lose profit on one, then they can get profit from another project. During my research, I visited some of the members to see how their coming together reflected on their enhancement from one stage to another, which we can call 'development.'

On the other hand, according to the IR-VICOBA members, there are church members who believe that being poor means being near to Jesus because Jesus said "Blessed are the poor." In a reflection on the Beatitude Matt 5:1-12, in response to the question, "What makes people poor in our society today?" one member said,

> Some groups and churches practise poverty so that they can inherit the Kingdom of God. This is self-deceit. Some members of those groups follow all those writings so that they can be on the side of Jesus, being poor. But they find cheating themselves, they suffer from many aspects of life while they live somehow longer in the world. They say Jesus did not use cars, shoes, or other clothes, and they avoid buying those luxurious goods.

The IR-VICOBA members reflected that, in Matt 5:3 and Luke 6:20, Jesus had another intent with "Blessed are the poor in spirit or the poor." As one person said during Contextual Bible Study, "Some people in some groups think being poor was a sign of being rich spiritually, and they preached to their members against material richness." The IR-VICOBA group was very much against that notion. They said that they believed that Jesus did not want them to be poor as the criteria for inheriting the Kingdom of Heaven, but that Jesus was consolating all downtrodden people; otherwise, he would not have encouraged them to work hard. The IR-VICOBA members also commented on Matt 6:33, where Jesus said, "But strive first for the Kingdom of God and his righteousness, and all these things will be given to you as well." Therefore, for the IR-VICOBA group, by making this intertextual comparison, they thought that Jesus aimed at the same notion of people trusting God in everything – and then other things like blessings would follow from that point.

5.1.2 The Dominating and Exploitative Nature of the Rich People in Society and the World

The question, "What causes people to be poor in society and how can such a situation be avoided?" led the IR-VICOBA members to discuss the dominative and exploitative nature of society and the world. Reading in the Bible study both the Matthean and Lukan Beatitudes (Matt 5:1-12; Luke 6:20-26), the parable of the rich man and poor Lazarus (Luke 16:19-31), and the parable of the rich man (Mark 10:17-22) made the IR-VICOBA members respond that some reasons for poverty lay in the domination and exploitative nature of the business with which they engage. Regarding their response to the issue of domination and exploitation in societies, the IR-VICOBA members indicated that Christians, as followers of Jesus, should live Christ-like lives where they had to fight all dominative and exploitative incidents. In their own words, they indicated that, "We should not dominate others and exploit them by any means and leave them poor or blind from knowledge." This response shows that many activities go on in society which they fight as part of their practice. This means that the one dominant hermeneutical tool for Bible interpretation is applying the text to the context. However, the IR-VICOBA members seem to look for an interpretation that gives sense to their reality in contemporary Tanzania. The texts give more power to the individuals and provide encouragement on how they are supposed to continue fighting those dominating and exploitative practises from people with power. One member argued:

> We should help people in our midst who want to be empowered and use our opportunities to profit from them instead of returning to being poor again. We should continue to help each other to get out of this situation, and therefore we should say goodbye to poverty. We have to use the education we get and the illumination on economic justice and legal justice. People who use their education and economic power for injustice should be told the truth, like Jesus said in the synagogue.

The IR-VICOBA members also say: "We want to be self-reliant, and the secret is to fight poverty until we die. Poverty makes us dependent, beggars, and looked upon as unfit living people in our society." The IR-VICOBA members use their context to interpret the text they are reading. They reflect on their socioeconomic reality and on how people have become beggars because of poverty, which is their war. The IR-VICOBA members say: "We are supposed to unite and make our own market system and work so that we can avoid other middlemen exploiting us. So, we ask our local government to interfere on this issue." This is a good way to show that they know they are being exploited and now want to have a voice to liberate themselves from the socioeconomic phenomenon that exploits them. Although it is a good start, it needs greater effort and investment. Raising one's voice is a good start, and the socioeconomic reality and the Word of God have enabled them to identify the problems that make them poor and to call for liberation. The Biblical text is thus *interpreted*, not in itself but as a tool to comment on challenges in current life.

5.1.3 Taking Care of the Needy: The Power of the Social Capital

As I mentioned earlier, caring for the needy was among the issues of interest when the IR-VICOBA members discussed the text and reflected on what they do every day. Taking care of each other, which I call the 'power of social capital,' is very important within the society of the poor. When the IR-VICOBA members mentioned it in their Contextual Bible Study, especially when they were reading Matt 5:1-12, Matt 25:31-46, and Luke 16:19-31, it was just a matter of contemplating something they do every day in their community; they do things in the community even though they are poor (e. g., contributing toward marriage ceremonies and burial expenses). In rural areas of Tanzania, a person depends on others in many ways. People contribute to each other's lives, and this is where the power of the social capital comes in, something one of the IR-VICOBA members referred to: "Jesus wants us to live a 'true love,' which requires all of us to become sheep and not goats. Jesus wants us to help our neighbors not only in hospitals and prisons but also in our neighborhood." These people knew that, without the power of social capital, as poor people they could not manage to confront the challenges in life they were passing through day after day.

While discussing different selected texts, the IR-VICOBA members reflected that Jesus taught them to help one another to be good followers of the Kingdom of God, as I have presented in Chapter 3. The members of the IR-VICOBA meant that serving one another was a requirement in the community of believers, with whom Jesus entrusted his mission. He meant that togetherness and the unity of power were other activities with many advantages. The togetherness of people, even among the downtrodden themselves, can be acquired by serving one another. I think this was what the IR-VICOBA members were referring to here.

However, I am a little bit unsure of whether the IR-VICOBA members here are sharing it *because* the Word of God has empowered them or whether 'caring about others' is a remnant of the teachings of *Ujamaa*, the Tanzanian ideology prevalent before the time of liberalized economy that is now being practiced in Tanzania. In Tanzania, *Ujamaa* ideology "aimed at building a nation of classless people, in unity, and cooperation as one family."[2] Communal life was given a high position in rural areas where people shared everything. In this case, their contemplation on this practice might simply be a continuation of something they are used to and stems not only from the influence of Bible study. Nevertheless, this way of life is well founded in Biblical teachings, and African traditions help them to continue to combat hardships, even now within the globalized economy.

In this case, social capital is a person's ability to capitalize on other poor people, hoping others will capitalize on them if they have economic and social problems. This is the way of poor people. They say in Swahili "*nguvu ya mnyonge ni umoja,*" literally "the power of the weak is unity." Poor people in Tanzania work toward that goal and expect other people to do the same for them when they need them in their challenges and problems. They are fulfilling the so-called 'golden rule': "In everything do to others as you would have them do to you; for this is the law and prophets" (Matt 7:12).

The act the IR-VICOBA members perform with social capital is what Jon Sobrino calls "a theology of solidarity." Sobrino describes that solidarity as not mere humanitarian aid, which reflects an ethical imperative, where a giver does not feel any personal commitment or any need to continue to aid; rather, authentic solidarity commits a person at a deeper level to continue giving, becoming a continuing process and not a contribution.[3] In their social setting as poor people, the IR-VICOBA members help each other, and this is a continuing process or even a life process. Their social capital involves mutual relations and is not a one-way process. As I discussed before, the poor and relatively poor or rich help one another in their community, which enhances the life of everyone within the society. This is a point that has made me think that social capital is similar to what Sobrino calls the "theology of solidarity," where people live together regardless of their situation. Rural people need this way of life to deal with the difficulties in their lives during an era of globalization, with the proliferation of poor people living in rural areas, like those areas in which the IR-VICOBA members live. In the description of theology of solidarity, Sobrino writes:

> The church's turn toward the world of the poor, whether in the universal church or in a particular church, is the basic solidarity of the church, that with which it carries out

---

[2] Njinga, *The Shift from Ujamaa to Globalization as a Challenge to Evangelical Lutheran Church in Tanzania*, p. 64.

[3] Sobrino, *The Principle of Mercy: Taking the Crucified People from the Cross*, pp. 145–146.

and maintains its identity. Moreover, it is this basic solidarity that begins to dissolve the isolation of local churches and establish new, positive relationships between local churches.[4]

This quotation reveals a solidarity that, in the Church of Christ, when members live that solidarity, they find themselves portraying a real meaning in life. Solidarity shows its real identity of the Church of Christ, which practise life-theology together in the world by reflecting the word of Christ. Thus, the church finds itself more powerful than the problems surrounding it. Reflecting more theologically, if the members *are* the church, then the community solves its problems and challenges by being a part of that believing community.

5.1.4 True Love Means Serving the Needy Neighbor

In their Bible study, the IR-VICOBA groups referred to the same steps of imitating Jesus in their daily lives. One member, referring to Matthew 25:31- 46, said, "Jesus taught about love, which requires people to share even when they have little in their homes, and Jesus wanted people to live that true love unconditionally." The emphasis was that people were supposed to assist other people in need even when they had very few resources of their own.

The IR-VICOBA members emphasized this because they too are poor people and need to help one another with the resources they have. This statement was a reflection on their own livelihoods; without the help of others, you cannot live in a world of limited resources. Regardless of being in the globalized economy, this attitude which the IR-VICOBA members emphasised as they read from the text about needy people is an influence of the Biblical teaching and is emphasised in socialism, which requires people to be self-reliant but to live together as communal beings, as I noted earlier.

Therefore, loving one's neighbors, whether locally or globally, can help and reflects God's love to many people in this world. The practices need to begin where people are situated. This is a move the IR-VICOBA members and other good Samaritans are making all over this world.

5.1.5 Loving Wealth More Than Loving God and Neighbors Is Sin

The IR-VICOBA members discussed people who love wealth more than loving God while reflecting on the rich man in Mark 10:17-31 and Luke 16:19-31, who do not even want to think about their neighbors because they are busy fighting

---

4 Ibid., pp. 151–152.

to accumulate wealth. Moreover, the IR-VICOBA members indicated that there were tendencies of people believing in and loving wealth more than anything. Some people would use any means to get that wealth, even if it meant dehumanizing other people. One member said, "There are people who respect their wealth more than God, or they do not want to go to church because they are busy with other activities or possessions." In another group, a member said,

> In the world we are living in today, some people have a lot of possessions, but God wants us to believe in him and not believe in possessions. We remember Job, Ibrahim, King David, and Solomon in the Bible, who were rich but still trusted God. We have to find the Kingdom of God first [then] other things will be added.

As we have seen earlier, the IR-VICOBA members are not against wealth per se and think that Jesus was not against wealth, either. However, to them, loving wealth more than God and neighbors is sinful. Loving God and neighbors is their number one commitment for any living human being.

Wealth cannot be the center of the life of a human being. The unjust business world wants to make wealth the center of human life, which is what the IR-VICOBA members were complaining about when they said that, in their society, people now believe more in wealth than in God. They were reflecting on the story of the rich man in Mark 10:17-22. Making wealth the center of human existence is very dangerous since, at present, it seems the way of the world is to uplift material things higher than God and to depend on them as sources of happiness. In response, the IR-VICOBA members reflected that, even though they are fighting poverty with all of their ability, as Christians they are not supposed to place wealth at the center of their lives because God is the Creator of everything. Moreover, people who center wealth in their hearts are not afraid of anybody, like the rich man in the story of Lazarus. This is discussed further in Chapter 7, where I examine the theology of the IR-VICOBA members.

5.1.6　　The Best Use of Resources: Empowering Through Teaching

In the section above, I discussed how the IR-VICOBA groups encourage people not to put wealth above God. However, they also made another point of being good stewards of the resources someone has acquired. Irresponsibly using resources like time, money, and land was another issue that arose during the IR-VICOBA participant-centered Bible study. Some people borrow money from financial institutions and fail to repay the principles and interests of their loans. The VICOBA group, while discussing Matt 25:31-41 about the sheep and goats, responded to the improvised question, "What makes people poor in your society?" by responding that some people become poor because of misuse of resources. One of them said, "There are people who take loans from VICOBA and other financial institutions and misuse the fund not daring to invest. These people consume other goods and ultimately find themselves going to prison and sometimes getting other diseases like BP because of those loans they take without a plan." On the same issue, another member added:

> Some people also take out unplanned loans, which they misspend and then find themselves unable to pay back the principles and interest.[5] Because of the financial institutions' regulations, once they fail to pay back their loans, these people are sent to court, and if they fail to pay back the collateral, and in most rural areas, their resources are confiscated, like houses, animals, cattle, and land, which are the main resources they have. People of this nature cause many problems to their families since they find themselves back at ground zero, begging from their relatives, friends, and sometimes going to town streets to beg.

People who misuse borrowed money do not know how to invest money. The notion the IR-VICOBA members made about having less knowledge and plans for investment stems from the fact that they use the money as if it is theirs, part of their own 'disposable income.' I think this is a tendency some poor people in rural areas do not think about when they have resources, and they do not dare to invest them but instead prefer to consume. These people, because of their misuse of money, find themselves losing their assets, which serve as collaterals for those financial institutions. Discussing this issue during Bible study, another member added: "Financial institutions set high percentage [rates] of interest, which makes people fail to pay back. I have heard some [financial institutions] come from abroad and unjustly take our money. Moreover, they make us poor and beggars when we fail to pay the loans." The problem here is not only the financial institutions, but the fact that people have little knowledge about how to use loans and cannot control their spending habits, misusing the resources they receive for future benefit.

It is true that most financial institutions in Tanzania are not Tanzanian; they come from abroad, or the government owns a percentage of the shares in those banks in Tanzania. Banks like the National Bank of Tanzania Ltd (NBC) are partly owned by South African Barclays African Group (55%), the Tanzanian Government (30%), and the World Bank Group (15%),[6] and some financial institutions are owned by international banks like CBA Banks. A few banks are owned by Tanzanians, like

---

5 Principle is the amount of money a person borrows from financial institutions, and interest is the cost of the borrowed money from the financial institution.
6 https://www.nbc.co.tz/en/about-us/.

the Postal Bank and the National Microfinance Bank. However, even these are owned as limited entities. Moreover, all the banks in Tanzania are regulated by the Central Bank of Tanzania. Nevertheless, they all still apply the same regulations and measures when someone takes out a loan from them. People who misuse the loans experience the same problems of losing their assets, which are sold by the bank, and the individuals find themselves poorer than before and sometimes even in prison.

Furthermore, there are microfinances like SACCOs (Savings and Credits Co-operatives), where a person becomes a member and is allowed to borrow money three times the cost of his shares, like VICOBA members. Still, these apply the same regulations and measures as banks to a person who takes out the loans. The main advantages of being a member of SACCOs or VICOBA are the low interest rates, receiving dividends from the profit, and people consuming responsibly while continuing to invest in SACCOs and VICOBA. Moreover, people are educated about investments and about how to return those loans and their interest.

One reason why people fail is that these banks from within and outside the country aim to create much profit for themselves, such that peasants fail to pay back the loans and high interest rates. Banks ask a person to pay 17% to 22% interest without adding insurance,[7] something they do not even mention when advocating their business. In addition, poor people have no knowledge about how to do business and pay off the loans and interest. Therefore, they often prolong poverty instead of alleviating it, given that people may end up homeless.

5.1.7   Laziness as a Cause of Poverty

The issue of laziness was another issue brought up by the IR-VICOBA members in response to the question of why some people were poor, sent to prison, naked, hungry, thirsty, and sick. During their participant-centered Bible study on Luke 16:19-31, one member said, "Laziness can cause people to be poor. There are people who steal so that they can get food, clothes, or anything else, which causes them to be sent to prison." For the IR-VICOBA members, poverty is a targeted enemy; therefore, regardless of what Jesus was saying on the issue of caring for needy people, they went as far as to ask why these people needed assistance from others. One member added, "These people do not want to work for their survival but prefer to steal other people's properties, and when they are captured by the owners, they find themselves brought to prison, where they live a poor life, requiring people and the government to support them." On this issue of being lazy, another member

---

[7] Samuel Kamndaya, "Why Tanzania Banks Now Banking on Personal Loans for Profit," *The Citizens* 29 May 2018.

also added, "Not only the imprisoned person but also their family members suffer much while they are in prison and sometimes the family ends up begging from their family and friends for support."

Informed by their own socioeconomic reality, this stance reflects the IR-VOCOBA members' own experience, which is not indicated in the text, even though they did contemplate it. Jesus did not mention lazy people. Possibly, other factors caused these individuals to be in that precarious situation, but the IR-VICOBA members thought more about people who are in desperate poverty because of laziness. In the context of the IR-VICOBA groups, where they have land for cultivation, lazy people are the ones who live more desperate livelihoods than them, although both are still poor. Nevertheless, the IR-VICOBA members, while resilient, are not rich; they try their best to fight the extreme poverty some of their neighbors are experiencing. As I mentioned earlier, these groups teach one another to fight laziness and make it their enemy, making people poor day after day.

Some IR-VICOBA members were like these people in the society, who are desperate before joining the IR-VICOBA groups. The IR-VICOBA groups have encouraged them to be very different from lazy people.

5.2 Conclusion

In this chapter, my main question has been: "How do the members of the IR-VICOBA groups understand the relationship between the Bible and socioeconomic reality?" This is reflected in the responses they gave in their Bible reading process. Many IR-VICOBA members indicate that socioeconomic reality is used to interpret the text. They come to the Bible with their own experience, the praxis they exhibit in society. Their responses in the Contextual Bible Study concretize those practices and how they continue to practise those practices. Many of their responses concern how to continue to avoid bad things in their society. This means that the hermeneutical principle used by the IR-VICOBA members is to interpret the Biblical texts according to their relevance for their social situation. Texts are valid if they give a response, a comment, or a critical reflection on the current social life condition. It seems, therefore, that the spirituality in their interpretation plays a role in whether the Bible is seen as Word of God because it gives sense to the actual life in the present.

All the exploitative and dominating acts in business must be fought and kept from being allowed within society. In addition, the IR-VICOBA members raised their voices on the socioeconomic phenomenon that engenders poor people in their midst, as seen in the context of the Bible texts. They reflected on whether they should raise their voices to the local government so that their members of Parliament could help them raise their voices to the central government.

The IR-VICOBA members explained how they viewed the issue of serving their neighbor and empowering themselves and their neighbor in their context. They discussed the issue of social capital and caring for the needy. As I mentioned earlier, I revisit this when discussing the theology practiced by the IR-VICOBA in their participant-centered Contextual Bible Study.

Other themes were also tackled here, like the habits that make people poor or live in precarious situations, including being lazy, misusing resources, and taking out loans that one cannot repay. The IR-VICOBA members reflected on those habitual characters, which lead some people to live in difficulty. Responding to their intellectual Bible-reading activity, they said those habits should be avoided by all means within society.

The IR-VICOBA members were also concerned more with the issue of people loving wealth than God. To them, wealth seems not to be a problem, and they defended their thought by saying that even Jesus was not against it; they thought God was the provider of all gifts in this world. He should be loved first, and then people will continue to enjoy the creation which God bestowed upon them (Matt 6:33).

Chapter 6: The Profile of the IR-VICOBA Members' Bible Reading in Tanzania: See-Judge-Act

In this chapter, I discuss the profile of the theology of the IR-VICOBA members, showing their stance, their similarities, and their differences with other contextual Bible profiles mentioned and discussed in this study. This chapter draws upon my reflections and interpretations of their reading of the Bible in their participant-centered Bible study. Therefore, to come up with my interpretation of their profile, I also discuss the presentation of the data in Chapter 3 and the analysis of that data from Chapter 4 and Chapter 5. The question I probe in this chapter relates to their profile: How do they differ from other people doing Contextual Bible Studies or liberation theology like the Ujamaa Contextual Bible Study and the Latin American liberation theologians? The difference and similarities in using the see-judge-act approach represent a critical point of departure and contribute to their theology in their Bible Studies. In this chapter, I look at how the IR-VICOBA members carry out see-judge-act for liberation and point to some important issues where they differ, especially from the Ujamaa Contextual Bible Study in South Africa.

6.1 See-Judge-Act

The three groups of liberation theology take different approaches; I presented the details in Chapter 1 above. According to West, the Ujamaa Centre deals with "see, judge, act."[1] In their method, the Ujamaa Centre's 'act' moment primarily begins with Bible study. In the following, I note that the IR-VICOBA groups are more similar in their approach to Latin American classical liberation theology. They use "See-Judge-Act" while distinguishing between the 'two acts' (the first and second acts): The first act and reflection are performed in their daily lives, and the second act is theologizing in their Contextual Bible Study. In my view, this is a significant difference from the Ujamaa Centre's interpretation practice.

The Ujamaa Contextual Bible Studies in South Africa perform "See-Judge-Act," but their emphasis on 'act' relates to an action taken *after* the Bible study. As already mentioned, all three stages are taken in the Bible study. Gerald West describes one of the Bible studies: "In addition to the renewed relevance of the Bible in the experience of individual workers, there is also the ongoing use of the Bible in the

---

1 West, "Locating Contextual Bible Study Within Praxis," pp. 43–48. Here, West describes that their liberation hermeneutics have been built in that notion of see, judge, then act.

See-Judge-Act structure of the [Young Christian Workers] YCW reflections."[2] For Gerald West, theology from below is a process of reflection from the Bible reading, and then the action comes from the Bible reading. People start to reflect on what to do *after* reading the Bible. They learn about the political, economic, and social situation in the Bible study and then take measures based on their reflections in the Bible study. In West's Contextual Bible Study, the emancipation of readers is envisioned primarily after the Bible study. West describes very openly that the 'see' moment is when they read the Bible and 'see' their own context through that reading. Only then do they judge what and how an action has to be taken. After that, they take measures, justification, and resolution of what action should be done.

Taking a quotation from the reading with the YCW, one can recognize that, in the future, the act comes before the theologizing (the Bible-reading process):

> The fundamental process of YCW group is the See-Judge-Act method. The young workers begin by analysing the conditions experienced by themselves and their friends at work, at home and at school (See). Then [they] assess the situation in light of the Gospel (Judge) and then try to improve the situation by taking appropriate action to change conditions (Act).[3]

This response reveals that the action of improving the situation occurs later as a corollary of the reading process and not as a reflection of what these YCW people are doing before the reading process. Critical reflection occurs within the Bible study venue, where the members discover that the hardships in their lives. This is why West writes:

> CBS uses the Bible as a substantive and 'subjective' companion to work for transformation; Transformation includes the transformation of the self and society, including the church (and the religious terrain in general; The primary focus of transformation is the structural and systemic, and primary terrain for transformation from the perspective of CBS is the ideo-theological.[4]

The See-Judge-Act routine is well stipulated on their website. They write:

---

[2] West, *Biblical Hermeneutics of Liberation: Modes of Reading the Bible in the South African Context*, 1, p. 185. The see-judge-act of *Ujamaa* has been well explained in the introductory chapter with the title "Liberation Theology in the Theology of Gerald West."
[3] Ibid., p. 188.
[4] West, 2Reading the Bible with the Marginalised: The Value/s of Contextual Bible Reading," p. 240.

Our primary resources for this work are Biblical and theological, making particular use of Contextual Bible Studies (CBS) and the See, Judge and Act method. We work, wherever possible, using the languages of the local communities with whom we collaborate.[5]

This makes a useful reference that the 'theology from below' by Gerald West starts with Bible reading: The action is a product of theologizing. For the IR-VICOBA groups, however, theologizing means reflecting on what they already reflect and practice (praxis) every day – the second 'act.' They do the first practice and reflection every day and then follow up with reflections and praxis—the second act of theologizing.[6]

The IR-VICOBA members follow the Latin American patterns of See-Judge-Act, reflecting on their own experience and commitment, their first act. Participants reflect on their experiences of what they have already done as the first 'Act.' The praxis of the IR-VICOBA groups before theologizing (judging in light of the Word of God), such as caring for the poor within their societies (solidarity with the poor) or caring for one another and 'empowering' one another when they confront challenges (such as burials, marriages, paying school fees, and other various economic dilemmas), are the sources of their theology in the Contextual Bible Study. They see, judge, and act first within their context. Their moment of 'judging' is a theologizing moment on what they can do in their society as the second 'act.'

This activity also produces many 'see' moments concerning new ideas, visions, objectives, and plans. For example, when they meet together and discuss the issue of fighting poverty, which they have already acted on by starting VICOBA, then they bring along some projects or ideas of how to start a project. In the IR-VICOBA groups, one hears reflections on the first act of undertaking their Bible study. The Bible reading strengthens and extends the practices they have already initiated. It means that the second act presumes the first act. And also, and even more important: The second act is part of the social reality given in the first act. The second act does not *add* a new act; it interprets the first act in light of the Word of God.

This explains one of the members' comments: "We should continue to empower each other regardless of our being poor, and we should learn to work hard so that we become capable economically." 'Continue' refers to what they do every day to empower each other. In the Contextual Bible Study, they discuss how to continue the practices they have already launched; they refer to their first reflection and action.

---

5 See http://ujamaa.ukzn.za/whatUJAMAAdoes.aspx.
6 There are nuances in West's publications. I comment on them in the concluding chapters. The essential point is that, even if the nuances hint at a less one-sided Biblical first act, the dominating system remains in West's latest writings.

On helping others, you hear them saying, "To be Christ-like, we need to continue to assist the needy people who are poor, assist the church when it starts the orphanage centers." Again, they use the term 'continue' to mean what they do in their lives, the first act of helping others. Nevertheless, they make another 'see' moment within the same Bible study. For example: "We are supposed to unite and make our market system work to avoid other middlemen to exploit us. So, we can ask our local government to interfere on this issue." The matter here is that these people work together as VICOBA, which is a unity. Their call of "we should unite" means continuing how they have already acted. They may also mean uniting with other peasants or groups to create unity, enabling economic liberation and economic emancipation.

On the side of classical Latin American liberation theologians, as I discussed in the Introduction, there are two acts. The first act is in a socioeconomic society where people live and commit themselves to reflecting on reality (seeing) by having passive and active judgment and actions, (praxis) which they call the first act, the praxis. Then, when they meet in the Bible study or do theology, they are doing the 'second act' of their praxis (reflecting and practising). The second act reflects upon and judges the reflections and actions that have been taken during the first act. Gutierrez writes:

> Theological reflection would then necessarily be a criticism of the society and the church in so far as they are called and addressed by the Word of God; it would be a critical theory, worked out in light of the Word of God accepted in faith and inspired by the practical purpose – and therefore indissolubly linked to historical praxis.[7]

A critical comparison of West and Gutierrez shows that the difference is that Gutierrez aims at another (implicit) interpretation of what the first act is. West comes from practice and wants to perform a new Biblical practice. West aims to produce a new liberation theology from Biblical perspectives. However, he forgets that the poor and downtrodden already have socioeconomic reflections, actions, and practices in their local community long before coming to the Contextual Bible Study. The IR-VICOBA groups come from practice but want to interpret the praxis they have already reflected and acted on as part of God's relation to humans and nature not only from the Biblical source. They use the Bible as a yardstick to measure and rectify those practices in light of the Word of God. This justification and rectification of their praxis ensure that the Bible remains an emancipatory tool.

On one occasion, a member argued, "We should continue to work hard so that we do not remain poor. When we have many things, we should be humble, for

---

7 Gutiérrez, Inda, and Eagleson, *A Theology of Liberation: History, Politics and Salvation*, p. 11.

we should treat poor people fairly and help them accordingly, because God is the one who enables us to build that economy." When they say we should continue to "work hard so that we do not remain poor," it shows a state of being at a stage where the members can continue to be liberated. Theologically, it means liberation has already taken place in their socioeconomic reality. After reading the text, they justify that it is an ethical practice that needs to continue. If I were to insert this into a good argument, they agree that it is theologically sound that this kind of solidarity is an ethical praxis. Nevertheless, the quotation also refers to the tendencies of rich people who may have become rich because of the outcome of their hard work, who treat others, especially poor people, unfairly and without helping them. In the Contextual Bible Study, the Word of God now systematically brings these people to a new level of argumentation, namely, that they should avoid these sorts of practices. As people of God, they reach another level, theologically: avoiding practices that put other people into the bondage of slavery and give them no chance for liberation.

6.2 IR-VICOBA Participant Bible Study 'See-Judge-Act' Is for Liberation

Above I have argued that, regarding theology from below, the IR-VICOBA members' reflections follow their reflections and actions (praxis) undertaken in their socioeconomic reality, which is the first act. For example, the IR-VICOBA *saw* that they were in hardship and *judged* and started the VICOBA, which, according to Gutierrez, was the first act.[8] Starting VICOBA was both a passive and active first act. As I mentioned in the Introduction, the IR-VICOBA groups commenced a group in which they contribute money (shares), so that someone can take out a loan with less interest than a standard bank would demand (about one-third of the cost) and invest in any project they find viable and fits their ability. A member returns the loan and interest little by little every week. All these actions are done in a socioeconomic area. The act of starting the VICOBA and continuing to contribute little by little to this fund is the first act. In the Bible study, they are now doing the 'second act,' reflecting on everything they have done in their lives in accordance with their faith. Now they reflect in light of the Word of God.

With this in mind, I continue to argue that the IR-VICOBA members in the participant-centered Bible Study are reflecting on what they have "acted"[9] on by starting the Village Community Banks (VICOBA) as a solution to their hardship.

---

8 Ibid., pp. 11–12. See also Brown, *Gustavo Gutiérrez: An Introduction to Liberation Theology*, pp. 65–68.
9 Using Stålsett's approach, this is a part of the active part of the first act – commitment to making changes of the reality, here being poor.

As I explained in Chapter 1 and Chapter 2,[10] the IR-VICOBA members reflected on texts relating to what they had done, which I call 'theologizing.' Then, they meet for Contextual Bible Study, for the second act, to theologize about what they have acted upon and what they do in their lives.

The second 'act' involves a 'judging and acting' moment to close the 'hermeneutical circle'[11] of see-judge-act. In one of the groups, the issue popped up of pursuing proper 'project management.' This moment of reflection and practice produces a new 'see' moment concerning how to manage a project, for example, by inviting an expert in project management to develop new 'judge and act' moments. In such a context, the following was said in one of the groups:

> We Lazaruses of today should not wish to have 'scraps' or the whole 'fish' but should look for 'nets.' We should be empowered to get our food. That would be good news for us. We are supposed to continue to work hard and empower one another by together learning how to fight poverty and come up with our strategy for self-empowerment.

Here, the 'second act' (the modern-day Lazaruses) strengthens and encourages empowerment among the group members. Empowerment represents their continuation to finding other ways of empowering themselves by learning to have a simple project and learning how to manage this project very well within the IR-VICOBA.

The Bible reading, then, pursues a theologizing that focuses on a greater level of liberation within their life situation. It is more of a judging stage (the second act) on what they see as a liberation praxis of their hardship. They want to continue to liberate themselves from the economic hardships that have pinned them to poverty. In the Contextual Bible Study, the IR-VICOBA members 'cement' and 'solidify' what they are doing in their lives, now in light of the Word of God. Nevertheless, they learn new ways and ideas for working on those measures, like how to be effective and efficient in using the money they acquire in loans or earn from small projects.

Moreover, they focus on how to continue to liberate on those issues society tends to neglect, like gender inequality, empowerment, and loving those in need. Therefore, Bible study cements and solidifies these ideas and prepares a way forward to liberate and emancipate the downtrodden, which is the task of 'liberation theology.' Contextual Bible Study also gives theological and faith-based recognition

---

10 This is the second act, according to Gutierrez. The poor are doing theology.

11 Jeanrond, *Theological Hermeneutics: Development and Significance*, pp. 5–6. Jeanrond writes that "we need some form of prior understanding in order to begin our engagement with the text or work of art. Naturally, these questions may be refined or even altered in the act of understanding itself. However, without any question, we are unable to structure our acts of reading or seeing. This is generally referred to as one dimension of the 'hermeneutical circle.'"

and significance to the praxis practice. Laypeople get a chance to theologize and decide about what they do and how they should continue to do things to improve the prospects of their own liberation. It works well because it is *for* them and *by* them. In addition to that, it impacts the whole society.

With this hermeneutical praxis, the IR-VICOBA groups also differ very much from other Bible study groups that take place in the same rural areas of Rungwe District in Tanzania.[12] In general, the IR-VICOBA members reflect on liberation, as one of them commented:

> We should continue to help people who like to be empowered in our midst and use our opportunities so that we do not go back to being poor again. We should continue helping each other to get out of this situation, and therefore we should say goodbye to poverty. We have to use the education we get and the illumination for economic justice and legal justice. People who use their education and economic power for injustice should be told the truth like what Jesus said in the synagogue.

Taking an example from the Bible study on the rich man and Lazarus, the IR-VICOBA member indicated:

> We poor people are treated like toys who have no voices. Now we want our voice to be listened to by everybody. You pastors tell the bishops, and we will tell the political leaders to fight for us so that those rich people do not take advantage of us, that we do not know the market, but they have to work for us in this regard. These wealthy businesspeople despise us like the rich man did poor Lazarus. They buy our bananas, tea, coffee, and other cash crops and pay us very little. They drive by in their gorgeous cars, which they get from cheating us. It is the same attitude as the rich man who gave poor Lazarus no food.

The IR-VICOBA members respond like that because they know their rights and want to fight for their liberation. They want their voices to be heard. They want to control the marketing of their products, and they want politicians and church leaders to be in solidarity with them as they call for liberation. They are tired of the agents and intermediates who benefit from their hard work. They are tired of being exploited by these people. Though the IR-VICOBA groups have taken action by starting the IR-VICOBA, they are more illuminated and empowered through

---

12 As I discussed in Chapter 1 about other Bible study taking place in Rungwe, like Alhamis Bible study, women and youth Bible study place more emphasis on spiritual matters than on dealing with other issues like social, political, and economic life.

the Bible. Now, they want to take a step forward, since liberation is a continuous activity.

When they discuss the corrupt pastors in some churches around them, the IR-VICOBA members understand that some people use the Bible to exploit and enslave others, making poor people even more impoverished. They fight to defeat these leaders regardless of where they come from. For example, the members indicated,

> Some fake pastors use witchcraft to teach the prosperity Gospel so that people can give more to them, and these pastors are wealthier than other pastors who teach the true Gospel of Jesus Christ. These pastors exploit members who remain poor. We ask the government and other church leaders to be aware of these pastors and not to imitate them in their teachings.

The IR-VICOBA groups want to be liberated from church leaders and preachers who use the Bible as an exploitative and enslaving tool to poor Christians. They do not stop at being illuminated themselves but go further. For example, in the quotation above, they alert their own church leaders as well as governmental leaders to take steps to fight these fake pastors/preachers. That is a stance of being liberated and fighting to liberate other people. They do not want anybody to impoverish them but fight against all such acts. So, why are there these fake pastors? The reason lies in the hardships: Some people have decided to live a dishonest life by cheating people using their faith. The outcome is that poor people become more impoverished.

6.2.1 The Fight for Economic Justice

In Chapter 4 and Chapter 5, I discussed how the IR-VICOBA members fight against all dominating and unjust socioeconomic structures in their midst, which is the outcome of their reflecting and acting in the first act. I also discussed how they reflect on these economic issues following their fight for liberation in their participant-centered Bible study.

Reflecting on the issue of injustice, one IR-VICOBA member said,

> Besides that, we grow cash crops like coffee, tea, and cocoa, but we are still poor. We grow crops for which we do not set the price. The company from afar buys our crops, but we do not set the price at all. Business companies come up with a new price every year, which makes us ever more miserable, and the government does not care about this at all.

To the IR-VICOBA members, their Bible study is the second act of reflection on getting themselves out of the precarious situations that they are experiencing. These arguments made by them clearly relate to what is going on in the socioeconomic reality of where they live, and inspire their first act of fighting poverty. It is empowering because God takes their side in the struggle in their socioeconomic reality, and now they listen to his word, weigh it, and place themselves in a position to continue to do it. Therefore, for the IR-VICOBA members, Bible study is a powerful tool to systematise their understanding of liberating knowledge, which teaches them and others like them how to live a life of liberty and how to continue fighting against all yolks of injustice and poverty. They want to fight whatever bad things they are experiencing.

Along a similar line, the Tanzanian theologian Laurent Magesa writes, "The Bible knows that when things are alienated from those to whom they belong, there can only be trouble, disorder and death. So God's justice at the outset has a dynamic, transformative quality. It causes things to change, and it expects that things must change if there is to be abundant life."[13] The VICOBA people seem to agree with this, albeit only on the condition that "transformative quality" implies a confirmation of the liberating practices already being done. Magesa, in a way, seems to agree when he claims: "Africans themselves have to deal with the problem of transforming their social structures to make them truly participatory, effective, and constructive for the welfare of their nations in particular and of their continent as a whole."[14] The IR-VICOBA members fight the cheating in those socioeconomic phenomena by working hard, fighting for a reasonable price, and trying to raise their voices. From that position, they cling to the Word of God, which they claim is more illuminating for them.

In their Contextual Bible Study, the IR-VICOBA members discussed what events put people in prisons or lead them to live a precarious life. As one member puts it,

> There are many cases of corrupt systems that lead people into precarious situations, as mentioned in the text. [For example,] people being in prison, beggars, being naked, hungry, and experiencing other adverse situations because they were under the colonial regime. I am sure some people exploited them even socially.

According to the IR-VICOBA members, beggars like Lazarus, the poor in the Beatitudes, and people without peace are the product of the negative socioeconomic

---

13 Robert J. Schreiter, *Faces of Jesus in Africa*, Faith and Cultures Series (Maryknoll, NY: Orbis Books, 1991). p. 155. In this article, Magesa gives some of the socioeconomic and sociopolitical realities that form the bases for Africans who are fighting for the justice and love of Christ. These realities include excessive wealth amid dehumanizing poverty and vice versa, the question of exploitation of the majority of African peoples by internal and external forces, questioning of political domination by domestic and international power brokers, and others.

14 Ibid., p. 157.

phenomenon in Jesus' Palestine.[15] The same situation happens today because many people find themselves as prisoners, beggars, naked, or hungry because of the prevailing socioeconomic difficulties in our world.

This notion of being empowered and empowering others on matters concerning justice and equality is essential to the IR-VICOBA members, as we saw in the discussion in Chapter 4. Another member of IR-VICOBA said,

> We should help people into praxis who want to be empowered and use the opportunities we have so that we do not go back to being poor again. We should be helping each other to exit this situation, and therefore we should say "goodbye" to poverty. We have to use the education we get and the illumination we possess for economic and legal justice. People who use their education and economic power for injustice should be told the truth, much like what Jesus said in the synagogue.

For the IR-VICOBA members, the 'second act' of their Bible study makes them systematically equipped to continue to fight against injustice. Reflecting on the story of the rich man in the Bible (Mark 10:17-31), the IR-VICOBA members saw that he did not understand the Commandments, although he boasted of knowing them from childhood. But he did not put the Commandments into practice. The IR-VICOBA members thought this possible the rich man in Mark acquired his wealth in dubious ways, which is why he did not understand the Commandments. One member said,

> This person had everything, and then Jesus asked him if he knew the Commandments. Possibly this man was stealing and squandering money from any organization. Possibly the person had enriched himself from evil sources and did not care for the poor and needy people in the society. Jesus was not against wealth, but [he was against] the rich man's attitude of selfishness, which is why Jesus asked if he knew the Commandments.

Therefore, for the IR-VICOBA members, the rich man was just like other wealthy people in their own society who acquire richness in evil and unjust ways. They thought this was why he had no compassion with the poor people, which would imply a sound understanding of the Commandments. The rich man was like the people they fought against in their own contexts because those individuals prolonged economic injustice within the society. Another member added, "Jesus was

---

15 The IR-VICOBA members were reflecting on the text and the historical background, which the facilitator gave them about the situation in Palestine. Using their own experience, they tried to connect with their context.

teaching people to be humble, to trust God, and to help people in their neighborhood. The test he gave to the rich man seemed difficult, but the lesson was already delivered by Jesus, who was a good teacher, according to the rich man." Then Jesus was an excellent teacher on how to put the Commandments in practice, the perception the IR-VICOBA have in their society to have a good and just society.

6.2.2   Social Justice and Gender Inequality in Society

Many women in African societies fight against many issues that undermine them in their context. Women participate in many gatherings that sometimes are empowered by activists and politicians against social injustice and gender inequality. Since these acts are done in their context, then they form a 'first act' of the Christian women. As a result of what they fight against within society, the IR-VICOBA members call and fight for liberation on many issues of inequality. The issue of gender inequality within their context is often discussed within the Contextual Bible Study and then becomes part of the second act discussed in light of the Word of God. Many women in the group call for continuing change. Unlike the classical liberation theologians, besides discussing the issue of poverty, the IR-VICOBA members became gender-sensitive, especially on the issue of gender inequality in decision-making. They connected the issue of poverty with gender inequality in decision-making within society. For example, when responding to the improvised question "What makes people in society poor?" following the reading of Beatitudes (Matt 5:1-12), the members responded that one reason lies in traditions. One woman said, "Some traditions make women in the African context be treated like property, for example, women are not allowed to possess wealth like land and cattle, only men, which is still going on in some rural areas." Within the hermeneutical context, one might say that the woman in the Bible study interprets (second acts) practices in their context, which is their first act. One needs a background in gender inequality in Tanzanian society to grasp the significance of what the woman said. When couples are both members of the IR-VICOBA, both gain new, gender-neutral knowledge by striving together to improve their family's resources and possessions. However, some male and female members are married to spouses who are not members of IR-VICOBA. Even though nonmember spouses are required to sign the loan contract when a spouse takes out a loan and agrees to use the money for the earmarked business, some nonmember husbands continue with the old system of oppressing women, believing that they alone are in control of all family finances and their use. In rural areas, where traditions prevail, in many marital relations women are seen as second-class people. Grabe and Dutt argue, "Traditional gender ideologies in most societies are linked to social constructions that portray men as leaders or heads of households ... Women, in contrast, are relegated more frequently to the unpaid domestic sphere, often resulting in financial dependence on male partners."[16] They continue that, "There is growing evidence linking institutionalized structural inequalities to traditional gender ideology in a manner that directly relates to men's disproportionate power and control over women."[17] Therefore, the argument of the IR-VICOBA woman above is well supported by other worldwide data that bad traditions are the main reason why women are treated in that way and remain poor. In their daily 'first acts' activities of fighting poverty – and as newly liberated people – the IR-VICOBA women are increasingly becoming the breadwinners; they work more than men do, and now, because of the VICOBA microcredits, they form businesses and fight poverty, which grants them equal chances with men. In doing so, they continue fighting for their position of equality. They do not need men misusing them; rather, they need men who accept them as equal partners and shareholders in the family. The question arises: Why should men have all the rights of ownership to things women produce? Or those things they produce together? The IR-VICOBA members continue to provide a way forward for women to fight for the rights of other women when they gather together in Bible study. The continuation here, the second act, puts their activities in society in light of the fight for those rights and to fight for the rights of other women when they gather together in Bible study. The continuation here, the second act, puts their activities in society in light of the Word of God.

According to the Gender Equality and Empowerment Programme II, other traditions and customary laws hinder women from property ownership. This is particularly the case of inheritance after the death of a spouse or after a divorce. On the matter of ownership of land, women own an estimated 19% of registered land, and their plots are less than half the size of those of their male counterparts.[18] The reason lies in traditions that do not allow women to own land in rural areas. Traditionally, a woman is expected to be married, whereupon her belongings shift to another family and she cannot inherit land from her parents. Nevertheless, while she is married, she remains a nonlandowner since all the land is in the name of her husband, even the land she has contributed, personally or jointly. Then, she finds herself out of land tenure.

Dowry and masculinity are traditions that prevail in the rural area of Tanzania such that they hinder some women from prospering. Empowered women resist the acts of men who practice those traditions when they use violence within their families. For example, when women, as a way of empowering themselves, start asking why men alone get to decide on assets or use the family resources they

---

16 A. Dutt and S. Grabe, "Gender Ideology and Social Transformation: Using Mixed Methods to Explore Processes of Ideological Change and the Promotion of Women's Human Rights in Tanzania," *Sex Roles* 77, no. 5–6 (2017), pp. 309–324 (p. 310).
17 Ibid.
18 Gender Equality and Empowerment Programme II-Tanzania, 2012–2014, p. 9.

have acquired together or that women alone have acquired, they suffer violence in those families. They are often beaten or asked to leave their families. What the IR-VICOBA women pointed out happens in society, and they show resistance. As one woman among the VICOBA members said, "Some traditions still treat women as tools for work and not as cocreations of God with the men in the family. In our neighborhood, some women are beaten by their husbands, and this happens because, they say, the women were bought since men must pay the bride price (dowry) for their wives, so they have no say in anything within the family."

This means that, traditionally, women have no say even regarding resources they have acquired together or alone within the family. Moreover, it brings forth another theological reflection of equality in God's creation, which most feminist theologians, as liberation theologians, fight for in Africa.[19] Musimbi R.A. Kanyoro writes that "Harmful traditional practises are passed on as 'cultural values' and therefore are not to be discussed, challenged and changed."[20] The harmful traditional practices mentioned by Musimbi here are like those mentioned by the IR-VICOBA members above: violence, depriving women of decision-making within the families and society and denying inheritance for female children. However, the list can also include denial of education, leadership position, health, and control of sexuality – all of which deprive a woman of being empowered in all spheres of life.

The violence mentioned by the IR-VICOBA member above is a side effect of this disempowering on asset ownership among women in rural Tanzania. Having no right to ownership of property also deprives them of being empowered, since women cannot access bank loans, which require fixed assets as collateral. Banks use fixed assets like land and houses as collateral that women do not possess. Once again, they find themselves being locked out of financial systems, which would enable them to have land and other properties. The financial institutions prolong the patriarchal system that deprives women of property ownership in Tanzania in one way or another.

The traditionalists and fundamentalists treat their women in that manner for several reasons. First, it may be linked to the tradition of paying a dowry; men think that, because they have paid a dowry, they can treat their wives any way they like. Second, some of them are illiterate and do not know the human rights and laws that tell them what they can and cannot do. Third, some treat their spouses the way

---

19 Rachel Angogo Kanyoro, *Introducing Feminist Cultural Hermeneutics* (Cleveland: Pilgrim Press, 2002), p. 64. See also Mercy Amba Oduyoye, *Introducing African Women's Theology*, vol. 6, *Introductions in Feminist Theology* (Sheffield: Sheffield Academic Press, 2001), p. 36. See also Mpyana Fulgence Nyengele, *African Women's Theology, Gender Relations, and Family Systems Theory: Pastoral Theological Considerations and Guidelines for Care and Counseling*, vol. 229, *American University Studies. Series 7, Theology and Religion* (New York: Peter Lang, 2004), p. 33.
20 Kanyoro, *Introducing Feminist Cultural Hermeneutics*, p. 159.

they do because of their own emotional character: They cannot tolerate it when their wives make mistakes. However, the law can bind those who are emotional for their misconduct. Fourth, some believe that the Bible indicates that men can treat women this way.

In addition, some men (and women) think that whatever women produce belongs to the man because he is the woman's husband. In their society, the IR-VICOBA members sometimes contemplate negative reflections and actions (first acts) committed by them or other people in society. One female member of the IR-VICOBA group advocated that the family should confiscate all of the assets of her sister-in-law after the death of her brother. She gave this testimony about this detrimental practice, which was done in their family: "I remember advocating persecution of my sister-in-law, who was asked to leave to our elder brother's (her husband) premises after his death. In the meanwhile, I have learned I would not advocate that as a woman because I know I was promoting persecution to other people, especially my fellow women." There are many instances similar to this in rural Tanzania, and people think this is right because these acts fulfill the requirements of their customary laws and traditions. Many women now fight against those practices in their society. In the Contextual Bible Study, such practices in society are reflected in light of the Word of God. As another member said, "If we want to be blessed by Jesus now and inherit the Kingdom of God, we are supposed to continue to lead people justly in different perspectives in our lives. We are not supposed to oppress anyone in our society but advocate for others if they are being persecuted." This is their attitude in their society, and that is why they say they should continue to lead people justly. In their daily lives, the IR-VICOBA members do not encourage people to exploit others. The testimony of the woman above justifies the attitude they have to not exploit others.

In society, women also fight against fundamentalist Christians who translate texts like Eph. 5:22-24 to be the Word of God that comes directly from God. Then, by applying the text in real life, they resort to the old traditions of subjecting a woman to persecution. The IR-VICOBA members are also against a traditional fundamentalist stance, which is why the woman above explained how she felt regret for her wrong actions toward her sister-in-law. One member, commenting on the issue of justice in the family, said, "We should continue helping people to fight for justice, and we should love one another." Reflecting theologically, 'to be subjective' does not mean being a slave. It is a matter of respect, where a person respects another person – here, a husband. To love is another way of respecting another person – here, a wife. Therefore, there is a need to consider Paul's use of the two terms, 'love' and to be 'subject' (Eph. 5:22, 25). He did not mean someone to be feared but someone to be loved. Whoever is subject to someone respectfully automatically loves that person, and whoever loves automatically is subjected to that person. The one term does not mean more than the other, but rather all of the terms here refer to being responsible toward one another.

Also discussed was the issue of men beating their wives, which causes women to be treated like animals without rights in their homes. The members indicated that "there [are] women who are beaten." This act of beating women and treating them as objects is against the righteous God, or should we say against God's justice and human rights. As mentioned earlier, in their Bible study the members came to understand that those practices are no longer fit to be carried out in the world they are living in since they represent injustice and are illogical within society. The IR-VICOBA members, both women and men, said they were against bad traditions and customary laws, which did not give room for a woman to own properties or to make decisions about those assets. They responded differently than traditionalists and fundamentalists on the issue of material assets ownership and decision-making because they were illuminated by the Word of God, which encouraged them to treat each other in godly love.

Moreover, the IR-VICOBA members also reflected on other matters concerning home affairs and family. This was why they were against disrespect among members of the community because of gender. One member reflecting on the Beatitudes on men who revile others (Matt 5:11) commented on the negatives practices of men toward women in some families: "In the world we are living in today, I think there is no need for men using their wives as tools or as a means for production. Men should stop beating their wives and using their masculinity to use the wealth at home the way they like and leave their wives and children suffering." Many IR-VICOBA members nodded their heads in agreement with their fellows' comments about the issue of violence and the negative traditions within their society.

A typical second act interpretation emerged when men in the group portrayed a drastic change in this issue of women's right to property ownership and decision-making in society. However, this interpretation is an indication of the outcome of the first acts done in society, where women together fight against those injustices and gender inequality. Their response provides a way forward for changes to involve both genders to have a significant impact on society.[21] However, they pursue this position as a Christian interpretation with a significant impact on human rights and equality. One of them argued, "If we want to be blessed by Jesus now and inherit the Kingdom of God, we should treat people justly in the different perspectives in our lives. We are not supposed to oppress anyone in our society but advocate for others if they are being persecuted." A second act interpretation here confirms the first act transformation: fighting gender inequality if we want to be blessed by Jesus.

---

21 Birch, "Christian Obligation for the Liberation of Nature." https://www.concern.net/.../engaging_men_on_gender_equality, p. 1.

One might ask whether the transformation is because of Contextual Bible Study only or because other sources made them respond this way. The first act contains both internal and external factors that have helped the IR-VICOBA members to respond so that they have to address the issue of ownership and decision-making on assets within the families. The external factors are a confluence of activists, lawyers, feminists, and womanists in their meetings; they teach the empowerment of women and gender inequality.[22] However, for the IR-VICOBA members, the second act, faith and the Word of God, illuminated them more, which is why you hear men in the group support such movements.

Implied in this second act position in the above quotation was the issue of being an advocate for others. As people empowered by the Word of God, the IR-VICOBA members claim to advocate for others. They have a call to be Christ-like individuals who are fully equipped to advocate within society for human rights concerning the ownership of assets to anyone due this in the eyes of their Bible Study. In the Bible study, they indicated, "We should also continue to empower each other so that we get out of this situation we are facing as poor people. The Word of God should illuminate how to be empowered economically." This attitude of the IR-VICOBA members finds support in 'the Word of God' (second act) to fight for women's rights without considering the dynamics of traditions and customary laws that, for many years, have hindered women. In their first acts, the IR-VICOBA members are ready to fight for other people deprived of their property, like land, houses, animals, and current resources. In their second act of Contextual Bible Study, they find support for all men and women, where the women are free to voice what they feel and where they are harmed in society.

Moreover, this attitude portrays the power of solving societal matters by involving men and women. Challenges are met when both genders together learn as the IR-VICOBA members do. Involving both genders enhances insufficiently structured regulations like those that the Tanzanian Presidential Commission of Inquiry made into Land Matters, which proceeded the 1999 Land Acts. These living laws of local communities are expressed and evolve into processes of social change, not codified customary laws.[23] Opportunities like these, where the law gives power to societies,

---

22 Demere Kitunga and Marjorie Mbilinyi, "Rooting Transformative Feminist Struggles in Tanzania at Grassroots," *Review of African Political Economy* 36, no. 121 (2009), ibid., pp. 433–441 (p. 434). See also Dutt and Grabe, "Gender Ideology and Social Transformation: Using Mixed Methods to Explore Processes of Ideological Change and the Promotion of Women's Human Rights in Tanzania," pp. 309–324 (here p. 309).

23 Issa G. Shivji and Tanzania, *Report of the Presidential Commission of Inquiry into Land Matters: 1: Land Policy and Land Tenure Structure*, vol. 1 (Uppsala: Ministry of Lands, Housing and Urban Development, Government of the United Republic of Tanzania, in cooperation with The Scandinavian Institute of African Studies, Uppsala, 1994), p. 252.

need many enlightened societies like those of the VICOBA members, who advocate justice in rural society. Otherwise, old traditions and customary laws will dominate and deprive women of owning assets and making decisions on those assets.

The IR-VICOBA members, although victims in many cases, also want to be agents of change by addressing so-called 'issues of social justice.' This may be seen when they said, "We should not dominate others and exploit them by any means and leave them poor or blind from knowledge." A member in another group said, "If we want to be blessed by Jesus now and inherit the Kingdom of God, we must lead people justly in different perspectives. We should not oppress anyone in our society but advocate for others if they are being persecuted." As I perceive it, by reflecting on the Word of God in that manner, they continue to fight for social justice. The IR-VICOBA members aim to change the world they live in as practical theologians from below. They use the Bible texts to reflect on the issues discussed in the context of current social justice and Bible study, and they make explicit a way forward on how to continue to help other members of society. I would argue that, with these positions, what they are doing is a theology of social justice from below. The critical perspective is that this theology from below distinguishes the first and second acts and often develops the second act to confirm and enrich the first.

6.2.3 The Issue of Ecology and Environment Conservation

In Chapter 5, I discussed how the IR-VICOBA members discussed environmental issues related to local poverty, particularly in response to the improvised question, "What makes people poor in society?" This discussion arose while reflecting on the narratives of the poor in both Beatitudes (Matt 5:3 and Luke 6:20) and of poor Lazarus and the rich man Luke (16:19-31). Environmentally destructive activities, actions, and practices are done in society as people fight against poverty and cause harm to the environment in order to survive. These human activities differ from place to place in developing countries: The destruction of natural vegetation as well as of sources of streams for horticultural and agricultural activities, overgrazing, and other poor farming practices have occurred, especially in rural areas. Some individuals within society, including some VICOBA members, have been making, and are using, charcoal and firewood themselves, which destroys the environment. Many teachings exist about the fight against bad land use, such as overgrazing and poor farming practices. In the fight against poverty, the IR-VICOBA members, as part of society, learn how to properly use land in farming and reduce the number of animals. Moreover, they learn about how to practice environmental conservation. These activities are part of 'first act' of the liberation theology, which in their context is done first.

In the Contextual Bible Study, where now they do the 'second act,' they continue with the education that started in their context, and they emphasize discussing these bad practices more. They agree that those bad practices need to be avoided, and some measures need to be taken for more liberation of nature. One member said,

> The environmental condition has made some poor, e. g., now we are experiencing very little rain compared with former times. In Tanzania, some regions experience drought, but in the central regions, people are poor because they have no rain because of the destruction of their environment. People cut many trees for firewood, and, in some areas, people raise cattle and overgraze.

Another member confirmed this view by giving examples in the nearby area: "In our neighboring village, there are people who sell charcoal, and the government does not take any steps to forbid it. In the same area, we see that droughts are increasing year after year, which is not a good sign."

Regarding the environment, the IR-VICOBA members mentioned how industrial globalization effectuated by the TNC within Tanzania pollutes the environment and endangers the population. They are referring to the coal industry and its impacts on people and fish in Lake Nyasa and Kiwira River. In their second act discussion, they mentioned a coal factory close to their neighborhoods which destroys the environment. One member mentioned,

> In the area nearby Tukuyu, coal extraction has polluted water, which is now unsuitable for use in that area. The river passing through it pours water into Lake Nyasa. No research has been done on whether the fish have some effect from the coal, but people continue to consume the fish from the lake and the river.

They also discussed issues concerning the pollution of the environment and the spreading of diseases, which accompany water pollution. Moreover, they discussed issues concerning environmental degradation, since most of the neighboring people are creating a semidesert by cutting trees to make charcoal and firewood. At the same time, the IR-VICOBA members also said *"mwanadamu ni mharibufu wa kwanza wa mazingira aliyoumba Mungu,"* meaning 'a human being is the first destructive creature of the creation of God.' By this, they once again develop a second-act argument, also in the context of environmental issues.

Human beings are destroying the environment, as discussed by the IR-VICOBA groups. Human beings in an era of globalization have been very destructive, causing many problems to society, like drought and diseases, as we have seen the discussions of the IR-VICOBA. Many mining industries from TNCs and companies abroad are interested only in minerals, and once they have extracted the minerals, they are not made responsible for caring for the hazards they caused as a result of the extraction process. For example, in Chapter 5, I discussed the IR-VICOBA's complaints about diseases and poverty caused by the chemicals used to purify those minerals. There are other effects, too, like the uncovered holes that enable the reproduction of mosquitoes which cause malaria, the leading killing disease in Tanzania or Africa in general, even more so than HIV/AIDS. Margaret Barker writes, "Many of the eco-disasters of our time are the result of human activity, a choice made without the Biblical vision, and so choices made with vision other than that of the original unity. The alternative vision or visions have not proved to be valuable or even viable."[24]

In addition, the vegetation tends to control the weather where it brings much rain, especially orographic rainfall. Deforestation causes the area to be too dry or a semidesert, which means people do not have enough food and must confront hunger and poverty, as agriculture is the cornerstone of their lives. Moreover, environmental degradation, as we have seen in the comments of the IR-VICOBA members and Gilarowski in Chapter 5, causes rivers and lakes to have little water, which in turn affects the production of good water and fishing activities. Moreover, water circulation, which causes rainfall, becomes impossible.

The IR-VICOBA members fight these adverse actions and practices in a society that fails to assist mother nature in caring for all of us. *Us* here means human beings and other living beings. The people of Busale and Ilima, most of whom are Christians, would learn from the second act reflections from IR-VICOBA members that salvation involves their dealing with the environment they are destroying. They have to make their environment pay them back by fighting poverty and hunger within the area and ceasing to destroy the vegetation.

6.2.4 The Issue of Caring for Others: Diaconia by the Victims of Poverty

As a community of faith, the IR-VICOBA cannot live in isolation from other people within society. Diaconia is part of the life of people who live as 'have-nots' with few possessions. This society has many dependent people who need assistance from each other. As part of the 'first act,' the IR-VICOBA members care for the needy in their society. Although poor themselves, they care for the poorest people in their community. Because of the African culture and their faith, they administer diaconia to other needy people.

Caring for others is another issue the IR-VICOBA members reflect on in the Contextual Bible Study as an outcome of their 'first act' in their society. In the second act, they reflect on those reflections and practices of caring for the poorest people, although they are also poor. In their reflection on the narratives on the needy from

---

24 Margaret Barker, *Creation: A Biblical Vision for the Environment* (London: T & T Clark, 2010), p. 6.

Matt 25:31-41 and Luke 16:19-31, the IR-VICOBA members had many responses to the texts. During Contextual Bible Study on Matt 25:31-41, one member said, "Jesus in the pericope teaches us that we have to care for one another even when we have few things; we can pray for them and share the Word of God with them." Another member from another group said, "Jesus wants us to live a 'true love,' which requires all of us to become sheep and not goats. Jesus wants us to help our neighbors, not only in hospitals and prisons but also in our neighborhood." Taking care of others in rural life is imperative because no one lives on their own. Therefore, from this perspective, many people are needy in one way or another, and they need a hand from the other person. From this perspective, caring and empowering each other becomes a diaconia[25] to one another, but more so to the neediest people.

The issues of being self-reliant and empowering other poor people were of much interest during the Bible study. Members were interested because, in many cases, they do these sort of practices and activities in their first act. In their response to the Bible study, they showed more concern about being self-reliant and empowering one another. One member said, "We should continue to empower each other regardless [of the fact] that we are poor, and we should learn to work hard to become economically capable." This attitude of the IR-VICOBA groups goes well with their objectives of fighting poverty by being self-empowered in whatever they do in their lives. They advocate working hard, regardless of other factors that make their efforts dwindle. Therefore, for the IR-VICOBA members, empowering each other is a number one priority to becoming free beings in this globalized economy.

Moreover, the IR-VICOBA members not only have the objective of self-empowering; they also want to empower other people, because they believe in liberating others by teaching good ways of combating poverty and other negative aspects in their lives. One member of the group typically commented, "To be Christ-like, we need to assist the needy people who are poor like us or more." This member of the IR-VICOBA spoke this way because they spend time organising other poor people into groups and teaching them how to start an IR-VICOBA group of their own in other areas. They do this because empowering others is another of their objectives, regardless their being poor themselves. The issue of Bible study fits well here because, in these Bible studies, they learn more than strictly the Bible, as I indicated earlier. In addition, they reflect on their daily reflections and practices about poverty and caring for other downtrodden people *and* receive Biblical confirmation that they do the right thing.

---

25 I use the term *diaconia* with the letter 'c' in the meaning of the practices and actions toward needy people or done by needy people themselves. Although the IR-VICOBA members are Christians, I am not going to use the more common term from Greek origin 'diakonia,' as this would be more ecclesiastic.

In the Contextual Bible Study of the IR-VICOBA, there is a good continuation of what they do in their daily lives as the first act. The IR-VICOBA members, after reflecting in light of God in Contextual Bible Study continue to empower each other by teaching, which is diaconal education. The IR-VICOBA members in the process of empowering themselves put diaconia into practice by educating other poor people in society. This education is a diaconia education given to other poor people.[26] For instance, if they learn how to keep livestock, produce cash crops, make soap, cook doughnuts, make fabrics and other handmade things, they ensure that they are teaching others to profit from such items. In the IR-VICOBA session, they learn more about how to practise these actions more systematically and generate profit. Moreover, from that standpoint, they proceed to teach other IR-VICOBA groups, so others can understand that simple technology. These people use money from their VICOBA fund and buy ingredients for whatever they want to learn how to make before they practice it in their homes. Those who learn from the first time become 'Trainer of Trainers' (T.O.T.) to other IR-VICOBA groups.

6.3 Conclusion

In this chapter, I have argued that the IR-VICOBA members build their profile of participant-centered Contextual Bible Study using the See-Judge-Act method. The IR-VICOBA groups use Bible reading as a liberating tool and a point from which to reflect on their hardship and fight in the political, economic, and social situations they are experiencing. Moreover, theologizing the economic hardship and social injustice they face daily exemplifies the first acts, which is their reason for starting the IR-VICOBA. I found that they differ from the Ujamaa Centre in South Africa, whose 'act' emerges from their reading of the Bible, the "See-Judge-Act." However, I found that the IR-VICOBA groups are similar to the Latin American liberation theologians, who reflect on their actions and commitments in their daily lives and then, in the Bible study, perform the "second act" of reflection in light of the Word of God.

I have seen that one case of their fight for liberation in their society was their fight for economic justice. They fight for the prices of their products, and I have discussed their perception and conception of ideas as they discussed in their Contextual Bible Study, which is their second act. They discussed the issue of fighting with people who exploit them by buying their products at very low prices, and they thought

---

26 Heinz Schimdt, "Empowering Education: A Diaconal Response T Poverty," *Diaconia* 2, no. 1 (2011), pp. 50–65. See also Reinhard Boettcher, *The Diaconal Ministry in the Mission of the Church*, vol. 2006, p. 1, Lwf Studies (Geneva: Lutheran World Federation, Department for Theology and Studies, 2006).

controlling their local market would be a further way of liberation by having reasonable prices. Moreover, the IR-VICOBA members discussed how to economically empower other poor people so that they also may become economically free beings. These are interpretations of their interpretation of the IR-VICOBA members' first act, now reflected in light of the Word of God as they do Bible study. It is their way of doing theology in their praxis, the first acts, and then reflecting on them.

Another issue dealt with here is freedom from social injustices. The case most discussed was that of women's empowerment and decision-making within the family. The IR-VICOBA members discussed the need to empower women to achieve gender equality and equal power in decision-making within their families. They discussed the fight against traditions and Biblical interpretations that deprive women of equality. Furthermore, they indicated that, when women are treated as equals, both men and women benefit within the family. Together with social justice, the issue of caring for the neediest people with diaconia was discussed, especially in terms of the "have-nots" and the "have little." These are part of their first act, which they perform in their society. In the Bible study, they reflect and do their theology on those issues, which is their second act. Nevertheless, in their intellectual activities – the second act – they come up with other ideas that sometimes make them go back to society for more reflections and practices, the first acts.

Finally, yet importantly, there is the issue of environmental degradation and ecology, which also exemplifies their first act. The IR-VICOBA members contemplated the issues of environmental degradation and how it produces poverty, destroys the ecology, and pollutes the environment. The central agent of all these problems is human beings. They reflected on how their own actions, and the acts of their neighbors at Ilima, have destroyed the environment. They now experience drought, which makes them more miserable and leads to hunger and death. However, across the entire world, we see issues like global warming as another effect of environmental degradation caused by human activities. Therefore, issues concerning the global environment, reflected in the theology of ecology and creation by the IR-VICOBA members, reflect more on global ecological issues. They show how the excellent Creator has made His creation in proper equilibrium, called ecology, which needs much redemption and salvation from people with evil intentions, whether they do this knowingly or unknowingly.

Chapter 7: See-Act-Judge: Theological Reflections on the Reading of the IR-VICOBA Groups

In the preceding chapter, I discussed the IR-VICOBA members' meeting in their contextual Bible study. I noted that, when they meet together, they reflect on issues they carry out in their daily activities. That is their societal praxis, the reflection and practice of their hardship in life being poor people. Moreover, I discussed how they relate with other poor people within the society who 'have little.' In their contextual Bible study, the IR-VICOBA members do theology. The question is: Are they doing theology from below, like the Ujamaa tradition? Or are they doing the so-called theology of nonperson, as Gutierrez called it? For Gutierrez, this is a theological reflection on the first act.[1] McAfee Brown writes about Gutierrez that, "Gustavo[Gutierrez] seems to suggest that theology is a 'critical reflection' on 'reflection and action' ... theology is a second reflection, so to speak, about what has already been going on – that is, the commitments we have made and the reflections we have engaged in about them."[2] This is what I analyzed and interpreted in the preceding chapter.

In this chapter, I go one step further and analyze the interpretive practices in the IR-VICOBA, to obtain the point of the view of the second act in the tradition of Gutierrez. The interesting perspective in such an interpretation will be whether the second act is less connected to the first act of interpretation. One might think that the second act takes up a less contextualized theology. However, in the following, it becomes clear that the second act is also contextualized: Is it also based on actions and practices from their socioeconomic reality. This means that their practices and reflections strongly influence the second act of empowering their path out of the poverty they live in.

Together with their pastors, the IR-VICOBA members read the Bible and work together with other poor people so that they can at least achieve a sense of resilience, which they have achieved now, although they have not totally exited poverty. In

---

[1] Gutiérrez, *The Power of the Poor in History: Selected Writings*, p. 60. Gutierrez describes theology as "a reflection in and on, faith as liberation praxis. It will be an understanding of faith from an option and commitment. It will be an understanding of faith from the point of departure in real. Effective solidarity with the exploited classes, oppressed, ethnic groups ad despised cultures of Latin America and from within their world." In the same way, the IR-VICOBA groups fight this situation from the exploiting bodies in their society and implicitly in the world. They make a theological reflection in their Bible studies.

[2] Brown, *Gustavo Gutiérrez: An Introduction to Liberation Theology*, p. 76.

the following sections, I discuss their Bible study and the theology they are making within the Contextual Bible Study.

7.1 The Theology of Love

As I discussed in the previous chapters, while doing their Contextual Bible Study, the IR-VICOBA members reflected on the issue of loving their neighbor and on their responsibility as Christians (Matt 25:31-46; Mark 10:17-31; Luke 16:19-20). In their daily lives, the IR-VICOBA members care for their neighbors and are also cared for by their neighbors in return.

The IR-VICOBA members reflected on the hungry, the prisoners, the naked, and the sick (the poor in a holistic meaning), who Jesus wanted others to care for in the texts. They also reflected on their own life experiences, as poor people, where they must be cared for. The society of the 'have-nots' and the 'have-little' need much love from their neighbors. The IR-VICOBA members think that believing in Christ means caring for your neighbor no matter the neighbor's situation. Take a comment from one member, who said during the Bible study, "We have to love God and our neighbors by sharing what we have. We are required not only to care for the needy because we are rich, but Jesus wants us to share even the little we have with the needy." The IR-VICOBA members reflected much on the love of God for them, which they said was supposed to be reflected in the love they give to their neighbors. In another group, one member indicated, "Jesus wants us to live a 'true love,' which requires all of us to become sheep and not goats. Jesus wants us to help our neighbors not only in hospitals and prisons but also in our neighborhood." The vertical love from God must have a horizontal reflection, which touches the lives of the neighbors. This reflection in the Bible study is their second reflection, their theology, on what they do in their lives every day.

Regarding their reflection of the pericope on the rich man and poor Lazarus, one member added, "Rich people who do not care for the poor people despise them in such a way that they dehumanize them to be very little or nothing, like the rich man did in the passage we read today." These words indicate that a reflected love from God toward them gives a way of humanizing them such that they need to appear to other people more humanely. A faithful Christian, according to them, is someone who shows love by caring for other people, especially people in need like Lazarus. This is the 'theology of love,' as I try to ponder the way they indicated during their Bible study.

Moreover, the IR-VICOBA members thought that love should not be conditional or one-directional. The love of a neighbor, which reflects the vertical love from God, should be for all people everywhere. As one member indicated, "Love should be to everybody, young or old, rich or poor, peasant, or official worker; everyone needs to be cared for when they need someone to assist them in their needy situation." Accordingly, this love does not involve age, race, status, or career but involves all people, especially when someone needs a helping hand.

In societies of 'have-nots,' like that of the IR-VICOBA members, understanding the 'theology of love' as portrayed here is very necessary, since many people live very miserable lives and need a hand to lift them up. The IR-VICOBA members accurately reflected that needy people need help from their neighborhood. Possibly, they took this stance because of the underprivileged situation they experience, where you cannot live on your own and need other people. Life in rural areas of Tanzania requires help from other people and their resources, which brings about a real and practical theology of love.

The theology of love is a practical theology that is necessary today. We need to care for our neighbors, as reflected by the IR-VICOBA members. Here, they call people into practicing this theology of love to be liberated from the bond of poverty. They call for changes within societies and the world in general.

Although the IR-VICOBA members are still deprived, when they convene they still go further to integrate with other poor by sharing and empowering them through teaching and providing them with what they have. When reflecting upon whether or not Jesus was against richness, one member said, "Jesus was not against wealth; he was against the bad character of the rich people [who were] not caring for the needy people, the poor among their societies. Jesus wanted blessed people to care for the people who were poor in society." They reflected that Jesus encouraged love among those who were blessed and those who were not. This means that the IR-VICOBA theology of love concerns a theology where the context strongly influences the content of the second act interpretation. The VICOBA people present a model of love that makes sense in their context of 'have-nots.'

7.2 Christological Approaches

While reflecting on the IR-VICOBA Contextual Bible Study, I found that the members spend much time reflecting on the character of Jesus based on the experiences from their social-cultural context. In their Contextual Bible Study, Jesus is viewed as a teacher, a provider, and a source of empowerment and hope. The basic point, however, is that all of these different aspects of Jesus develop from practice. Jesus is a teacher, provider, etc., because his way of approaching people and communities deepens the interpretation of the social reality and context. The IR-VICOBA members were confronted with the questions Jesus asked his disciples: "Who do you say I am?" and "Who do people think I am?" (Mark 8:27-29). These questions often portray a Christological reflection about Jesus' identity among the needy today. Quoting Taylor, Christopher Magezi and Jacob T. Igba put the same question in the African context: "If Christ was to appear as the answer to the questions that Africans are asking, what would he look like?"[3]

Many African theologians have argued that Jesus would be perceived Christologically as an elder brother,[4] liberator,[5] protoancestor,[6] chief or king.[7] Christology, according to Nyamiti, is where Africans can break new grounds in African theology.[8] Writing on the theology of Nyamiti, Tanzanian theologian Stephen Munga deduces that Nyamiti's method of doing theology is grounded in the two sources of African theology. In this way, the task of theologians is to Christianize the African beliefs and cultures and not to Africanize Christianity.[9] Magezi and Igbo write that the issue of Christologies in Africa is divided into two groups: those who perform inculturation starting from the Bible and those who start with the African culture and traditions to do their Christology. However, they write that those who start with the African cultures and traditions are in danger of belittling the place of Christ and encouraging syncretism.[10] The theologians who support it are

---

3 Christopher Magezi and Jacob T. Igba, "African Theology and African Christology: Difficulty and Complexity in Contemporary Definitions and Methodological Frameworks. (Essay)," *HTS Teologiese Studies* 74, no. 1 (2018), p. 4.
4 Schreiter, *Faces of Jesus in Africa*, pp. 116–127 (here p. 116).
5 John Parratt, *A Reader in African Christian Theology*, rev. ed., vol. 23, Spck International Study Guide (London: SPCK, 1997), p. 74.
6 Bénézet Bujo, *African Theology in Its Social Context*, Afrikanische Theologie in ihrem gesellschaftlichen Kontext (Maryknoll, NY: Orbis Books, 1992), p. 77. According to most African religions, ancestors are a 'living dead' who have control of blessing and power to the 'living.' They are unseen people who have passed away and who live with the living, empowering and blessing them in whatever circumstances these people are experiencing. The ancestors are venerated among Africans. However, Jesus is more than that since, according to the IR-VICOBA members, he is God and is therefore worshipped.
7 Schreiter, *Faces of Jesus in Africa*, pp. 103–115.
8 Charles Nyamiti, "African Christologies Today," in *Faces of Jesus in Africa*, ed. Robert J. Schreiter (Maryknoll Orbis, 1998), pp. 3–23. In his view, Nyamiti argues that African theology has two sources that are Christian, namely, the Bible and traditions; non-Christian sources are African culture, traditions, and sociopolitical situations. Nyamiti agrees with the view of the EATWOT theologians who met in the Dar es Salaam Conference where he attended (Torres and Fabella, *The Emergent Gospel: Theology from the Underside of History: Papers from the Ecumenical Dialogue of Third World Theologians, Dar Es Salaam, August 5–12, 1976*.). This was also the case in a concert of the African theologians who met in Accra Ghana in 1977, which he also attended. Kofi Appiah-Kubi and Sergio Torres, *African Theology En Route: Papers from the Pan-African Conference of Third World Theologians, December 17–23, 1977, Accra, Ghana* (Maryknoll, NY: Orbis Books, 1979), pp. 192–193.
9 Stephen I. Munga, "Beyond the Controversy: A Study of African Theologies of Inculturation and Liberation" (Lund University Press, 1998), p. 124. See also Godwin Akper, "The Person of Jesus Christ in Contemporary African Christological Discourse," *Religion and Theology* 14, no. 3–4 (2007), p. 226.
10 Magezi and Igba, "African Theology and African Christology: Difficulty and Complexity in Contemporary Definitions and Methodological Frameworks. (Essay)," p. 5.

Nyamiti,[11] Bujo,[12] Wanamaker,[13] and others. This is the more employed methodology. The theologian who supports starting from the Bible before moving on to culture and traditions is Bediako. However, this is arguable. Most theologians find themselves doing both, either putting the Bible and Christian tradition at the center or finding themselves pulled by their African beliefs and culture to be at the center.

My research on the Contextual Bible Study in the context of IR-VICOBA takes another perspective and direction. The study deals largely with poor people's (self-)liberation and very little with African cultures and traditions. The Christologies developed in the IR-VICOBA context reflect the IR-VICOBA members' reading of Scripture. Nevertheless, their reflections are based on their socioeconomic reality; in most cases, the text is used to measure their reflections and actions in their own societies as well as their commitment and practices. For example, reflecting on the poor, the mourning, the weeping, and the hungry in the Beatitudes, the IR-VICOBA members perceived Jesus as relating with these people but in connection with their context. One of them argued:

> I think Jesus saw these people were poor, hungry, crying, and in desperate situations, [and he] also saw other people who were rich, eating, and celebrating. Those who were rich, with everything, did not care for other people, and they took care of themselves, like the society we are living in today, where rich people assist themselves and do not care about the poor, crying, and despised people.

The phrase "like the society we are living in today" indicates that the IR-VICOBA members perceive Jesus' character and teachings in relation to their own society. They ponder about Jesus, who is close to the poor from the perspective of their society. In their daily praxis, the first act, the IR-VICOBA members take the issue of assisting the needy seriously. To give further emphasis, the IR-VICOBA members think Jesus fought for the rights of the needy and was against other people who were not performing the right social practices. As one member put it,

> The poor, the hungry, the crying people were despised and mocked by the rich, those who needed assistance from the rich. Jesus would not be angry such that he gave those harsh and woeful words. I am sure he did not intend to give woe to the rich, but he wanted them to be more responsible. Otherwise, woe was their share in the Kingdom of God.

---

11 J. N. K. Mugambi and Laurenti Magesa, *Jesus in African Christianity: Experimentation and Diversity in African Christology* (Nairobi: Initiatives Publishers, 1989), pp. 17–39.
12 Bujo, *African Theology in Its Social Context*, p. 79.
13 Charles A. Wanamaker, "Jesus the Ancestor: Reading the Story of Jesus from an African Christian Perspective," *Scriptura* 62, no. 0 (2012), pp. 281–298.

For the IR-VICOBA members, Jesus lives in society and is perceived to deal with people's hardships and to make ways to get them out of such situations by teaching the right solutions. Jesus shows who he is to these needy people in society. Below, I reflect on those Christological reflections by the IR-VICOBA groups, as I perceived and conceived them during their Bible study.

7.2.1   Jesus, the Empowerer and Liberator

Among the practices of the IR-VICOBA members in their societies are self-empowering and empowering other poor people, a liberating attitude. Based on this 'first act' in society, they perceive Jesus in the same way as they do in their Contextual Bible Study, where they do their 'second act' by doing theology. Jesus, the empowerer and liberator, is a theological perception of the IR-VICOBA members. Their perspective starts from their context and then reflects on the text they are reading, which confirms that Jesus is their liberator and empowerer. Reflecting on the Lukan Beatitudes (Luke 6:20-26), the IR-VICOBA members perceived Jesus as a liberator and empowerer. One of them said,

> Jesus wanted to empower the poor since they were in a difficult situation. Jesus did not want them to get out of the world, but he said by believing in him and his kingdom, they are blessed, meaning that Jesus aimed at redeeming them from the difficult situation they were passing through. The blessedness was to start from where they were and continue up to heaven in future.

The above quotation from the IR-VICOBA members shows their understanding of who Jesus was and is to the people in the pericope and to them. In their socioeconomic lives, they view Jesus as the one living with them and intending to liberate them, as he did in Palestine when he was on Earth. They emphasized the present life (present Kingdom of God) in their societies without quickly turning to the future Kingdom of God. Thus, Jesus liberates and empowers them from the difficult situations they are currently experiencing.

Many theologians from Africa hold similar perceptions. Beghela, wrote about the source of liberation theology of the eminent African theologian on liberation theologies outside of South Africa, Jean-Marc Ela from Cameroun. Ela was troubled with the Christological question of "What does God mean for people in a situation of poverty, drought, famine, injustice, and oppression?"[14] Stinton also quotes Ela, who maintains, "It is impossible to attempt an overall interpretation of the Good

---

14 Philemon Beghela, "Rethinking African Theology: Exploring the God Who Liberates' by Jean-Marc Ela," *Studia Historiae Ecclesiasticae* 38, suppl 1 (2012), p. 3.

News from our African situation without making liberation the fundamental axis of theology which comes from our people."[15] Ela continues, "It is necessary for us to discover the Gospel by returning to the life of the believers to rethink the faith which concerns the totality of the realities of concrete societal existence where God meets them. Such a context becomes relevant to the living revelation."[16] In most cases, African Christians and theologians in oppressive, difficult situations of injustice have had that question on their minds.[17] It is these sorts of situations that one hears from the IR-VICOBA members as they interpret the Bible in the Contextual Bible Study. In my view, therefore, the "Christologies" in the context of IR-VICOBA are significantly different from the one developed by Bediako (see above). Bediako's position starts from the Bible, although that is not what the IR-VICOBA group believes: They claim that Jesus did not start from Scripture but rather from the context of the people. He was speaking to them.

In their Contextual Bible Study, they reflected on how they perceive and act in their society, thinking as poor people in that society. They ask who Jesus is as part of their daily lives, especially when faced with challenges. While reflecting on the Beatitudes, the IR-VICOBA members thought about Jesus as the one who empowers and gives hope to the poor. They denied that Jesus had a preference only for the poor when he said, "Blessed are the poor." Their stance was that Jesus was giving them words of empowerment and hope. Empowerment means supporting poor people striving to improve their lives. Jesus did this by giving them several blessings, e. g., they will inherit the Earth, receive mercy, see God, be called children of God, and receive the Kingdom of Heaven (cf. Matt 5:3-12). One member said,

> I think Jesus was giving encouragement and hope to the poor and the mourning because being poor, as we are, is not a good thing, though it sounds like a curse. I think Jesus aimed to tell them that, because they believed in him, they would enter the kingdom of the assured, where they would be happy, filled, and empowered.

---

15 Diane B. Stinton, *Jesus of Africa: Voices of Contemporary African Christology, Faith and Cultures Series* (Maryknoll, NY: Orbis Books, 2004), p. 195. In this quotation, Ela explains why liberation should be the axis of African theology. It is this time when most of the African countries had much 'flag' independence, then mostly controlled by their former colonial master from Europe. This was the time of neocolonialization. Nevertheless, if the same attitude were expressed today, we would still need liberation theology in contemporary Africa due to world injustice in a global economy where the rich take more, as reflected by the IR-VICOBA in their Contextual Bible Study.
16 Beghela, "'Rethinking African Theology: Exploring the God Who Liberates' by Jean-Marc Ela."
17 Stinton, *Jesus of Africa: Voices of Contemporary African Christology*, pp. 192–193. Stinton writes that the African theology as Liberation Theology proposed by Jean-Marc Ela was received by African theologians who met in Accra in 1977. They agreed together that "We stand against oppression in any form because the Gospel of Jesus Christ demands our participation in the struggle to free people from all forms of dehumanization."

The IR-VICOBA members' understanding of Jesus is, therefore, that he is giving people hope and empowerment in their own societies. This means that the Christologies start in real life and are reflected from the position of these life experiences. It is possible to think of empowerment as something that describes freedom from hardship, rather than just being a Christological term. However, how I have seen the IR-VICOBA members use this term portrays who Jesus was and is to them. In the world of the poor, holistically speaking, their perception of Jesus Christ in this way is significant since Jesus becomes part of their struggle and liberation. One member said, "The message of Jesus was one of liberation from poverty, empowering new knowledge, and making them exercise freedom, especially for people under colonial regime and the power of the Devil." Therefore, according to the IR-VICOBA members, Jesus shows the way to make changes, by giving the message of liberation and empowering them in their world. This perception is also held by another Tanzanian theologian, Magesa, who maintains that, "as a necessary corollary to the liberation of the poor (because his salvation is intended for all), Jesus is the liberator of the rich, the proud, the intellectually conceited, the satiated."[18] Therefore, according to the IR-VICOBA members and Magesa, Jesus as a liberator is not confined to the poor but also includes the rich. This position is crucial, and it comes from their first-act experiences, where all kinds of people need liberation.

In this study, IR-VICOBA members perceive Jesus as the one who empowers people in need to take steps forward in their everyday lives. They also thought believers should think about inheriting not only the coming Kingdom of God but also the present Kingdom of God. They view Jesus as the one who was close to the needy and who gave them a way forward. In my view, the IR-VICOBA members conceived Jesus as providing the 'ability to do things' or 'give power' in many aspects of life, as I discussed in Chapter 4 and Chapter 5 above. Their arguments here are similar to those of Tanzanian theologian Laurenti Magesa, who writes,

> Precisely because Jesus' qualities and life-orientation are beyond our full comprehension and complete emulation, they evoke our profound admiration. Jesus becomes in the life of the Christian the supreme exemplar, the ultimate beacon that anchors the faith, the courage and the hope to appropriate in the circumstance of present existence what he was and what he stood for.[19]

---

18 Schreiter, *Faces of Jesus in Africa*, p. 157.
19 Ibid., p. 152. Laureti Magesa, in his article "Christ the Liberator and Africa Today," writes how the attributes of God-man, Jesus, epitomize the perfection of the Godhead in the proclamation of the reign of God. Being disciples of Jesus requires entering into continual instances of this work by his helping hand.

For instance, in the Beatitudes, if you do not have land and someone tells you that you will receive land, this is empowerment. If you have no mercy and someone tells you that you will have mercy, or if you have no peace and someone tells you that you will have peace, or security, or food (be filled), all of these words from that person will empower you. To them, Jesus becomes 'the empowerer' of the poor people who makes them free to develop and be ready to fight for their rights. The IR-VICOBA groups' Contextual Bible Study portrays how they view Jesus as a liberator and empowerer in their everyday lives. With a similar perception, Magesa writes, "When we speak of Jesus as a liberator, then we refer to his assurance of solidarity with us, particularly but not exclusively as a church, in the struggle – his struggle – to diminish poverty among masses of the people."[20] Therefore, according to the IR-VICOBA members – and not only after reading the Bible texts – Jesus is a liberator of daily struggles. He does this in the same way he empowered people in the streets of Palestine. He empowers people in their socioeconomic reality. He is the Jesus who lives with them in their society, not just by hearing his Word.

7.2.2 Jesus, the Teacher

Another Christological term that would fit the description the IR-VICOBA members gave to Jesus is that of "teacher." In fact, this is also a reflection from what they do in their daily life as teachers of other poor people in society as followers of Jesus. The IR-VICOBA members portrayed Jesus as a good teacher in their daily lives and the Kingdom of God. The IR-VICOBA members conceived Jesus as a teacher who teaches them the good news, even today. They viewed Jesus as the one who enlightens them through his word and empowers them to change their lives, as he did in the text they were reading.

Regarding the Kingdom of God, the IR-VICOBA members portrayed Jesus as a good teacher who taught about the Kingdom. One member commented, "Jesus was teaching how people could inherit the Kingdom of God here on Earth and in heaven; Jesus in the Beatitudes gave all the descriptions on how to live on Earth and in heaven." The important thing is that the teachings of Jesus, in the IR-VICOBA discussions, also connect to life in the here and now. The Kingdom is a heavenly one, but it is also present in the here and now, and Jesus is the one who teaches that present Kingdom. One might see this as a way of seeing Jesus the teacher from the perspective of the first act. The IR-VICOBA groups already perform liberating practices in their everyday lives. Now they see Jesus as the teacher who confirms and supports their socioeconomic liberation.

---

20 Ibid., p. 158.

7.3 The IR-VICOBA Members' Theology on Poverty

The IR-VICOBA members have even changed how they view the relationship of poverty with the Kingdom of God. They find that God deals with both the rich and the miserable on the issue of the needy within their society. One of the IR-VICOBA members in the Bible study said, "Love should be [given] to everybody, whether young or old, rich or poor, peasant or official worker. Everyone needs to be cared for when they need someone to assist them in their needy situation." Another member of the other group said, "We have to love God and our neighbors by sharing what we have. We are required not only to care for the needy because we are rich; Jesus wants us to share with the needy even the little we have." The difference between poor and rich to them is not a big issue; the important issue is the care of the 'needy,' who can be poor or rich.

Their socioeconomic reality, the act of starting VICOBA, and being economically empowered over even a small amount have made the members very keen in their interpretation about the poor and poverty. Jesus said, "Blessed are the poor," but the IR-VICOBA members did not take the interpretation that God was referring only to the poor literally. Many passages in the Bible describe how God requires the rich to care for the poor and the downtrodden, for example, Isaiah 42:5-8 and 1 Tim 6:17-19. These passages require the rich to care for the poor and not depend on their richness or be selfish with it. In this way, the IR-VICOBA members read the Kingdom of God passages in light of their own experiences (first act) in daily life.

How the first act influences their Bible reading also leads to a different perception of poverty than other liberation theologians. Jon Sobrino writes:

> Since the poor are those to whom Jesus' mission was primarily directed, they ask the fundamental questions of faith and so with power to move and activate the whole community in the process of learning what Christ is. Because they are God's preferred, and because of the difference between their faith and the faith of the non-poor, the poor, within the faith community, question Christological faith and give it its fundamental direction.[21]

Compared with Sobrino's way of privileging the poor, the IR-VICOBA think differently because of their experiences in the first act. For them, Jesus must have another meaning, not one indicating that the poor are blessed. In the Contextual Bible Study on Mark 10:17-22, about the rich man who was told to sell everything and give to the poor, the IR-VICOBA members developed a position that one might see as

---

21 Sobrino, *Jesus the Liberator: A Historical-Theological Reading of Jesus of Nazareth*, p. 30. See also Gutiérrez, *A Theology of Liberation: History, Politics, and Salvation*, pp. 162–165.

their theological stance on poverty. One of the members asked some questions: "Why did Jesus ask the rich man to sell everything he had? Does it mean he wanted this person to go to ground zero and become poor? Does this mean that it is a sin to have wealth? Does it mean that, when someone needs to inherit the Kingdom of God, they should be poor?" It is very plausible that they interpret things this way because they spend most of their daily lives resisting poverty and saving something to have more money to live on. From that background, it is unacceptable to end up with an interpretation similar to Sobrino's. In society in their first act, poverty is not blessed; poverty is something that needs to be fought, like they claim Jesus did. One member said,

> Jesus' answer to the rich man was not to require him to sell everything; otherwise, this young man would become poor and a beggar. Jesus was testing the faith of this man. It is like when God tested Abraham [asking him] to sacrifice his son; but when he agreed, God gave the sheep instead of sacrificing the child. Besides, he would not allow this rich man to become poor, as we know being poor is a bad option. Jesus knew that this man depended much on his wealth regardless of saying that he knew all of the Commandments.

This represents one more way of reflecting the same argument as stated above: God does not want the rich man to sell everything. From their life experience, the members know that selling everything means starting from zero and risking extreme poverty. According to them, as one of them said during Bible study, Jesus had another intention or meaning by saying, "Blessed are the poor." Their stance was, "Jesus was not against the wealth; he was against the bad character of the rich people not caring for the needy and poor in their societies. Jesus wanted people who had been blessed to care for people who were poor." This was their stance since almost all indicated agreement by nodding their heads. Therefore, to them, a theology of poverty is a theology that recognizes the resistance to poverty made in the everyday social context.

From their life experiences, they know that poverty is a human-made thing. Human beings have created poverty such that some people live in challenging situations. This human-made poverty is what they always fight against it in their society. On this, one member said,

> God did not create humans to be poor; we make poverty among ourselves. Some systems have created some people to be poor and some to be rich. Both spiritual and physical poverty have a connection with these systems, which do not go according to God's purposes of creation.

Here, the IR-VICOBA members also reflect a theology based on the knowledge that the sources of poverty are not only individual or everyday. The (second act) theology reflects a (first act) knowledge that poverty is also social and systemic. One way of making this second-act theology is to say that people who are resilient within society have to care for the neediest people. In the discussion, one hears such voices: "Take an example of business people who buy our coffee, or tea, or cocoa by cheating us and giving a low price so that they get more profit in the market where they sell it in what they call the 'world market.' People like these must be rich from exploiting peasants like us." Based on such first-act experiences, making people miserable is a (second-act) sin of cheating.

Some intermediaries cheat peasants in business, as evidenced by a case recorded by the *Ippmedia* on 14 May 2018, which portrays the whole story of how peasants in rural areas in Tanzania are cheated:

> One farmer by the name Ngurume had weighed the cottonseeds on the village council scale earlier that morning, and it had come 550 kg, now [on the agent's scale] it was just 500 kg. He says this is common, being cheated by agents' middlemen who buy farmers' cotton and sell it on to ginneries, where cotton is processed into lint for export.[22]

This is the (first-act) reason why the IR-VICOBA members (second act) think that Jesus was not against wealth, except when gained by dishonest means, like the example given above. If people become rich in such ways, then they are cheating others, which is against the 8th Commandment of God, "You should not steal." The members do their theology from below. One of them said, "We should use the opportunities we have to continue to help people who like to be empowered in our midst so that no one goes back to being poor again. We should be helping each other to get out of this situation, and therefore we should say goodbye to poverty."

7.4   The Theology of Solidarity

Based on the practices through which the IR-VICOBA members help one another, they develop a (second-act) theology of solidarity. For example, in their Contextual Bible Study, they discussed their own situations compared with those in the text,

---

22 "The Farmer and the Middlemen: The buying agent loosed the stopper on the scale as Raphael Ngurime's bulging bag of cotton swing from the hook," 14th May 2018, at https://www.ippmedia.com/en/news/farmers-and-middlemen. This incident happened in another rural area in the Western zone of Tanzania. However, this can be applied to all places where intermediaries are involved in buying cash-crops from peasants. The complaints of IR-VICOBA members here coincide with this example in the Western zone. The intermediaries behave this way to get profit for themselves.

and one member said, "We should also continue to empower each other so that we can get out of this situation we are facing as poor people. The Word of God should illuminate us to know how to be empowered economically." The 'getting together and empowering each other' shows that they want to unite their energy and come together for the economic solution to the problems they are experiencing. The term 'continue,' as used here, refers to something these people are doing in their midst, in their socioeconomic reality. Thus, the IR-VICOBA members in their society, because of their impoverished situation, come up with 'to help one another and help the poor people who are more miserable than they are.' This is their daily praxis. The first acts of solidarity means solidarity among themselves as poor people as well as solidarity with other poor people in society to be liberated from such situations.

One Bible study member said, "We are supposed to unite and make our market system work so that we can avoid other middlemen exploiting us. So, we can ask our local government to interfere on this issue." To them, solidarity empowers them to develop their market system or strategy to avoid people who exploit them. This was a good idea, though it might take much time until they actually succeed in having the necessary system in place to sell their products fairly. However, when they are theologizing in their participant-centered Contextual Bible Study, they build on the already acquired knowledge of how to go together, in solidarity, to liberate themselves and others from that injustice.

There are two directions here of the theology of solidarity. One is situated among the poor themselves, the second among people with authority having solidarity with the poor. When they say, "We are supposed to unite and make our market," they are referring to the local market, where the intermediaries cheat them. They aim to fight the injustice done in their localities. They came together to have their VICOBA, and now they have paved the way to go further for the market of their products, which the intermediaries exploit. The market must be liberated, and it can only be liberated when the poor peasants are in solidarity among themselves – then come other people with authority to join in solidarity with them.

For the IR-VICOBA members, solidarity with other poor people also involved teaching others to be responsible for their own lives. During the discussion on this issue, a member said, "We should continue to help one another but also teach other people to be working hard … We need to empower the needy to work hard, although we are supposed to assist them on their needs." The IR-VICOBA members believe living in solidarity with others is the path God has destined them to take. When they say we should continue to 'help one another,' they express a 'second act': their theology of solidarity. In the discussion on the Markan Beatitudes, one member said,

> A point to note is that we must have a good relationship with God and others to maintain this relationship. We need to care for the needy and care for the work of spreading the Gospel and humanitarian activities. Only then is our richness be on the side of God, and we are practicing the Kingdom of God in the world we are living.

This member was referring to the relationship with God and their neighbors, which indicates their solidarity with both. Besides mentioning the Gospel and humanitarian activities, these people knew that they were assured of a good result when they entered into solidarity with divine and human beings in their first act. On the same understanding, reflecting on how to be in solidarity with other people referred to the teaching of Jesus, which is their second act, one of them said, "Jesus taught us that we have to care for and help each other so that we become his good followers and inheritors of the Kingdom of God now and in the last day [we are] found to be sheep on the right-hand side of Son of Man." Adding more emphasis on solidarity with God in whatever they do in their discussion on Luke 16:19-31, one IR-VICOBA member said, "Our relationship with God is shown by how we relate with our neighbors. The vertical relationship with God is of much meaning to human beings' relationship with our creator, and a horizontal relationship with our neighbor manifests this first relationship." They indicated that this was a teaching of Jesus to people in Palestine and to them as they interpreted the Gospel by reflecting on their context. This is a theology of solidarity of the IR-VICOBA, evidenced by their being in a relationship with Jesus and God. This relationship is important and requires them to be in solidarity with other people who are poor, exploited, and suffering as they continue to practice it. Examples of their practice include their fight for justice, equality, and liberation from poverty.

As for their epistemological-hermeneutics, the IR-VICOBA groups refer to God and Jesus, who are in solidarity with them in whatever they do in their daily lives. They also refer to the solidarity they share with other poor people. In this way, they also enter into soteriological and liberation praxis in solidarity with their God, much as Jesus was in solidarity with God in the Synoptic pericopes. The theology of solidarity is a reflection of the IR-VICOBA members working together with God and Jesus for the betterment of the whole society. Therefore, for the IR-VICOBA groups, solidarity with God in their living society enables true liberation to happen.

7.5   The Struggle Against Money-Theism

In Chapter 4, I discussed how the IR-VICOBA members were very skeptical of people who put money above God and other human beings. Theologically, this is called 'money-theism.'[23] Within their society, the IR-VICOBA members, being believers, fight against this attitude of money-theism among themselves and in other people. Reflecting on Mark 10:17-31 and Luke 16:19-31, the IR-VICOBA members theologized about people who put money first. Though the IR-VICOBA members aimed at fighting poverty, which by definition involves having some money rather than none, their stance was quite different from that of people like the rich man. Their stance is to prioritize God first, as they pondered Matt 6:33 and those passages mentioned above. Money was among the things which are an additional but not a fundamental thing: God comes first. "There is a tendency of rich people to love wealth more than anything and misusing that wealth. They do not even want to give or show their wives what they have because they love their wealth more than God and their families." This reflection by the IR-VICOBA members is a 'second act' theological issue dealing with money. It presupposes the negative experiences in the first act, which they fight against within society, in which rich people exploit the poor.

As the IR-VICOBA members were discussing why the rich man became unhappy when told to sell everything he had and give the proceeds to the poor, they reflected on the issue of the first commandment, which states:

> I am the Lord your God, who brought you out of the land of Egypt, out of the house of slavery, you shall have no other God besides me. You shall not make for yourself an idol, whether, in the form, anything that is in heaven above, or that is on the Earth beneath, or that is in the water under the Earth. You shall not bow to them or worship them for I, the Lord your God, am a jealous God. (Exod 20:2-5; cf. Deut 5:6-8)

These words made the IR-VICOBA think about the rich man, who knew that Commandment but loved wealth more than God such that he did not think of God at all in action but only in words. According to the IR-VICOBA members, having wealth is not sinful, though misusing it is. As one member said,

> Having wealth is not a sin, but the only problem is that rich people fail to share with others the richness they have, and it is here where sin starts. However, God provides everything to a human being, but he also wants others to get a share of that possession. Sometimes the rich despise and degrade others because of their richness.

They continued discussing that in their society. As another member puts it:

---

23 Groody, *Globalization, Spirituality, and Justice: Navigating the Path to Peace*, p. 22. Groody writes that money-theism is idolatry against true God. It represents the idolization of capital, expressed as the worship of the gods of the marketplace and is often practiced through the rituals of the marketplace.

Wealth has become their God. Some rich people torment poor people because of their wealth. Even in our neighborhood, some rich people have affairs with poor people's wives because they are rich. That goes against God's commandment and worshipping wealth; as a result, they spread HIV-AIDS. We should not trust wealth but believe in God, the Creator of everything.

When the poor, like the IR-VICOBA members, theologize in that way, they develop a second-act grassroots theology. Theology comes from the people, not just from the intellectual enterprise of elite theologians. In Chapter 4 and Chapter 5, I discussed how the IR-VICOBA members put self-empowerment and the empowerment of other poor people in their surroundings into practice. To do that, they hoped to start a market for their products to avoid people who exploit them and to use political leaders in their area to change some of the exploitative actions happening in their context. All of those initiatives intend to ensure that they avoid degradation of humanity in this world heaped upon them by wealthy people. That is how they connect the narratives of the rich man who mistreated Lazarus (Luke 16:19-33) or the rich man who did not want to share his wealth with the poor when Jesus tested him (Mark 10:17-22) with their own social reality.

They want to fight poverty by stopping others from profiting from the efforts of less fortunate people. Business intermediaries believe in money and making a profit without considering the concomitants. In this way, the theology of money-theism is based on the first-act daily experiences of business practices and the war against the injustice of the IR-VICOBA members. In their contextual Bible study, they theologize against money-theism. Their theology is a theology of ethical-praxis. In their societies, the poor IR-VICOBA members are devoted to God and not just to the marvel of creation. They show their devotion by taking their limited resources to serve other poor without making money the foundation of their faith. Nevertheless, they still work hard to strengthen their economy by fighting poverty.

7.6   Salvation Includes Human and Nonhuman Living Beings

7.6.1   Enhancing Life

In Chapter 4 and Chapter 5, I discussed that the IR-VICOBA members referred to the unjust systems in their societies, which cause precarious and perilous situations for the poor. Such poor fail to get even a piece of bread every day and sometimes find themselves in other difficult situations, like contracting diseases, being imprisoned, and having nowhere to stay. In the discussion of the events that lead people to be in perilous situations, one member said,

> The corrupt socioeconomic system is another instance that leads people into precarious situations, like those mentioned in the text. [For example,] people being in prison, becoming a beggar, being naked or hungry, and other adverse situations, because they were under the colonial regime. I am sure some people exploited them even socially.

According to the IR-VICOBA members, the corrupt socioeconomic system does not enhance some people's lives. In fact, it can actually promote death for some people. Being jailed and hungry and living miserable lives is a sign of death. They went on to discuss the situation in their own context. One member said,

> Sometimes these international companies cause many people to be jailed because the government sides with them, trusting that they apply the proper laws and regulations, so that ordinary people, peasants, and town vendors find themselves jailed. They do not know the laws and regulations, and since they are poor, they do not have money to pay for advocates in courts of law. The government and legal institutions trust companies from abroad a lot, and sometimes at the cost of their people because companies from abroad use their money and cause people to be imprisoned.

The IR-VICOBA group also mentioned how judicial systems operated in favor of the rich. One member said, "People who are rich can change justice even in the court by bribing lawyers. The poor are sent to jail even without justice to take part in the court."

This is the social situation the IR-VICOBA members are very well aware of and fight against in their society. Reflected theologically within their Contextual Bible Study, this context represents the second act concept of salvation, which is relevant and useful. People need to be saved from that situation. Moreover, those systems must also be liberated to stop producing more downtrodden people. Responding to that situation, the IR-VICOBA members discussed the situation of characters in the texts whom Jesus was teaching about the Kingdom of God. For example, while discussing the Beatitudes in Matthew and the interpretation of the blessedness, one member said, "The message was a message of liberation from poverty, empowering new knowledge and making them exercise freedom, especially for people who were under the colonial regime." When they argue like that, the IR-VICOBA members are theologizing on the Kingdom of God and the poor. They theologize on how Jesus, who was God and also human, dealt with a situation like the one they experience and fight against, which needs salvation and redemption. As one of them put it, "We should also learn to empower each other to get out of this situation we are facing as poor people. The Word of God should illuminate us more to be empowered economically." For the IR-VICOBA, salvation is a theological second act referring to the acts of God, who confirms empowerment for poor people.

7.7 Conclusion

In this chapter, I have illustrated different theological approaches of the IR-VICOBA members referring to their socioeconomic reality. The IR-VICOBA members theologize about what they do in their first act in their society. The IR-VICOBA theologizes, meaning they put everything they reflect on, commit to, and practice systematically according to the Word of God. Their praxis – their commitments and actions in their societies – is what they reflect on in light of the Word of God. Thus, the second act is also an act of contextualization. The second act reflects the first act and serves to interpret the Bible so that the need for first-act liberation is supported and enhanced through second-act reading and interpretation. As their theological response to what they act and practice, they find a way to continue doing those practices, albeit now well-structured and in light of the Word of God. In this way, they create their unique theology(ies) on those issues they tackle in their Contextual Bible Study. As argued elsewhere, their theology starts from the context and not from the texts.

In this pursuit, the beginning of the Village Community Bank (VICOBA) has been a way forward to fight poverty and other injustices in the situation they experience. Their Bible study is their systematic placing of those reflections and practice, and that is where they measure and weigh whatever they reflect on and do in their lives. They use the Word of God as a yardstick to measure those practices to avoid wrong reflections and practices and continue right reflections and actions.

The IR-VICOBA members, being poor people, do theology from below, practicing a theology of nonpersons as a way of reflecting on what they have already done in their life. They reflect in light of the Word of God on who Jesus is to them, as people surrounded by challenges stemming from poverty. In this perspective, I have found that, during their Bible study, the members meet together to reflect on the theology of love, something they do every day, and the theology of solidarity within their own group and with other poor people who deal with environmental and socioeconomic hardships. This is a 'second-act' theology from below.

A Christological approach to Jesus is another theological reflection by the members of IR-VICOBA. They perceived Jesus as an 'empowerer' and teacher. Reflecting on their own poverty, they perceived Jesus as someone who teaches how people should live in their context and empowers them to do so. Jesus is the one who sides with the poor by liberating them from all unjust socioeconomic structures, as he did during his time in Palestine.

Salvation theology includes human beings, nonhuman beings, and inanimate things. Therefore, the redemption the incarnate Son of God offers includes all human beings and nonhuman living things. Any system that does not enhance the lives of living things should be resisted – and be saved and redeemed.

Chapter 8: Liberation Theology of the IR-VICOBA Members and the Tension Between the First and the Second Act

8.1 IR-VICOBA Members Do Liberation Theology from Below

This project aimed to answer the question: "How do poor Christians in the South-Western part of Tanzania reflect the relations between text and context in their Contextual Bible reading?" It studied the IR-VICOBA members (men and women) who read the Bible together with their pastors. The members are poor people fighting poverty. Moreover, the study investigated the impact of the interpretations of these poor people within their context. The project questions applied are the following: "1. How do the members of the IR-VICOBA groups relate the relationship between the Bible and social reality? 2. What kind of Contextual Bible Study is practised in the IR-VICOBA groups? 3. What are the main topics in their implied theology of the Bible readings?" In this concluding chapter, I first summarize the responses to the three research questions. I then give a concluding response to the project questions, formulated above.

8.1.1 The Relationship Between the Text and the Bible in the IR-VICOBA Groups

In response to the first project question, "How do the members of the IR-VICOBA groups relate the relationship between the Bible and the social reality?," the preceding chapters showed that the IR-VICOBA members allow their social reality to influence their Bible reading. They do not accept Bible readings that do not confirm or relate to their own social reality of poverty. Taking the example of their reflection on Mark 10:17-22 (the rich man Jesus asked to sell all he has and to give the proceeds to the poor), the IR-VICOBA members seriously reputed that Jesus truly wanted this person to become as poor as those in poverty in the society they are living in. One of them said, "Jesus was not against the wealth; he was against the bad character of the rich people for not caring for the needy people, the poor. Jesus wanted people who had been blessed to care for the people who were poor in society." That interpretation, as we saw in Chapter 4, implies that, with reference to their society, Jesus wanted the rich to care for the poor, but he did not intend to make people poor. Taking care and teaching other poor people is what they do as poor people to liberate them from becoming poor again.

During their Contextual Bible Study, the IR-VICOBA members used the Bible as a tool to liberate themselves from the perilous situation of poverty they are facing. Their interpretation was discussed in Chapter 3 to Chapter 5. Regarding texts like Matt 5:3 and Mark 10:21, which show that Jesus said, "Blessed are the poor" or "Go, sell what you own, and give the money to the poor, and you will have treasure in heaven; then come and follow me," the IR-VICOBA asked difficult questions, and in many cases, they repudiated that Jesus had a partial preference to those who were economically underprivileged. Rather, he had another meaning of blessedness to the poor. However, they emphasized Jesus was giving power and hope (empowerment) to the poor in those pericopes.

In their reflections on those texts in general, the IR-VICOBA members came up with themes that reflected on those characters for the selected texts who were in situations of impoverishment, much as they were. First, they viewed Jesus as the main character in those texts. Second, they looked at how Jesus related to the characters in the texts, especially those who were downtrodden because of their precarious situations. The study found that the IR-VICOBA members, and possibly many other poor people in rural Tanzania, do not think that being poor in their context guarantees inheriting the present and future Kingdom of God. However, they viewed Jesus as having a preference for the poor, which put them in a position to serve other people, although they were poor themselves. They saw this position as a response to the Word of God and strived to build the Kingdom of God in the world today. Their praxis in society led them to place great emphasis on liberating themselves and others like them. In this study, having solidarity and caring for the needy exemplify these praxes and connect them with the work of Jesus within society. They are the body of Christ working in society.

The Contextual Bible Study of the IR-VICOBA Groups

The second research question asks, "What kind of Contextual Bible Study is practised in the IR-VICOBA groups?" The study has found that the IR-VICOBA members use the See-Judge-Act method more in the sense of the Latin American theologians than in the tradition of the Ujamaa Centre under Gerald West in South Africa. In the contextual Bible study, they reflect on the Kingdom of God from the perspective of what they act and commit in their lives, their praxis, now in light of the Word of God. In this way, they differ substantially from the Ujamaa, which does not distinguish between the first and second acts in the same way as we have seen in the IR-VICOBA groups. In the Ujamaa, the Bible is the lens through which one understands social reality; for the IR-VICOBA groups, the socioeconomic reality is the lens through which one reads the Bible.

Because of this tendency, the IR-VICOBA also interprets poverty differently from the Sobrino tradition. The IR-VICOBA members know from their own experience that assisting each other to overcome poverty is an important aspect of their daily life. Because of that, they do not, like Sobrino, conclude that poverty is a blessed and sacred situation. The IR-VICOBA groups believe the opposite to be true. When their social experience involves people trying to assist and be in solidarity with one another, the Bible interpretations must also live up to such positions. Poverty is something to resist, so the Bible reading must give sense to this view on poverty. When Jesus says, "Blessed are the poor," that was not taken literally by the IR-VICOBA members, and they did not interpret this to mean that God had preference only for the poor. For them, in many places, the Bible shows that God works with all people who believe and serve him. There are many passages in the Bible that describe how God requires the rich to care for the poor and the downtrodden, for example, Isa 42:5-8 and 1 Tim 6:17-19. These passages require the rich to care for the poor and not to depend on their richness or be selfish. If they care for the needy, then they will be in line with God, the Creator of heaven and Earth, to whom the downtrodden people belong.

Poverty calls for self-liberation and the liberation of others. It involves the responsibility of taking care. One finds this in one of the members of IR-VICOBA's quotation: "Jesus taught us that we have to look out for each other and help each other to become his good followers and inheritors of the Kingdom of God, now and in the last day. [We will be] found to be sheep on the right-hand side of the Son of Man." Another group indicated, "Whatever economic move we are doing is connected to our God, whom we trust to be our source of blessing. Therefore, we should not despise the downtrodden but serve them as a way to serve our God." Because of their experience of bringing people out of poverty, they do not view the poor as bringers of salvation.

The IR-VICOBA members are Protestants, and most of them are Lutherans. Their focus on the responsibility of everyone to share a social life and goods with all people might be a reflection of Lutheran tradition.[1] This is one example of how the context influences the Bible reading among the IR-VICOBA groups. As one member indicated during Bible study, "Love should be shown to everybody, whether young or old, rich or poor, peasant or official worker; everyone needs to be cared for when they need someone to assist them in their needy situation." They practice this in their social life. In their Bible reading, they implement what they resolve from their interpretations.

Conclusively, I want to address their difference with the Ujamaa Centre from South Africa, which does all three stages (see, judge, act) within the Bible study venue. In this study, I have argued that the IR-VICOBA members use the method of

---

[1] This area needs a more research looking on the reading of the IR VICOBA members and the Lutheran tradition, which might be one of the influence of their Bible interpretations of these groups.

see-act-judge like the liberation theologians from Latin America and South Africa. But I have also shown how they differ from them. West places more emphasis on the acts carried out as a result of the Bible reading and makes this process the source of liberation theology of downtrodden people.

The Main Topics of the IR-VICOBA Member' Contextual Bible Study

Reflecting on the third research question, "What are the main topics in their implied theology of the Bible reading?" the study found that the IR-VICOBA members do theology from below. Their theology is a theology of the victims of the unjust socioeconomic system in this world. In Chapter 7, I discussed some theological themes the members do as they read the Bible. The study has found that, as they undertake their Contextual Bible Study, they do a theology of love, a theology of poverty, a theology of solidarity, and a theology of social justice. They also fight against money-theism, and they encourage the practice of soteriology, which includes both human and nonhuman beings.

The IR-VICOBA members perceived that Jesus, who lived in Palestine, was also living among them and still liberates the downtrodden. The decisive point, however, is that this interpretation of Jesus comes out of an interpretation where Jesus supports the liberation struggle the IR-VICOBA already has taken on in their lives.

The IR-VICOBA members refer more to the center of the church's mission. The church must exist for the service of others, by bringing life to many people. This was and is the mission of the incarnate love of God-Jesus. This mission should be seen in society, not only from believers but from all people. It cannot be seen except through the praxis of believers like the IR-VICOBA. One conceives this as they discuss this theology: "Whatever economic moves we make is connected to our God whom we trust to be our source of blessing, and therefore we should not despise the downtrodden but serve them as a means of serving our God." Serving is the mission of the church toward itself and toward others. The IR-VICOBA members indicate that this service has a connection with their God, through Jesus Christ. Serving one's neighbor is a service to one's God.

As the body of Christ, they are called to be Christ-like people to self-liberate and to liberate others who are put down by different socioeconomic injustices within their society. In this study, the IR-VICOBA members want their voices against the socioeconomic injustice within their society to be heard by the world. The IR-VICOBA members, and possibly many other poor people, believe that poverty should be fought, in the global economy, not praised or uplifted as some people of faith do when they misread Biblical texts. In doing so, they greatly emphasize poverty having a connection with the inheritance of the Kingdom of God. In those texts, like Matt. 5:3 and Luke 6:20, which caused ambiguity among readers, the study found that the IR-VICOBA members strongly believe that Jesus has another meaning than praising poverty or letting someone be so poor that they find themselves at ground zero. Their emphasis lies on God being the source of all blessings, so he cannot deprive anybody of from utilising those resources. They gave examples from the Old Testament, where God is referred to as a source of all blessings, like Deut 28:1-14. Moreover, they gave examples of characters from the Bible who were rich and were called friends of God, like Abraham, Isaac, Jacob, Job, David, and Solomon.

The theology of love is another theme reflecting the third research question. The love of Christ is shown in society and not in the Bible study venue. His body (the believers) portrays Jesus, who loves them as they practice love toward the needy in society. This is the incarnate love of Jesus, given through his body in the world, to victims of socioeconomic injustice. According to the IR-VICOBA members, caring for the needy means presenting Jesus closer to the victims. Nevertheless, it becomes better understood when the victims, like the IR-VICOBA members, are involved in bringing Jesus to the needy. Taking care of the downtrodden goes deep into the heart of God, is on the side of God, and is having God on your side.

Reflecting theologically, hearing from the IR-VICOBA members, one can say the transcendent and the immanent meet together through this love of God, which can be shared with the world. First, it brings God very close to both the needy and the rich because all know that God has enshrined them with many gifts, and all of them are called to share. Second, it gives people inner peace since they form a good relationship with God, the Creator of heaven and Earth, who wants them to share their gifts. Third, it makes the world an excellent place to live in when people live in harmony with their neighbors. Fourth, because God calls all to serve him, people can serve God by serving their neighbors, both rich and poor, destroying all class boundaries, status, and hegemonic approaches to fellow human beings. Therefore, people are called to abolish all class thinking and destroy status if they want to be good followers of Christ and want to live in a peaceful world by doing theology of love.

For the IR-VICOBA groups, poverty is a sign of responsibility to the Church of Christ. They aim to become wealthier to emancipate themselves and continue to redeem others with whom they have solidarity within society. This is easily hearkened by the IR-VICOBA members as they discuss how to be closer to other poor people and how to have solidarity with them throughout their difficulties, etc. The poor are ready to work in solidarity with other poor people as a way of responding to difficulties they are experiencing. The IR-VICOBA members accentuate this attitude through their life choices and how they teach others who are more miserable than they are. They see this as a response to their reading of the Bible, which obligates them to participate in God's mission to help the needy in the same way Jesus did and taught. They go further by empowering other people who are poorer, so that they too can be illuminated to see the possibilities for change in their precarious situations.

Therefore, as victims of socioeconomic phenomena themselves, the poor know the proper ways of liberating others. Following their practices is an excellent way for the world to learn about eradicating poverty. The liberation theology of the IR-VICOBA members may be found in praxis as well as in the reflection and practices done in society, here referred to as the first act and well formulated or measured in the Contextual Bible Study venue in light of the Word of God. This is something the IR-VICOBA shares with the classical Latin American theologians.

Text and Context in the IR-VICOBA Groups

While reflecting on the main project question: "How do poor Christians in the South-Western part of Tanzania reflect the relations between text and context in their Contextual Bible reading?" I came to realize that there is a significant change in interpretation. When I started this research, I aimed to investigate how the IR-VICOBA move from the text toward the context. The finding has proved that moving from the text to the context was not the only approach to their interpretation. The IR-VICOBA interpret the Bible texts using their experiences of faith, commitment (which is their daily reflection), and practice (praxis).

In most cases, they read and interpret the texts from the perspective of their own context. In other words, their context informs their interpretation of the texts. They compare the context of the Biblical texts and their own context. In all Biblical texts they read, their interpretation reflects what is happening in their midst, their struggles, commitment, faith, practices, and reflections. The important aspect is that they critically analyze the traditional teachings about the Kingdom of God, emphasizing the coming Kingdom of God and glorifying poverty. Their own interpretations reflect their situation, focusing on the causes, challenges, and responses of a community of believers reflecting in light of the Word of God. They relate their social reality with the realities Jesus, the main character in those pericopes, was confronted with. One sees this specific profile, when the VICOBA position is discussed and compared to the liberation theology of other liberation theologians. These theologians are Per Frostin, who wrote on the liberation theology of Tanzanian *Ujamaa*, Gerald West and the Ujamaa Centre from South Africa, and Gutierrez and Sobrino, the classical liberation theologians. For example, the texts inform the context of Gerald West and Ujamaa Centre as we have seen in Chapter 6: They act after seeing and judging according to the Word of God. For Gutierrez and Sobrino, there are double acts, like the IR-VICOBA, where the see, judge and first act is done first in their context. When they meet in the Bible study, it is reflection according to the Word of God, which is the second act.

The study found that there has been a change in how some rural people, like the IR-VICOBA members, read and interpret the Bible. They read the Bible in a more emancipatory manner, not like they did when they were under Tanzanian *Ujamaa* ideology. I discussed *Ujamaa* ideology as liberation in the Introduction. This understanding has been a stance of Per Frostin in his work on liberation theology in Tanzania and South Africa, who maintained that this *Ujamaa* ideology was an ethic of liberation, emphasizing values essential to the struggle against colonialism and neocolonialism. He chose to call this liberation "the third-world experience" and held that it was the common denominator of various liberation theologies.[2] Other Tanzanian theologians had the same perspective, as I also discussed in the Introduction. Nevertheless, the readings of the IR-VICOBA members show some change in ideology and way of life within the context.

The VICOBA members start from their context and their practices, not from an intellectually conceived ideology. Therefore, the liberation theology of the IR-VICOBA members is quite different from what Per Frostin proposed in the 1980s. For Frostin, *Ujamaa* was a way to do liberation theology. But even if the goal was liberation, the inspiration came from above, from theologians and politicians and their respective writings.[3] In this way, Per Frostin did *Ujamaa* liberation theology from above. Politicians and theologians are the ones who would connect *Ujamaa* ideology and liberation, not the people from below. However, Frostin writes: "As suggested by the analysis of *epistemological ruptura*, the development of African liberation theology will be seen as a process, formed by a dialectic between the experience of the oppressed and intellectual reflection."[4] His research mostly dealt with intellectuals, not with people from below.

Frostin is right in arguing that *Ujamaa* was an Africa Liberation theology that formed between the experience of the oppressed and intellectuals. Nevertheless, this perception of theology of the oppressed and intellectuals is still valid but now in a more structured sense, with the oppressed and intellectuals reading the Bible together and struggling together to fight the poverty they face in society. Like the *Ujamaa* ideology in Tanzania during research done by Frostin, the IR-VICOBA members see their praxis in their society. During the *Ujamaa* ideology, the struggle was carried out by Christians in the villages. These people had no Bible study but applied Bible teachings in their societies, especially on issues concerning love, unity, peace, and struggle. Moreover, in the Ujamaa villages, these Christians

---

2 Frostin, *Liberation Theology in Tanzania and South Africa: A First World Interpretation*, 42, p. 184.
3 This notion can be justified by reading the Acknowledgements in his book, where he mentions different people. Moreover, Frostin mentions Makumira *Ujamaa* of the College members and the Christian community of the *mama wa Mateso* (mother of pain) not referring to their theology but as communities.
4 Frostin, *Liberation Theology in Tanzania and South Africa: A First World Interpretation*, 42, pp. 13–14.

lived with people of other faiths. That is the situation Frostin found while doing research on *Ujamaa* ideology as a liberation theology. This situation made Frostin do his research from above, dealing with politicians and theologians on the issues concerning the oppressed and poor, the fighters of poverty in villages.

The IR-VICOBA people do liberation theology from a position of socioeconomic difficulty because of the liberalization of trade, which is their socioeconomic reality and experience. Further, it is a grassroots theology of poor people – a theology from below. With the exception of a few learned people in their groups, all of the poor IR-VICOBA members perform liberation theology by fighting their shared enemies – poverty and disease – and tackling issues of wealth, business, and the accumulation of wealth.

During *Ujamaa* in Tanzania, the central government controlled everything, even the prices of products. During socialism, they talked about egalitarian ownership and how to liberate themselves as a single unit.

In this new phenomenon called globalization, the poor have other problems; the phenomenon is a source of poverty, ignorance, and diseases, albeit differently than during *Ujamaa*. These problems are possible because people currently live in a country that follows trade liberalization, which has caused their interpretation of Biblical texts to be different than they were during the time of socialism (called *Ujamaa*). Now, they talk much more about freedom for poor peasants who cannot predict the price of their own products. They fight against negative socioeconomic phenomena, which are full of injustice. The rich and the powerful in the world dominate the market and exploit the poor. This is easily perceived if one listens to the IR-VICOBA groups reading the Bible. They discuss the 'interpretation of the victims' of the unjust socioeconomic phenomenon they are facing. When they talk about low prices of the products they grow and make, although it sounds like they are referring only to local issues, the problems actually reflect a bigger picture of injustice across the global economy. Their voice has an implicit echo of injustice within the world today. That is their socioeconomic reality, where they practice their commitment and faith as a community of believers.

These changes have negatively impacted the IR-VICOBA members; however, in most cases, as one hears from their Bible studies, they complain that they are not making enough profit to escape poverty, because many factors hinder them. In their Bible reading, you hear complaints of injustice in business, whether local or global. They try to fight poverty and teach each other ways of liberation. As a community of believers during the Contextual Bible Study, they reflect upon the light of the Word of God and do their theology by reflecting on these difficulties and their daily practices. The IR-VICOBA members perform a theology of love and a theology of solidarity. They do praxis theology of how to liberate themselves and how to liberate other poor people. The Gospel they read together is interpreted in light of their own socioeconomic reality, and they use their practical experiences to interpret the Gospel. The theology of love and the theology of solidarity with the needy, the poor, and the downtrodden is a required practical theology in this socioeconomic reality.

In reflecting on people in impoverished situations, the IR-VICOBA members interpret the texts using their own praxis, experiences, and context: the Tanzanian context. They read the texts by referring to the economic, social, and religious situations they are experiencing.

In the Introduction to this thesis, I referred to Werner Jeanrond and his position on hermeneutics:

> Hermeneutics is more interested in the analysis of the dialectic between the reader and the text and in the effect of this dialectic for the self-understanding of the individual reader or groups of readers. Thus, hermeneutics reflects activities done through language rather than upon the history and grammar of particular historical languages.[5]

The results of the research above make a lot of sense as a follow-up to Jeanrond's position. The Bible study I discovered and interpreted is definitely a dialectic "between the reader and the text and in the effect of this dialectic for the self-understanding of the individual reader or groups of readers." Contextual Bible Study as it takes place in South-Western Tanzania gives a strong prominence to the reader-text relationship. In this way, it is a concrete case of a hermeneutical Bible reading.

Jeanrond's second criterion, however, does not match the practice in the IR-VICOBA: "... hermeneutics reflects activities done through language rather than upon history and grammar of particular historical languages." My thesis is about Contextual Bible Studies and not about hermeneutics in itself. Nevertheless, in conclusion, it is interesting to observe that the hermeneutics of the IR-VICOBA is not necessarily an activity only through "language." Rather, it is a hermeneutics that fundamentally involves the relation between reader and text. At the same time, this relationship also fundamentally develops from the relationship between history, the reader, and the text. It is a relationship negotiated not only in language; it is a relationship deeply influenced by history, the first act. This might be the specific contribution to liberation theology emerging from the IR-VICOBA practices.

Gutierrez and Sobrino, the classical Latin American theologians, take Bible reading or doing theology as a reflection on praxis. That is why, in "A Theology of Liberation," Gutierrez wrote the following:

---

5 Werner G. Jeanrond, *Theological Hermeneutics: Development and Significance* (London: SCM Press, 1994), p. 7.

This book is an attempt at reflection, based on the Gospel and experience of men and women committed to the process of liberation in the oppressed and exploited land of Latin America. It is a theological reflection born of the experience and of shared efforts to abolish the current unjust situation to build a different society, freer and more human.[6]

Reading and theologizing are born of nonpersons, according to Gutierrez, or the crucified, according to Sobrino. Their experience and shared efforts to abolish the current unjust situation to build a different society of men and women include their praxis in their society, which is their first act. Then, when they convene, similar praxis among the IR-VICOBA groups in Tanzania, they do in light of the Word of God as to make a good theology, which is their second act. If we compare this with the quotation from Werner Jeanrond on hermeneutics above, we see they still establish a dialectic between reader, text, and history, which is their first act to come with a good theological interpretation of the text for their understanding, which is their second act.

The Bible reading of West, as I have interpreted in this work, seems to put more emphasis on transformation *after* reading the Bible. It regards very little of the grassroots practices and poor people before coming to the Bible study. One might claim that West belongs more to the text-reader hermeneutics of Jeanrond than history-reader-text hermeneutics. It emphasises the acts only after reading the Word of God. However, it is questionable what West calls "the experience of the poor" means. In my understanding, especially from the knowledge I have acquired from Gutierrez and Sobrino, together with the IR-VICOBA members, the experience includes the faith, commitment, and practices of the poor people even before coming to the Bible study. Liberation occurs in the context either before the Bible study, which some like Sobrino and Gutierrez calls the first act, and after the Bible study, which is the second act. Regarding liberation only after reading the Bible would undermine the power, faith, and commitment of the poor in liberation theology.

8.2 From Local Perspective Liberation Theology to the Broad Perspective

The study indicates that Contextual Bible Study is one of the best ways to read the Bible since all members participate in doing theology – a theology of the people – and interpreting the Bible, even though they are not rich in theological education.

---

6 Gustavo Gutierrez, *A Theology of Liberation: History, Politics and Salvation* (London: SCM Press, 1994), p. ix.

Their richness lies in their daily contextual experience, which is enough to make changes within African Bible reading. The ELCT and other churches should adapt this approach to reading Biblical texts and encourage their members to use it to better the entire church.

I argue this way because the Church built in Contextual Bible Study, reflected in this study, is one that makes arises in solidarity because it is formatted by the expectations of justice developed in the IR-VICOBA members' own experiences. It is a church built in love, solidarity, and unity, aiming at fully self-liberating the economically, socially, and politically underprivileged people. When the learned theologians and the underprivileged meet together in Bible study, they formulate a very powerful theology from below, where both have many things to learn from each other. The church built in that unity has a powerful impact on society. Their service also in society illuminates the whole of society. The ecclesiology made in contextual Bible study, this community of believers who live Christ-like lives, makes the Kingdom of God visible in society. Their praxis makes the Kingdom of God which rises up against the injustices within their society. Moreover, the theology that liberates the entire society in their Contextual Bible Study is more reflected and well put.

Contextual Bible Study increases the opportunities to make decisions, since many people can now be involved in issues that arise within society and which are contemplated during the Contextual Bible Study. Different challenges can also be discussed within the Bible study and attain resolution, the second acts.

The findings of this study show that the Bible is a liberating tool (though I am aware that it can also be used as an enslaving tool) that has been used to empower and make heard the voice of economically underprivileged people. Implicitly, harkening to the voice of the IR-VICOBA members, one recognises that learned theologians have somehow enslaved lay people through their Bible interpretation. Although their presence is significant, I think the lay Christians are still being silenced on many issues concerning Biblical interpretation. Therefore, when they are given an opportunity and power to interpret, one hears their voice and how they want to liberate themselves and others from that cage in which the learned theologians haves confined them. Contextual Bible Study is the right way to make theologians learn more from lay Christians than using only the tools they have learned in universities, seminaries, and theological colleges.

The practice in the IR-VICOBA groups of contributing money by buying shares, which is part of the VICOBA, is another way of empowering the poor. I think the practice works well because it curbs the problem of poverty and makes members more active as they discuss their commitment and faith while having a way forward toward building up capital for small economic projects and social liberation. The church and society should make more effort to use this method of building capital to make liberation a praxis and not mere words. As a means of supporting the economically underprivileged to gain capital empowers them, and for more liberation, this method self-economically empowers them since they do not rely on anyone to give them the capital but contribute enough capital, some of which they can then borrow. Having the economic ability to borrow from the group makes economically underprivileged people also socially free: They do not need to depend on the banking system or rich people to borrow money. That is their liberation.

Contextual Bible Study should be given more room in theological universities and colleges. Theologians should be equipped to move away from the old methods of preaching and teaching, rendering theologians the only Bible experts. Contextual Bible Study empowers other people to participate in doing theology from below. The learned theologians become 'participant facilitators' rather than experts, which means they do not use, as Freire calls it, "the banking concept of education" so commonly used in most churches and educational institutions, an inheritance from the colonial era. By doing that, the church equips lay Christians to stand on real teachings and fight with some difficult traditions emerging from the Bible or church traditions. Contextual Bible Study is the right way to 'reconceive' theologies that are outdated in more participatory ways.

Contextual Bible Study can also be the right way to solve social issues like gender inequality and youth problems, which have their foundation in African traditions. Moreover, it can help to find solutions to challenging issues like unemployment, simple economics, planning, and other spiritual and religious issues. For example, when the IR-VICOBA members discussed decision-making within the family, they indicated that most families have problems because men think they own everything, while women are the most significant producers of assets within those families. Interestingly, the IR-VICOBA members include both men and women in their discussion, such that the issues are solved easily compared to the banking concept of educational teaching done by some activities, theologians, and politicians, which produce fights. Contextual Bible Study serves as another criticism of the romantic inculturation hermeneutics, which does not interfere with some traditions, especially those that undermine the role of women in the African context.

In their Bible study, the IR-VICOBA members mentioned the issue of changing unjust phenomena so that they could also benefit from their own hard work. However, they reflect more on local matters, without knowing that these matters actually belong to an economic phenomenon called the global economy. There is a need for much change in this regard, especially if people want to change the lives of other poor people or reduce poverty.

As a way forward, empowering the poor and developing countries worldwide is very important if we are to obtain a humanized and just world. The world needs to empower peasants so that they can increase the value of their own products. For instance, in the Rungwe District, where I did my research, coffee, cocoa, tea, avocados, bananas, and other crops are all produced, as I discussed in Chapters 3–5.

From the time they started growing those crops, they have only sold their products raw, whereas it would be better if they could start factories to produce chocolate, juices from different fruits, banana crisps, etc. Surprisingly, there are some peasants in that area who grow cocoa yet do not know what chocolate looks like or how it tastes: If you ask them about chocolate, they ask "What is that?" To empower these peasants, the rich and the governments would need to assist them in increasing the value of their products, which will have a significant 'multiplying effect.' As a result, it would increase their income. Therefore, increasing the value of the product empowers the poor in the world they are living in.

Such increased income would stimulate their economy and give them social relief. Moreover, some people within the area would work in the factories, which would increase the disposable income of many. Many others could generate a good income from that multiplying effect. The prices of their bananas, or other fruits like avocados and mangoes and cereals, would increase since the disposable income would increase. The churches would have more people to support their functions and performance in public.

In their Contextual Bible Study, the IR-VICOBA members also discussed the issue of people becoming poor because of environmental problems, like people cutting down trees and destroying the environment. Many find themselves facing a situation of poverty because Mother Nature cannot produce favorable conditions for agriculture and for enhancing the lives of other organisms. The IR-VICOBA members interpreted the texts and responded to the question, "What causes people to be poor in their context?" They reflected on the nearby village of Ilima, which sometimes fails to have any rainfall, leaving the villagers to live miserable lives of poverty. The Tanzanian government needs to become serious about the issue of environmental conservation since the village mentioned by the IR-VICOBA members lies in Rungwe District, among the dense, wet districts of Tanzania. If deforestation can cause all those problems, then it is a problem that the government should be worried about. The government should work on sustaining the environment like encouraging people to use gas and other energy alternatives and discouraging charcoal use.

The IR-VICOBA members must use a lot of effort when they teach the other IR-VICOBA groups near them. Their teaching can make significant changes that might help solve the repercussions of environmental degradation. Since the IR-VICOBA members fight poverty to the best of their ability, it is possible to see that environmental knowledge has many advantages by teaching people to stop destroying their natural environment. This knowledge plays a major role in their lives and is of greater importance than teaching simple economies. This is a challenge posed by the IR-VICOBA members to society and the local government.

Moreover, the issue of ecology is a global issue. In the globalised world, global organizations should work with the local government to ensure that they raise awareness and incentivize local people, like the people of Ilima, to plant more trees. The planting of trees would help not only with the local climate but also with the issue of global warming, which local people like the IR-VICOBA members know very little about.

8.3　A Call for Further Research

I call for other researchers to research how the Bible can be used as a tool for liberating the downtrodden and as a contextual method of doing theology from below. This empirical research should involve people at the grassroots level to enable their experiencing real life; a true reading of the Bible can be of much benefit. Many areas can be researched at the grassroots level, for instance, issues concerning Christians and politics, economy, social life, justice, love, discrimination of all kinds, gender inequality, and other bad traditions. Although these issues are broadly discussed in this dissertation, researchers can still go deeper into these subjects.

Bibliography

Akper, Godwin. "The Person of Jesus Christ in Contemporary African Christological Discourse." *Religion and Theology* 14, no. 3-4 (2007): 224-43.

Appiah-Kubi, Kofi, and Sergio Torres. *African Theology En Route: Papers from the Pan-African Conference of Third World Theologians, December 17-23, 1977, Accra, Ghana.* Maryknoll, NY: Orbis Books, 1979.

Bandara, Lars Osberg and Amarakoon. "Why Poverty Remains High in Tanzania: and What to Do About It?" *REPOA Special Paper*, January 2011-2012.

Barker, Margaret. *Creation: A Biblical Vision for the Environment.* London: T & T Clark, 2010.

Beghela, Philemon. "'Rethinking African Theology: Exploring the God Who Liberates' by Jean-Marc Ela." *Studia Historiae Ecclesiasticae* 38, no. suppl 1 (2012): 1-9.

Bevans, Stephen B. *Models of Contextual Theology.* Faith and Cultures Series. Rev. and expanded ed. Maryknoll, NY: Orbis, 2002.

Bevans, Stephen B., and Katalina Tahaafe-Williams. *Contextual Theology for the Twenty-First Century.* Cambridge: James Clarke, 2012.

Birch, Charles. "Christian Obligation for the Liberation of Nature." In *Liberating Life: Contemporary Approaches to Ecological Theology.* Maryknoll, NY: Orbis Books, 1990.

Boettcher, Reinhard. *The Diaconal Ministry in the Mission of the Church.* Lwf Studies. Vol. 2006:1, Geneva: Lutheran World Federation, Department for Theology and Studies, 2006.

Boff, Leonardo, Clodovis Boff, and Paul Burns. *Introducing Liberation Theology.* Como Fazer Teologia Da Libertaçao. Vol. 1, Tunbridge Wells, Kent: Burns & Oates, 1987.

Brown, Robert McAfee. *Gustavo Gutiérrez: An Introduction to Liberation Theology.* Maryknoll, NY: Orbis Books, 1990.

Bujo, Bénézet. *African Theology in Its Social Context.* Afrikanische Theologie in Ihrem Gesellschaftlichen Kontext. Maryknoll, NY: Orbis Books, 1992.

Cadorette, Curt. *From the Heart of the People: The Theology of Gustavo Gutiérrez.* Oak Park, IL: Meyer Stone Books, 1988.

Chavez, Christina. "Conceptualizing from the Inside: Advantages, Complications, and Demands on Insider Positionality." *Qualitative Report* 13, no. 3 (2008): 474-94.

Creswell, John W. and Cheryl N. Poth. *Qualitative Inquiry & Research Design: Choosing among Five Approaches.* Qualitative Inquiry and Research Design. 4th ed., International Student Ed. Thousand Oaks, CA: Sage, 2018.

Davidson, Christina. "Transcription: Imperatives for Qualitative Research." *International Journal of Qualitative Methods* 8, no. 2 (2009): 35-52.

Dickson, Kwesi A. *Theology in Africa.* Maryknoll, NY: Orbis, 1984.

Draper, J. A. "African Contextual Hermeneutics: Readers, Reading Communities, and Their Options between Text and Context." 3–22, 2015.

Dutt, A., and S. Grabe. "Gender Ideology and Social Transformation: Using Mixed Methods to Explore Processes of Ideological Change and the Promotion of Women's Human Rights in Tanzania." *Sex Roles* 77, no. 5–6 (2017): 309–24.

Engelke, Matthew. *A Problem of Presence: Beyond Scripture in an African Church*. The Anthropology of Christianity. Vol. 2, Berkeley, CA: University of California Press, 2007.

Engelke, Matthew. "Text and Performance in an African Church: The Book, 'Live and Direct.'" *American Ethnologist* 31, no. 1 (2004): 76–91.

Freire, Paulo. *Pedagogy of Commitment*. Series in Critical Narrative. Boulder, CO: Paradigm Publ., 2014.

Freire, Paulo. *Pedagogy of the Oppressed*. Pedagogia Del Oprimido. New rev. 20th-anniversary ed. NY: Continuum, 1993.

Freire, Paulo, and Ira Shor. *A Pedagogy for Liberation: Dialogues on Transforming Education*. London: Macmillan, 1987.

Frostin, Per. *Liberation Theology in Tanzania and South Africa: A First World Interpretation*. Studia Theologica Lundensia. Vol. 42, Lund: Lund University Press, 1988.

García, José Luis Sánchez. "Sustainability as an Innovative Key Element, Another Perspective to Rethink the Problem of Hunger and Poverty in the World." *Journal of Innovation & Knowledge* 3, no. 2 (2018): 59–60.

Gibellini, Rosino. *Paths of African Theology*. Percorsi Di Teologia Africana. London: SCM Press, 1994.

Groody, Daniel G. *Globalization, Spirituality, and Justice: Navigating the Path to Peace*. Theology in Global Perspective Series. Maryknoll, NY: Orbis Books, 2007.

Gutiérrez, Gustavo. *The Power of the Poor in History: Selected Writings*. Fuerza Histórica De Los Pobres. London: SCM Press, 1983.

Gutiérrez, Gustavo. *A Theology of Liberation: History, Politics, and Salvation*. Teología De La Liberación. Revised version. ed. London: SCM Press, 1988.

Gutiérrez, Gustavo. *The Truth Shall Make You Free: Confrontations*. Verdad Los Hará Libres. Maryknoll, NY: Orbis Books, 1990.

Gutiérrez, Gustavo, Caridad Inda, and John Eagleson. *A Theology of Liberation: History, Politics and Salvation*. Teologia De La Liberacion, Perspectivas. London: SCM Press, 1974.

Gutiérrez, Gustavo, Robert A. Krieg, James B. Nickoloff, and Gerhard Ludwig Müller. *On the Side of the Poor: The Theology of Liberation*. An Der Seite Der Armen. Maryknoll, NY: Orbis Books, 2015.

Gutierrez, Judith, and Judith Condor. *The Task and Content of Liberation Theology*. 2007. doi: 10.1017/CCOL0521868831.002

Hasu, Päivi. "World Bank & Heavenly Bank in Poverty & Prosperity: The Case of Tanzanian Faith Gospel 1." *Review of African Political Economy* 33, no. 110 (2006): 679–92.

Hatcher, Karen M. "In Gold We Trust: The Parable of the Rich Man and Lazarus (Luke 16:19–31)." *Review & Expositor* 109, no. 2 (2012): 277–83.

Hennelly, Alfred T. *Liberation Theology: A Documentary History.* Maryknoll, NY: Orbis Books, 1990.

Hewitt, Marsha Aileen. *From Theology to Social Theory: Juan Luis Segundo and the Theology of Liberation.* American University Studies. Series 7, Theology and Religion. Vol. 73, NY: P. Lang, 1990.

Hoel, Nina. "Embodying the Field: A Researcher's Reflections on Power Dynamics, Positionality and the Nature of Research Relationships." *Fieldwork in Religion* 8, no. 1 (2013): 27–49.

Holladay, Carl R. *The Beatitudes: Happiness and the Kingdom of God.* 2013. doi: 10.1093/acprof:oso/9780199795734.003.0006

Jeanrond, Werner G. *Theological Hermeneutics: Development and Significance.* London: SCM Press, 1994.

Justin, Sands. "Introducing Cardinal Cardijn's See–Judge–Act as an Interdisciplinary Method to Move Theory into Practice." *Religions* 9, no. 4 (2018): 129.

Kamndaya, Samuel. "Why Tanzania Banks Now Banking on Personal Loans for Profit." *The Citizens*, 29 May 2018.

Kanyoro, Musimbi. "Reading the Bible from an African Perspective." *Ecumenical Review* 51, no. 1 (1999): 18–24.

Kanyoro, Rachel Angogo. *Introducing Feminist Cultural Hermeneutics.* Cleveland, OH: Pilgrim Press, 2002.

Kitunga, Demere, and Marjorie Mbilinyi. "Rooting Transformative Feminist Struggles in Tanzania at Grassroots." *Review of African Political Economy* 36, no. 121 (2009): 433–41.

Kusini, Kanisa la Kiinjili la Kilutheri Tanzania-Ukanda wa. *Karne Ya Kwanza Ya Injili (1891–1991).* Dar Es Salaam: Dar es salaam University Press, 1991.

Luther, Martin, and John Nicholas Lenker. *Luther's Large Catechism: God's Call to Repentance, Faith and Prayer, the Bible Plan of Salvation Explained.* Minneapolis, MN: The Luther Press, 1908.

Magezi, Christopher, and Jacob T. Igba. "African Theology and African Christology: Difficulty and Complexity in Contemporary Definitions and Methodological Frameworks (Original Research, Essay)." *HTS Teologiese Studies* 74, no. 1 (2018): 1.

Mbiti, John S. *Bible and Theology in African Christianity.* Nairobi: Oxford University Press, 1986.

Mbiti, John S. *Introduction to African Religion.* London: Heinemann, 1975.

Meilaender, Gilbert. "The Decalogue as the Law of Christ (Essay)." *Pro Ecclesia: A Journal of Catholic and Evangelical Theology* 27, no. 3 (2018): 338.

Messerschmidt, Donald A. *Anthropologists at Home in North America: Methods and Issues in the Study of One's Own Society.* Cambridge: Cambridge University Press, 1981.

Mligo, Elia Shabani. "Jesus and the Stigmatized: Reading the Gospel of John in a Context of HIV/AIDS-Related Stigmatization in Tanzania." 2009.

Moxnes, Halvor. *The Economy of the Kingdom: Social Conflict and Economic Relations in Luke's Gospel.* Overtures to Biblical Theology. Philadelphia: Fortress Press, 1988.

Mugambi, J. N. K., and Laurenti Magesa. *Jesus in African Christianity: Experimentation and Diversity in African Christology.* Nairobi: Initiatives Publishers, 1989.

Munga, Stephen I. "Beyond the Controversy: A Study of African Theologies of Inculturation and Liberation." Lund University Press, 1998.

Niwagila, Wilson. *From the Catacomb to Self-Governing Church: A Case Study of the African Initiative and Participation of the Foreign Missions in the History of the Northwestern Diocese of the Evangelical Lutheran Church in Tanzania 1890–1965.* Hamburg: Verlag an der Lottbek 1991.

Njinga, Meshack Edward. *The Shift from Ujamaa to Globalization as a Challenge to Evangelical Lutheran Church in Tanzania.* 1 vol. Oslo: Theology Faculty, 2003.

Nyamiti, Charles. "African Christologies Today." In *Faces of Jesus in Africa*, edited by Robert J. Schreiter, 3–23. Maryknoll Orbis, 1998.

Nyengele, Mpyana Fulgence. *African Women's Theology, Gender Relations, and Family Systems Theory: Pastoral Theological Considerations and Guidelines for Care and Counseling.* American University Studies. Series 7, Theology and Religion. Vol. 229, NY: Peter Lang, 2004.

Nyerere, Julius K. *Education for Self-Reliance.* Dar es Salaam, Nairobi, London, NY: Oxford University Press, 1968.

Nyerere, Julius K. *Freedom and Socialism = Uhuru Na Ujamaa: A Selection from Writings and Speeches 1965–1967.* Eastern Africa. Dar es Salaam: Oxford University Press, 1968.

Nyerere, Julius K. *Ujamaa: Essays on Socialism.* Ujamaa. London: Oxford University Press, 1968.

Oduyoye, Mercy Amba. *Introducing African Women's Theology.* Introductions in Feminist Theology. Vol. 6, Sheffield: Sheffield Academic Press, 2001.

Parratt, John. *A Reader in African Christian Theology.* Spck International Study Guide. Rev. ed. Vol. 23, London: SPCK, 1997.

Peter A. S.Kijanga. *Ujamaa and the Role of the Church in Tanzania.* Arusha: Evangelical Lutheran Church in Tanzania, 1978.

Peters, Pam. "The Cambridge Dictionary of English Grammar." viii, 391: CUP, 2013.

Pilario, Daniel Franklin. *Globalization and the Church of the Poor.* Concilium. Vol. 2015/3, London: SCM Press, 2015.

Schimdt, Heinz. "Empowering Education: A Diaconal Response T Poverty." *Diaconia* 2, no. 1 (2011): 50–65.

Schreiter, Robert J. *Faces of Jesus in Africa.* Faith and Cultures Series. Maryknoll, NY: Orbis Books, 1991.

Scott, James C. *Domination and the Arts of Resistance: Hidden Transcripts.* New Haven: Yale University Press, 1990.

Shivji, Issa G., and Tanzania. *Report of the Presidential Commission of Inquiry into Land Matters: 1: Land Policy and Land Tenure Structure.* Vol. 1, Uppsala: Published by The Ministry of Lands, Housing and Urban Development, Government of the United Republic of Tanzania in cooperation with The Scandinavian Institute of African Studies, Uppsala, 1994.

Silverman, David. *Qualitative Research*. 4th ed. Los Angeles, CA: Sage, 2016.

Sobrino, Jon. *Jesus the Liberator: A Historical-Theological Reading of Jesus of Nazareth*. Jesucristo Liberador. Maryknoll, NY: Orbis Books, 1993.

Sobrino, Jon. *No Salvation Outside the Poor: Prophetic-Utopian Essays*. Maryknoll, NY: Orbis Books, 2008.

Sobrino, Jon. *The Principle of Mercy: Taking the Crucified People from the Cross*. Principio-Misercordia. Maryknoll, NY: Orbis Books, 1994.

Stake, Robert E. *Qualitative Research: Studying How Things Work*. NY: Guilford Press, 2010.

Stausberg, Michael, and Steven Engler. *The Routledge Handbook of Research Methods in the Study of Religion*. London/NY: Routledge, 2011.

Stausberg, Michael, and Steven Engler. *The Routledge Handbook of Research Methods in the Study of Religion*. Handbook of Research Methods in the Study of Religion. London: Routledge, 2011.

Stiglitz, Joseph E. *Globalization and Its Discontents*. NY: W.W. Norton & Co., 2002.

Stinton, Diane B. *Jesus of Africa: Voices of Contemporary African Christology*. Faith and Cultures Series. Maryknoll, NY: Orbis Books, 2004.

Stålsett, Sturla J. *The Crucified and the Crucified: A Study in the Liberation Christology of Jon Sobrino*. Bern: Peter Lang, 2003.

Stålsett, Sturla J. *The Crucified and the Crucified: A Study in the Liberation Christology of Jon Sobrino*. Universitetet i Oslo, 1997.

Tanzania, Kanisa La Kiinjili la Kilutheri. *Ibada Za Nyumba Kwa Nyumba*. Moshi: Moshi Pulishing Press, 2017.

Tanzania, Kanisa La Kiinjili la Kilutheri. *Nyumba Kwa Nyumba: Mwongozo Wa Masomo Ya Ibada, 2015*. Moshi: Moshi Printing Press, 2015.

Torres, Sergio, and Virginia Fabella. *The Emergent Gospel: Theology from the Underside of History: Papers from the Ecumenical Dialogue of Third World Theologians, Dar Es Salaam, August 5–12, 1976*. Maryknoll, NY: Orbis Books, 1978.

Wanamaker, Charles A. "Jesus the Ancestor: Reading the Story of Jesus from an African Christian Perspective." *Scriptura* 62, no. 0 (2012): 281.

Weber, Max, and Anthony Giddens. *The Protestant Ethic and the Spirit of Capitalism*. Die Protestantische Ethik und der Geist des Kapitalismus. London: Routledge, 1992.

West, Gerald. "Locating Contextual Bible Study within Praxis." *Diaconia* 4, no. 1 (2013): 43–48.

West, Gerald. "Reading the Bible with the Marginalised: The Value/s of Contextual Bible Reading." *Stellenbosch Theological Journal* 1, no. 2 (2015): 235–61.

West, Gerald. "Tracing the Kairos Trajectory from South Africa (1985) to Palestine (2009), Discerning Continuities and Differences." *Journal of Theology for Southern African*, no. 143 (2012): 4–22.

West, Gerald O. *The Academy of the Poor: Towards a Dialogical Reading of the Bible.* Interventions. Vol. 2, Sheffield: Sheffield Academic Press, 1999.

West, Gerald O. *Biblical Hermeneutics of Liberation: Modes of Reading the Bible in the South African Context.* Cluster Monograph Series. Vol. 1, Pietermaritzburg: Cluster, 1991.

West, Gerald O. *Contextual Bible Study.* Pietermarizburg: Cluster Publication, 1993.

West, Gerald O. "Locating 'Contextual Bible Study' within Biblical Liberation Hermeneutics and Intercultural Biblical Hermeneutics: Original Research." 70, no. 1 (2014): 275–10.

West, Gerald O. *Reading Other-Wise: Socially Engaged Biblical Scholars Reading with Their Local Communities.* Semeia Studies. Vol. 62, Leiden: Brill, 2007.

West, Gerald O. *The Stolen Bible: From Tool of Imperialism to African Icon.* Biblical Interpretation Series. Vol. volume 144, Leiden: Brill, 2016.

Westlund, David. *Ujamaa Na Dini: A Study of Some Aspects of Society and Religion in Tanzania.* Stockholm: University of Stockholm, 1980.

Wilfred, Felix, and Jon Sobrino. *Globalization and Its Victims.* Concilium. Vol. 2001/5, London: SCM Press, 2001.

Appendices

Appendices

Appendix 1: Letter from NSD

Meshack Edward Njinga
Det teologiske fakultet
Universitetet i Oslo Postboks 1023 Blindern
0315 OSLO

Vår dato: 15.11.2016   Vår ref: 50611 / 3 / STM   Deres dato: Deres ref:
TILBAKEMELDING PÅ MELDING OM BEHANDLING AV
PERSONOPPLYSNINGER
Vi viser til melding om behandling av personopplysninger, mottatt 17.10.2016. Meldingen gjelder prosjektet:

50611	*The Kingdom of God and the Poor: An Investigation of the Impacts of Globalization to Poor Christians in the Tanzania*
Behandlingsansvarlig	Universitetet i Oslo, ved institusjonens øverste leder Daglig ansvarlig
	Meshack Edward Njinga

Personvernombudet har vurdert prosjektet, og finner at behandlingen av personopplysninger vil være regulert av § 7-27 i personopplysningsforskriften. Personvernombudet tilrår at prosjektet gjennomføres.

Personvernombudets tilråding forutsetter at prosjektet gjennomføres i tråd med opplysningene gitt i meldeskjemaet, korrespondanse med ombudet, ombudets kommentarer samt personopplysningsloven og helseregisterloven med forskrifter. Behandlingen av personopplysninger kan settes i gang.

Det gjøres oppmerksom på at det skal gis ny melding dersom behandlingen endres i forhold til de opplysninger som ligger til grunn for personvernombudets vurdering. Endringsmeldinger gis via et eget skjema, http://www.nsd.uib.no/personvern/meldeplikt/skjema.html. Det skal også gis melding etter tre år dersom prosjektet fortsatt pågår. Meldinger skal skje skriftlig til ombudet.

Personvernombudet har lagt ut opplysninger om prosjektet i en offentlig database, http://pvo.nsd.no/prosjekt.

Personvernombudet vil ved prosjektets avslutning, 15.12.2019, rette en henvendelse angående status for behandlingen av personopplysninger.

Vennlig hilsen

Kjersti Haugstvedt
Siri Tenden Myklebust

Kontaktperson: Siri Tenden Myklebust tlf: 55 58 22 68 Vedlegg: Prosjektvurdering

Personvernombudet for forskning
Prosjektvurdering – Kommentar

Prosjektnr: 50611

The Data Protection Official presupposes that the research is conducted in line with laws and ethical guidelines in Tanzania.

PURPOSE
This study aims at investigating the impacts of globalization on poor Christians in the third world. This study focuses mainly on how the teaching of the Kingdom of God and the poor relates to globalization in the context of the third world compared to the destitution globalization leaves to these people of third world regardless of the claim made by its perpetrators that it provides many opportunities.

SAMPLE
The sample consists of members from the IR-VICOBA Bible study groups, gatekeepers from each group, and church leaders.

For information about research on vulnerable groups, please see: https://www.etikkom.no/en/library/topics/research-on-particular-groups/vulnerable-groups/

RECRUITMENT
The sample will be recruited through the group leaders. The Data Protection Official presupposes that the recruitment process is conducted in a manner that fulfils the requirement of voluntarily participation and confidentiality.

INFORMATION AND CONSENT

We presuppose that information is given to the participants in a language they fully understand. The participants receive written information about the project, and give written consent. The information letter is somewhat incomplete, and we ask that the following changes are made:

- The date the project is scheduled to be completed is 15.12.2019.
- The following information must be revised: "Also, after all work has been done, the voice recorder will be kept by the University's Research Office that will in due course destroy the recordings as stipulated by the laws of research ethics of the Norwegian state." Instead you can write that all voice recordings will be deleted, and all other personal information will be anonymi or deleted, when the project ends.
- We ask that the revised information letter is sent to The Data Protection Official for Research before distribution, personvernombudet@nsd.no

METHODS

The data material is collected through personal interviews as well as observation during the Bible study group.

Appendix 2: The Consent Form of the IR-VICOBA Groups

University of Oslo, Faculty of Theology
Informed Consent Form
I bring you greetings from the Faculty of Theology in the University of Oslo and most especially from my supervisors and myself.

I am a Tanzanian and a Ph.D. student in the above-mentioned institution currently doing my fieldwork in the Mbeya region in Rungwe District to IR-VICOBA Bible study groups. My supervisors and I want to thank you for accepting to be part of this project as a Tanzanian Christian/pastor/church leader who directly or indirectly faces the impacts of globalization. This study concentrates on how the Kingdom of God teachings affect the poor and relate to Bible readings in the context of third-world countries like Tanzania. The information you are about to share in this study remains very useful and valued in the development of this project and most especially for the contextualization of theological reflections with the grassroots people.

Confidentiality and Ethical Issues in the Interview/Bible Study
Dear participant(s), all the information you will share with me during this interview/Bible study will be kept confidential by the researcher and my supervisors, who will then read your verbatim reports after I have transcribed them. Each Bible study takes an hour every time we meet, and it meets every day you meet for VICOBA session. Only one session a month is scheduled for research, and all other Bible studies continue as you are used to convening every week.

The audio recordings of your Bible study are kept only for this research. The information I record forms part of my academic publications and presentations of your Bible-reading experience. Also, the voice recordings will be deleted, and all other personal information will be anonymised or deleted, when the project ends as stipulated by the laws of research ethics of the Norwegian state. This will mean that no other person has access to your information or can otherwise make use of it.

This research is not a provision of any economic empowerment project. However, during the Bible study, many economic questions may appear that may be a way forward to eradicate poverty. However, my supervisors and I believe that this research will make an important contribution in examining the relationship between the Church and the Kingdom of God and the poor in Tanzania and in other third-world countries.

Please, if there are any portions of this form you do not understand, let me know, and I will explain them again before you sign this form.

- I Mr./Mrs./Rev. ……………………………………………………….have read this form, and I am willing to participate in this project.

- I have been informed by the researcher (Meshack Edward Njinga) about the nature, conduct benefits, and risks involved in this project.

- I give my permission to attend the Bible study and use an audio recorder/mobile phone.

- I have understood after reading the form that the information I give will be processed anonymously in academic publications and presentations.

- I have the right at any stage of the interview to withdraw without prejudice.

- I have had enough opportunity to ask questions for clarification, without pressure from any person to accept being a participant of this study.

- Below is my signature as evidence my willingness to participate in the project described above.

Signature of participant and first name ………………………… Date …………..

As the researcher, I have contacted these participants and discussed the purpose of the study. It is my evaluation that the participants have understood all that is involved in their participating in a research of this magnitude and have offered their consent to take part in the study.

Name and signature of person obtaining consent ……………….. Date ……………

Index

A

African Christianity   48, 63, 65, 197
African context   48, 49, 95, 148, 181, 196, 222
African cultures   196, 197
African theology   196, 199
agribusiness   159

B

Beatitudes   26, 61, 62, 76, 78, 79, 85, 87, 88, 90, 94, 96–98, 128–132, 140, 150, 152, 153, 162, 179, 181, 185, 187, 197–199, 201, 205, 209
Bible as a tool for liberation   50

C

Campesinos   41, 43–46
charismatic groups   88, 95, 130, 144, 145
Christological reflections   198
Christology   16, 31, 33–35, 39, 196, 197, 199
Church Theology   50
classical Latin American liberation theologians   37, 174
colonial type of Bible study   51
Commandments   99–101, 120, 125, 137–139, 180, 203
commitment   23, 30, 31, 38, 39, 50, 51, 53, 74, 124, 133, 155, 164, 166, 173, 175, 193, 197, 216, 218, 220, 221
communal   32, 50, 51, 80, 165
Communal life   164
community sharing   42
concept of salvation   209
contextual assessment   101, 139

Contextual Bible Study   7, 15–18, 20, 29, 38, 47–58, 61–65, 71, 74, 76, 78, 79, 83, 85, 104, 108, 119–121, 123–125, 132, 133, 155, 157, 158, 160, 161, 163, 169–176, 179, 181, 184, 186, 187, 189, 191, 194, 195, 197–199, 201, 202, 204, 205, 209–212, 214, 216, 218–223, 229
contextual Bible study   17, 43, 47, 49, 50, 53, 193, 208, 212, 221
critical   6, 30–32, 36–40, 47, 51–55, 58, 59, 62, 64, 65, 77, 87, 169, 171, 174, 187, 193
Critical reflection   172
critical reflection on praxis   30

D

Decalogue   100, 137–139
degradation of humanity   208
diaconia   119, 189–192
disposable income   167, 223
domination   135, 162, 179
downtrodden   33, 35, 48, 63, 64, 87, 91, 96, 104, 115, 124, 127, 128, 130–132, 135, 137, 142, 159, 161, 163, 174, 176, 190, 202, 209, 212–215, 219, 224

E

elder brother   96, 184, 196
emancipated   135, 136
empowerment   15, 18, 53, 62, 79, 118, 130, 137, 157–159, 161, 176, 186, 192, 195, 199–201, 208, 209, 212, 236
environmental degradation   150, 151, 188, 189, 192, 223
Ernesto Cardenal   16
exploitation   22, 23, 36, 92, 94, 120, 135, 139–141, 162, 179

F

facilitator   19, 26, 53, 54, 61, 77–79, 87–90, 108, 180
familyhood   22, 48
future Kingdom of God   101, 119, 198

G

gender inequality   146, 176, 181, 185, 186, 222, 224
Gerald West   16, 29, 30, 47, 48, 50–54, 56, 62, 78, 171–173, 212, 216
globalization   143, 153, 154, 164, 188, 218, 234, 236
Gustavo Gutierrez   16, 23, 29, 35, 36, 40, 220

H

hidden transcript   154

I

inculturation   196, 222
intellectual Bible-reading   170
IR-VICOBA   6, 7, 15–21, 29, 33, 42, 46, 47, 54–66, 68–79, 81, 83–121, 123–155, 157–171, 173–181, 183–202, 204–224, 234, 236

J

Jon Sobrino   16, 29–31, 33–35, 37, 39, 127, 143, 164, 202

K

Kairos Document   50
Kingdom of God   7, 17, 26, 34, 35, 43, 44, 49, 56, 58, 60–65, 76, 79, 85, 88, 89, 91, 96, 99–101, 106, 109, 111, 119, 120, 125, 127–130, 134, 158, 161–163, 166, 184, 185, 187, 197, 198, 200–203, 206, 209, 212–214, 216, 221, 233, 234, 236
Kingdom of Heaven   86–89, 91, 120, 128, 129, 161, 199

L

liberating justification   157
liberation theology   21, 24, 29, 30, 32, 33, 35–41, 48, 56, 171, 174, 176, 187, 198, 199, 214, 216–220
liberator   16, 29, 37, 133, 196, 198, 200, 201
love of money   45, 46, 116
love of richness   115, 116, 121

M

marginalized   33, 35, 38, 51, 59, 63, 74
masculinity   97, 182, 185
materially poor   88, 89, 127, 128
Members of Parliament   98
misuse of the Bible   48

N

neocolonization   154
Nyerere   21–24

O

ordinary readers   51–53, 60

P

peasants   15, 20, 24, 25, 42, 60, 67, 68, 70–72, 93, 94, 101, 102, 111–114, 117, 135, 139–141, 153–155, 159, 168, 174, 204, 205, 209, 218, 222
Pentecostal churches   27, 95, 105, 144, 145
Per Frostin   21, 23, 24, 61, 216, 217
perilous   45, 128, 208, 212
poor   7, 15–17, 20, 21, 23–27, 29, 30, 32–41, 43–66, 74–76, 78, 79, 85–95, 97–109, 111–121, 124–147, 149, 150, 152–155, 157–170, 173–181, 186–195, 197–216, 218, 220–223, 234, 236
Positive thinking   136
praxis   16, 29, 30, 32–35, 37–39, 41, 46, 49, 51, 65, 71, 157–160, 169, 173–177, 180, 192, 193, 197, 205, 206, 208, 210, 212, 214, 216–221

precarious   38, 44, 121, 129, 130, 133, 142, 150, 151, 169, 170, 178, 179, 208, 209, 212, 216
present Kingdom of God   101, 200
Prophetic Theology   50
prosperity gospel   121, 145
Prostitution   142
protoancestor   196

R
reflection and action   32, 173, 193

S
SACCOs   168
See-Judge-Act   39, 54, 171–173, 175, 191, 212
see-judge-act   30, 39, 40, 47, 55, 56, 171, 172, 176
self-reliant   121, 158, 162, 165, 190
social capital   157, 163, 164, 170
social transformation   49, 51, 53
Socially engaged Biblical scholars   53, 59
socioeconomic injustices   214
socioeconomic phenomenon   163, 169, 180, 218
socioeconomic reality   17, 30, 38, 56, 123–126, 135, 140, 155, 163, 169, 175, 179, 193, 197, 201, 202, 205, 210, 212, 218
solidarity   40, 62, 164, 165, 173, 175, 177, 193, 201, 204–206, 210, 212–215, 218, 221
spirit of equality   42
Spiritual poverty   89
spiritual poverty   88, 89, 120, 127
spiritually rich   88, 91, 128
State Theology   50
Synoptic Gospels   17, 61, 76, 83, 121, 123, 147

T
the crucified   16, 34, 35, 38, 220
the holistic meaning of the poor   127
theology from below   16, 30, 47, 56, 61, 172, 173, 175, 187, 193, 204, 210, 214, 218, 221, 222, 224
theology of love   194, 195, 210, 214, 215, 218
theology of money-theism   208
theology of nonperson   193
theology of nonpersons   16, 38, 210
theology of poverty   203, 214
theology of solidarity   164, 205, 206, 219
theology of the poor   33, 38
trade liberalization   25, 93, 218
traditionalists   148, 183, 185
trained theologians   51, 59, 63
Trainers of Trainees   160
Transnational Corporations   141
true love   157, 163, 165, 190, 194

U
Ujamaa   21–25, 29, 47–49, 51–54, 56, 62, 93, 138, 164, 171, 172, 191, 193, 212, 213, 216–218

W
water pollution   148, 149, 188
witchcraft   111, 114, 117, 178
Word of God   25, 26, 28, 30–32, 37, 39, 41, 48, 52, 56, 88, 95, 97, 116, 117, 121, 130, 134, 136, 147, 154, 158, 160, 163, 169, 173–176, 179, 181, 184–187, 190–192, 205, 209, 210, 212, 216, 218, 220
world economy   65, 141, 154